Beliefs, Values & Traditions

SECOND EDITION

ANN LOVELACE & JOY WHITE

Heinemann

EDUCATIONAL RESOURCE SERVICE

Heinemann Educational Publishers
Halley Court, Jordan Hill, Oxford OX2 8EJ
a division of Reed Educational & Professional
Publishing Ltd

OXFORD MELBOURNE AUCKLAND
JOHANNESBURG BLANTYRE GABORONE
IBADAN PORTSMOUTH NH(USA) CHICAGO

© Ann Lovelace and Joy White, 1996, 2002

First Published 1996
New edition 2002
04 03 02
6 5 4 3 2 1

284917

British Library Cataloguing in Publication Data
A catalogue record for this book is available from
the British Library
ISBN 0 435 30261 2

Designed and typeset by Artistix, Oxon
Illustrated by Artistix, Ed Dovey, Oxford Illustrators,
Simon Girling Associates and Specs Art
Cover designed by Threefold Design
Printed and bound in Great Britain by Bath Press
Colourbooks, Glasgow

Acknowledgments

This book is dedicated to Ruth Tayler who has loyally supported the authors over many years and who exemplifies all that is best in the teaching of RE.

The authors would like to thank the following for their help and encouragement: Angela Connors, Alistair Christie and Sue Walton, Hilary Eve, Jennifer Johnson, Violet and George Longworth, Linda James and Frank Shorter, Bob Potter, Moses White.

The publishers would like to thank E. H. Bladon, W. Owen Cole and Arye Forta for commenting on the manuscript.

The publishers would like to thank the following for the copyright material reproduced in this book.
Amnesty International United Kingdom for the extract on p. 147; Les Barton for the cartoon on p. 56; Richard Curtis for the extract from *The Vicar of Dibley* on p. 44; BBC Television for the text from an advert for the film *Priest* on p. 29; Beacon Press for the quote by Rabbi Sue Wasserman 'When Laura was raped...' from *Four Centuries of Jewish Women's Spirituality* by V. Ashton on p. 182; Bloomsbury Publishers Ltd for the extract from *Arab and Jew* by David Shipler on p. 209; Bono for the extract from *Rattle and Hum*, reproduced by permission of Reed Books, on p. 50; British Muslims for the logo on p. 126; CAFOD for the logo on p. 54; Carlin Music for the lyrics from the song 'If I were a rich man' on p. 186, music by Jerry Bock and words by Sheldon Harnick, © 1964 Alley Music Co. Inc. and Trio Music Co. Inc., copyright renewed 1992 by Jerry Bock and S. Harnick, lyrics reproduced by kind permission of Carlin Music Corp, UK administrator; the Catholic Association for Racial Justice for the logo on p. 60; the Central Board of Finance of the Church of England for the extracts from *The Alternative Service Book* on pp. 32, 55, 75 and 84; Chabad Lubivitch for the leaflet cover 'If you're looking for G-d...' on p. 169; Christian Aid for the logo on p. 54; Christian Ecology Link for the logo on p. 54; the Christian Research Association for the statistics on p. 36; *the Church Times* for the cartoon by Noel Ford on p. 40 and the cartoon by Ron on p. 65; the Community Research Unit of the Board of Deputies of British Jews for the graph on p. 168, adapted from a Jewish Continuity publication, and for the letter on p. 173 taken from *Jams Zone*, Issue 1, published by Jewish Continuity; Tom Coop for the cartoons on p. 5; the Council of Christians and Jews for the logo and *Common Ground* cover on p. 197; the *Croydon Advertiser* for the extracts on pp. 96 ('Sisters battle...'), 129 (both); the *Croydon Guardian* for the extract on p. 151; the *Croydon Post* for the headline on p. 39; Edwina Currie for the quote on p. 171;

© *Daily Mail*/Solo Syndication for the quotations on p. 117; the *Daily Telegraph* for the quote by Prince Charles, reproduced by permission of Ewan MacNaughton Associates, on p. 125; *Eastern Eye* for the extracts on pp. 97, 124 ('Pig's Head Jibe'); Exley Publications Ltd for the poem from *Cry for Our Beautiful World* by Helen Exley on p. 130; Fellowship of Reconciliation, England, The Eirene Centre, The Old School House, Clopton, Northants NN16 3DZ for the original cartoons from which the cartoons on p. 73 have been redrawn; Roger Frith for the poem on p. 21; Janis Goodman for the Hanukkah card on p. 172, reproduced by permission of Leeds Postcards; *The Guardian* for the headline 'More than 90 per cent...' on p. 80 and the extract on p. 134; © copyright 1952 (renewed), 1953 (renewed), Hampshire House Publishing Corp., New York, USA, assigned to TRO Essex Music Ltd, London SW10 0SZ; HarperCollins Publishers Ltd for the extract from *Audacity to Believe* by Sheila Cassidy on p. 79, and for the quote from *A Backdoor to Heaven* by Rabbi Lionel Blue on p. 165; Barry Holtz for the poem on p. 176; Investment Option Ltd for the advert on p. 47; the Islamic Foundation for the poem by Mymona Hendricks, from *Muslim Poems for Children*, on p. 135; Islamic Relief for the logo on p. 138; the Jewish Aids Trust, HIV Educational Unit, Colindale Hospital, Colindale Avenue, London NW9 5HG, tel. 0181 200 0369 for permission to reproduce the poster on p. 163; the *Jewish Chronicle* for the Kerber cartoon on p. 160 and the extracts on pp. 160, 172, 175, 205; Jewish Continuity for the logo on p. 173; the Jewish Lesbian and Gay Helpline for the poster on p. 164; © Joel Kauffman for the cartoons on pp. 48 and 80; the Imran Khan Cancer Appeal for the illustration and Zakah Fund information on p. 149; Kingsbury United Synagogue for the advert on p. 182; Kingsway Publications for the quote from *Give Us This Day* by Fiona Castle on p. 8; David Kossoff for the extract on p. 213; Frances Lawrence for the quote on p. 72; LARCAA, 23 Clarence St., Liverpool, for the poem by Suliaman El Hadi, taken from *Decade of the African Child* on p. 95; Sarah Leveten for the Shalom illustration on p. 211; the Liverpool *Daily Post* for the statistics on p. 64; © 1995 MAYC World Action, 2 Chester House, Pages Lane, Muswell Hill London N10 1PR for the extract from *Colour Me Blind* on p. 58; Macmillan Books Ltd for the extracts from *Rape, My Story* by Jill Saward on p. 71 and from *The Kurt Cobain Story* by Dave Thompson on p. 82; *Marie Claire* for the extract 'Dead Centre' on p. 83; Melody Maker for the quote by Ian Brown on p. 146; *Muslim News* for the extracts on pp. 124 ('Attacks on Muslims continue'), *New Internationalist* for the cartoon by Polyp on p. 74; Newspaper Publishing plc for the extracts from *The Independent* on pp. 33, 87, 128; *The Observer* for the extracts on pp. 45, 94, 112; Pan Books Ltd for the extract from *Now and Then* by Roy Castle on p. 76; *Parentwise* magazine for the extract on p. 35 ('Family rites...'); PEANUTS cartoon © UFS, Inc. on p. 72; Penguin Books Ltd for the extracts from *The Autobiography of Malcolm X* on p. 122 and from *Forced Out* on p. 143; Quiller Press for the quote by Father Serrini on p. 57; the *Reigate & Banstead Independent* for the extract on p. 204; Rosedale Publishing for the quote by Linford Christie on p. 36; Richard L. Rubenstein and John K. Roth for *Approaches to Auschwitz* published and reproduced by permission of SCM Press © 1987, on p. 191; Singapore Press Holdings Ltd for the extract from the *Straits Times* on p. 114; © Spellbound Card Co. Ltd, Dublin for the cartoon by John Byrne on p. 42; Cath Tate Cards for the cartoon on p. 28, © Angela Martin; Tearfund for the poster and logo on p. 51 and the cartoon on p. 53; © Times Newspapers Ltd for the extract from *The Times* on p. 35 ('Bride back at church...'); Steve Turner for the poem on p. 48; the United Reform Church for 'Rainbow Covenant' on p. 57 and the quote on p. 74; Veritas (Dublin) Ltd for the second two quotes by Desmond Tutu, taken from *Desmond Tutu: Black Africa's Man of Destiny* by Patrick Comerford, on p. 61 and also the quote on p. 87; Virago Press Ltd for the extract from *Winter in the Morning*, © Janina Bauman 1986, on p. 211; Virgin Publishing Ltd for the extracts from *The Meaning of Life* on pp. 19, 120, 207; *Vogue* magazine for the quote by Jemima Khan on p. 108; the Voluntary Euthanasia Society for the medical emergency card on p. 81; Colin Wheeler for the cartoon on p. 24 which first appeared in *The Independent*, 11 December 1995; Wickes Building Supplies Ltd. for the advert headline on p. 200; Elie Wiesel for the poem of p. 194; the WWF – The Global Environment Network for the quote by Rabbi Hertzberg from *Faith and Nature* on p. 198 and the cartoon from *When Humans Roamed the Earth* on p. 199; Yad Vashem, Israel for the logo on p. 193; the Yearly Meeting of the Religious Society of Friends in Britain (Quakers) for the extracts on pp. 28 and 75. Quotations from the Bible in the Christianity section of the book are taken from *The Good News Bible*, published by the Bible Society/HarperCollins Publishers Ltd, UK © American Bible Society, 1966, 1971, 1976, 1992. Quotations from the Qur'an are taken from *The Meaning of the Holy Qur'an* new edition with revised translation and commentary by Abdullah Yusuf Ali, published by the Amana Corporation, Maryland, USA. Quotations from the Tenakh in the Judaism section are taken from *A New Translation of the Holy Scriptures* published by the Jewish Publication Society, Philadelphia.

Photo acknowledgements appear on p. 224.

Cover: Illustration © The artist Ibrahim Brian Thompson Tel: (0151) 7345398.

The publishers have made every effort to trace copyright holders. However, if any material has been incorrectly acknowledged, we would be pleased to correct this at the earliest opportunity.

Contents

Notes for teachers

Beliefs, Values & Traditions is designed for Key Stage 4 students doing a GCSE Religious Education (Short Course) or a general non-examination course. It addresses issues in three religions: Christianity, Islam and Judaism. Also available is *Beliefs, Values & Traditions Resource and Activity File*, a photocopiable pack designed to support *Beliefs, Values & Traditions.*

How it fits in with the GCSE Religious Education (Short Course)

- Its subject content supports many of the syllabuses.
- It follows the examination criteria.
- It uses the QCA glossary spellings and definitions of terms.
- It contains GCSE-type questions with a mark allocation guide.
- It provides scope for evaluation through discussion questions.

How it meets the needs of non-examination courses

- It uses stimulating material about relevant issues of today.
- It follows the two QCA Model Syllabus Attainment Targets – Learning about religions and Learning from religion.
- It allows differentiation through a variety of stimuli and questions.
- It consolidates learning in earlier Key Stages.

How to use the book

In addition to the issues-based chapters which make up the majority of the book, there are important sections which students will need to read and frequently refer to. These include:

- general information on belief and morality common to the three religions (pages 6-13).
- outlines on the history and beliefs specific to each religion (pages 14-17, 90-3 and 154-7).
- a comprehensive index (pages 222-4).

Each of these features plays an essential part in helping students both to answer questions and to increase their knowledge and understanding. For some issues, general information is given in the Christianity section, to which pupils can cross-refer. Throughout, it is a useful exercise to refer to parallel chapters of those religions not currently being studied. Interesting comparisons can be made and further ideas for questions can be used or adapted. Each topic follows the following pattern:

- Opening stimulus material followed by a Get Talking activity which can be done in pairs or through general class discussion. The questions are designed to get students started and to encourage student evaluation. They can also be used for written work.

- Fact Files – these give specific religious teaching on the topic, with textual references. They are supported by other relevant features, such as extracts from newspaper articles.

- Questions are set for students to recall, select, explain and evaluate the material. The mark allocations give an indication of the amount of information needed.

- Creative assignments – these can be done without extra material but they will often be enhanced with additional materials. Reference books can be supplemented by newspapers and magazines, including those from faith communities.

- Re-examine – questions are set at the end of each group of linking topics to give opportunities for more developed answers.

Notes for students

Welcome to *Beliefs, Values & Traditions* which is written to help you discover that religion is not just about the past but is very much alive and part of today's world. Whether you are studying for GCSE or doing general RE, you will find that this book contains a great deal about the important issues that face all people at different stages of their lives. Your teacher will help you get the most out of the book. You might find it helpful to read the notes on the opposite page.

Practical tips

- **Do** take time to read about the religions you are not actually studying. You can discover a lot that will interest you. It can also provide a useful alternative viewpoint.
- **Do** look in magazines for articles and features about the issues you are studying. Bring them to school for discussion or for display. Keep a folder of them.
- **Do** write off to organizations. The information you receive will support your work and help you with your creative assignments.
- **Do** try to visit places of worship – you can learn so much. You may even discover some useful information just by reading the notice-board outside!
- **Do** ask friends and family who are going abroad to bring you back pictures and information about the faiths you are studying. Remember, these are world religions and they cross many cultures.
- **Do** take a camera when you go away yourself.

How to answer questions

- **RE**fer to the number in brackets after each question. This shows how many marks are awarded and will give you an idea of the depth of answer needed.
- **RE**fer to the Fact Files, features and pictures in the section.
- **RE**fer to all the introduction sections.
- **RE**fer to the index.
- **RE**fer to your teacher.

But to some questions there are no answers:

Why did those all-night revision sessions seem such a good idea at the time?

Why doesn't even your favourite mascot guarantee the topics you've revised come up?

Why is some bright spark on his third sheet of paper when you've hardly started?

Why do some invigilators insist on eating garlic the night before?

And finally ...

- **Don't** be blinkered about religion. Keep an open mind and respect people's views, even if you don't share them. Many of the world's problems are caused by intolerance brought about through lack of knowledge and understanding. When you leave school you will be constantly meeting and mixing with people whose beliefs, values and traditions may be different from your own.

Belief

What do you believe?

'I believe above the storm the smallest prayer will still be heard.
I believe that someone in the great somewhere hears every word.'

These lines are from a song that was in the charts in the 1990's. Your parents (and even grandparents!) could tell you that it was popular before. It was first a hit over forty years ago and has been successfully revived twice since. It seems that the subject of what people believe is of recurring interest to different generations. People usually like to create new music for themselves and, to use a phrase from the 1990's, it wouldn't do a great deal for one's 'street cred' to have one's parents singing along to the same tunes! So what does 'street cred' actually mean? The word 'cred' is short for 'credibility', which brings us to where we started – belief. The term 'street cred' generally refers to those whom others tend to follow because of what they stand for – how they dress and act etc. In Latin, the word 'credere' means 'to believe' and it is from this that we also get the word **'creed'** which is often used in religion to describe what people stand for and believe.

What is belief?

A belief is an idea that one accepts as true – with or without proof. Even without proof, most people would say that evidence is needed for belief.

 Get talking

- **What things do you believe in as being true for which you have no proof?**
- **Do you have evidence for these beliefs?**

Religious belief

For religious belief, the word 'faith' is often used. To some people the two words 'faith' and 'belief' mean the same thing, but to understand religious faith it might be helpful to see 'faith' as going a step further than 'belief'.

- Belief is accepting that something is true.
- Faith is being able to put trust in that belief.

A simple comparison might be parachuting.

You might believe totally that the parachute has been well-made and that the instructor knows their job *but* you may not have the faith to put trust in those beliefs.

People who are religious believe in a force or God in whom they feel able to put their trust. This faith may vary and waver at different times but for many it will direct their actions and give a purpose and meaning to their lives.

Christians, Muslims and Jews each have their own beliefs, values and traditions as is shown later in the book. However, there are also some beliefs about God that they have in common.

Shared beliefs

One God	Monotheism	There is only one God.

who is…

All-powerful	Omnipotent	God is the 'First Cause' and through him all life first came into existence. He creates and controls all of nature.

All-knowing	Omniscient	God has unlimited knowledge about everything. Nothing can be hidden from him.

Beyond	Transcendant	God exists outside the created world and is not bound by the same limits as humans who live in time and space.

Within	Immanent	God is also ever-present everywhere within the universe.

Many people see God's hand in the power of nature

How is God revealed?

At some time in our lives most of us have feelings of awe and wonder at the power or beauty of nature. Sometimes in these situations people are aware of an unseen (spiritual) force which they cannot explain. Others see the created world as evidence of 'God's hand' and they feel his presence around and within them.

Many great religious leaders have experienced God in places of great natural power. When **Moses** received the **Ten Commandments** he was alone on a mountain. The prophet **Muhammad** was in a desert cave when the first **revelations** from **Allah** came to him.

Miracles

A miracle is an event believed to have a supernatural cause. Even if we don't believe in such happenings we often use the word to describe something that has amazed us or which seems to go against what is usual or expected. Many people with religious faith believe that God performs **miracles**.

When he was fifteen, Daniel, the son of Fiona and the late Roy Castle, had a serious accident and remained unconscious for several days.

We stood around his bed and prayed ... at the end of the prayer, he opened his eyes and looked up and said quite clearly, 'Amen'. The nursing he received was magnificent ... but I still believe that his healing was a miracle. We knew that God had everything in control, because he was in control of our lives.
(Fiona Castle)

Prayer

Many people communicate with God through prayer.

A Christian at prayer

Conversion

Some people experience God in their lives in quite a sudden and dramatic way, which often means a change in attitude and lifestyle. Sometimes God speaks through their thoughts or in dreams and visions. At other times he is revealed through the words from holy books.

Cat Stevens was a successful pop star who gave up his recording career, sold his gold discs and took up a new life as a religious educator under the name of Yusuf Islam. His conversion came after being given a copy of the Qur'an in English.

'A feeling of belonging ran through me. I was a stream that had found its ocean.'

Yusuf Islam

Other people find faith in a more gradual way. Stephanie Cook, Olympic gold medallist in the year 2000, says that her faith began to blossom when she was a teenager and was persuaded by a friend to go to a church youth group.

'There was no particular moment, just a gradual realization.'

Stephanie Cook

 Creative assignment

Describe a time in your life when you felt a sense of wonder or mystery. It could be a straightforward account or in the form of a poem or piece of art.

Stars are born: a photograph from the Hubble telescope showing newly forming suns from pillars of dust and gas as they looked seven millenia ago

Not everyone, of course, has religious beliefs.

- An **atheist** believes that there is no God.
- An **agnostic** believes it is impossible to know if God exists.
- A **humanist** is an agnostic or atheist who believes in the importance of living life fully for the welfare of others.

These people will accept other theories as to how the Earth and life came into being.

The Big Bang

This is a widely-held belief and it states that, at the beginning of time, there was a large explosion which resulted in the releasing and scattering of matter. This eventually formed into stars and planets. Followers of this belief say that on our own particular planet the conditions needed for life developed because certain chemicals happened to come together in the right combination. This suggests that it was a matter of chance that life began. The evolution of that life, including that of humans, has taken billions of years.

Do science and religion contradict each other?

Scientists are concerned with *how* things work. They are not involved in finding out *why* we are here and whether there is a God. Some scientists say that their work leads them to believe that God cannot exist. Others say that all knowledge and science come from God. To them God is still 'the First Cause' responsible for 'the Big Bang' when it happened.

Morality

Baiting foxes: wanton cruelty

Lord Soper collapses. The crowd rushes to help

 Get talking

- What have been the biggest influences in your life in teaching you right from wrong?

The meaning of morality

Morality is concerned with right and wrong behaviour.

Most people have some belief and understanding of what is considered to be right and wrong.

- A moral action is one that is thought to be right.
- An immoral action is one that is thought to be wrong.
- An amoral action is one that shows no understanding of the difference.

Is right always right and wrong always wrong?

Absolute morality

The photos above show examples of situations where there is little doubt about the actions being right or wrong. Some actions are thought to be good 'in themselves'. They are right in an absolute way, regardless of the motive for doing them or what the consequences of doing them might be.

Relative morality

Most actions are good or bad in relation to other factors. Morality is not always a simple matter and we often find ourselves in a situation where we have to weigh up everything and decide what is right in the circumstances. Sometimes an action can seem wrong by some standards but the intention is good, or it might be the lesser of two evils. For instance, it is wrong to break the rules of the road, but there might be an occasion when it seems the right thing to do. An example of this might be parents rushing a sick child to hospital who decide not to stop at a red light.

Which way?

How do we learn the right path to take in life?

My family

I always knew that as long as I owned up it would be okay. I still had a lecture and my pocket money stopped, though.

My friends

She had that way of making me feel guilty if I suggested things like bunking off school. It used to annoy me but I guess I should be grateful to her really.

My school

Now I'm a student teacher I often think of Mr Williams because he was always fair and listened to everyone's point of view. He used to do some brilliant assemblies. I try to copy him when things get tough.

The society I live in

I'm certainly not going to drink and drive and risk losing my licence.

My religion

I learned about the Ten Commandments at Sunday School and I've never really forgotten them. I still think they're important.

My conscience

Everybody called me 'Chicken' for not joining in but it just didn't seem right somehow.

What is a conscience?

A conscience is an inner feeling which seems to 'speak' to us about what is right and wrong. Although many people say they have a conscience inside them, it does not automatically appear to be part of everyone, like a limb or an artery. Its existence is very much determined by all the influences around us. Some people's consciences seem to develop or be neglected regardless of what they are taught.

Reasons for making moral decisions

- Humanists and many other atheists and agnostics believe that humans should be responsible for their actions and should apply the **golden rule** of treating others as they would want to be treated themselves.

- People with religious faith share these views but they are also influenced by the teachings of their faith. They not only learn that it is their duty to live in obedience to God's will but they receive inspiration and guidance to do so from their holy books, leaders and teachers.

A moral dilemma

Recall, explain and evaluate

1 Write two different responses the girl in the drawing might give to her parents:
a showing absolute morality
b showing relative morality. **(2)**

2 Explain what she would consider before deciding what to do or say. **(3)**

3 'Honesty is always the best policy.' Do you agree? Give reasons for your answer, showing you have considered other points of view. **(5)**

YOUR MOTHER HAD SUCH A JOB KEEPING IT A SECRET. SHE'S BEEN WORKING ON IT FOR WEEKS. WE WANTED YOU TO HAVE SOMETHING NICE FOR THE LEAVING PARTY AS YOU'VE DONE SO WELL.

WHAT AM I GOING TO SAY?

Christians

Christianity came from the religion of Judaism 2000 years ago in the Middle Eastern country of Israel, known then as Palestine. It has the largest following of any religion, with people from almost every country in the world.

There are many different groups of Christians. These groups are usually known as **Churches**. The word refers both to the community of followers as well as to the place of worship. The largest group of Christians are the **Roman Catholics**. These Christians make up over half the total from around the world. Their leader is the Bishop of Rome, known as the Pope. The other two main groups are the **Orthodox Church** and the **Protestants**. The Orthodox Church is a worldwide group of Churches orginating in the Middle East. The largest of these today are the Russian, Romanian, Greek and Serbian churches.

The Protestant Church has been divided over the centuries into a large number of denominations and includes the Anglican Church, to which the Church of England belongs. Other Protestant Churches, often referred to as non-conformists or **Free Churches**, consist of a very large number of denominations and include Baptists, Methodists, the Religious Society of Friends (Quakers), the Salvation Army and the United Reform and Pentecostal Churches.

Although Christianity is diverse in its traditions, Christians are united in their belief in Jesus Christ as the Son of God.

Jesus

Jesus is thought to have been born in Bethlehem, during the time of the Roman occupation. He was the son of Joseph and Mary and won a large following among his fellow Jews who saw him as the fulfilment of the prophecies that God would send a **Messiah** to redeem (save) humankind. With his twelve chosen **disciples** Jesus travelled around the country preaching the **gospel** (good news) that he had brought the **Kingdom of God** to all who followed his teaching and believed in him. His fame spread and many miracles of healing and power over nature were attributed to him. He taught and showed by example the importance of love and compassion for the poor and rejected. His outspoken criticism of the religious authorities of his day made him enemies who eventually persuaded the Roman Governor of the province, **Pontius Pilate**, to agree to his execution. His suffering and death on the cross, known as the **Passion**, and his **Resurrection** three days later are fundamental to Christian belief and are marked at the main Christian festival of **Easter**.

Worship

Jesus predicted his death at his **Last Supper**, the night before he died. He instructed his disciples to share bread and wine with him, which he blessed and said represented his body and blood. This is regularly re-enacted in many Christian Churches as a **sacrament** – a visible and outward sign of God's blessing. In the Orthodox, Roman Catholic and Anglican Churches it is the most important part of worship and is known as the **Eucharist**, **Holy Communion** or **Holy Mass** and may be held several times a week. Other Churches celebrate it less frequently and some, including the Religious Society of Friends and the Salvation Army do not use it in their worship.

Public and private prayer is an important part of being Christian. Many Churches follow a set pattern of prayer and praise in their worship which is known as **liturgy**. Other Churches follow a more informal and free approach.

The Bible

The written source of authority for Christians is the Bible. This is divided into **Old** and **New Testaments**. The Old Testament begins with accounts of God's creation of the world, gives a history of the Jews and the unfolding account of their relationship with God and contains the **Ten Commandments**. The New Testament contains the four accounts of the life and teaching of Jesus from Matthew, Mark, Luke and John. These are known as the **Gospels**. They focus mainly on the events of the last week of Jesus' life and were not written until at least twenty years after his death. The New Testament also includes the account of the continuation of Jesus' work by his followers and the founding of the first Christian Churches. It records that shortly after his death, the disciples received God's divine presence, the Holy Spirit. This gave them power to follow Jesus' instructions to go out and preach his word. Many Christians today testify to the power of the **Holy Spirit** (**Paraclete**) guiding them in their lives. The spreading of the Christian message, **evangelism**, is still seen as an important mission and some Churches such as Baptists place particular stress on it.

The spread of the faith

Under Jesus' appointed leader, Peter, the disciples formed the first Church and together with a fast-growing band of followers began spreading the teachings of Jesus. They were joined by a man who had been their opponent and persecutor. His name was Saul – later known as **Paul**. On a journey to Damascus, Saul underwent a dramatic experience when Jesus spoke to him in a vision. This resulted in his **conversion** to Christianity and he became an important Christian of the time, devoting his life to travelling throughout the northern Mediterranean countries establishing Christian Churches. His letters (**epistles**) to many of these churches are also contained in the New Testament and they give detailed interpretations of Jesus' teaching.

As Christianity spread, the Romans were afraid of its power and tried to stamp it out. Persecution raged for 300 years. An important reminder of this time is the widely-used Christian symbol of the fish. The Greek word for fish is **icthus**. Each of the letters in this word is the first letter of one of Jesus' titles in Greek: Jesus Christ, Son of God, Saviour. The drawing of a fish became a secret code for the early, persecuted Christians when they wanted to pass messages to each other or arrange meetings without the Romans knowing. Many Christians were tortured and executed at this time.

Finally **Emperor Constantine** gave Christianity its freedom and it became the official religion of the Roman Empire.

Divisions and unity

Christianity waxed and waned over the centuries and it became divided. The first big split (the **Great Schism**) came in the eleventh century when the Western and the Eastern Church (now the Orthodox Church) separated. The second major division happened during the Reformation when protestors against the corruption in the Church in Rome broke away and formed the Protestant Church.

In the twentieth century, the **ecumenical movement** was established to bring unity among Christians. The **World Council of Churches** was founded in 1948 and a measure of co-operation exists between Churches on local, national and international levels.

Although the Church's power has declined in recent years, both in numbers of followers and in its standing in many communities, it is still a powerful force for good. It plays an important part in giving meaning to the lives of millions of people throughout the world.

The nature of God

Christians believe in one God who is all-powerful and all-knowing. He has created humankind for a purpose and each person's destiny is known to him. Alongside this belief is the teaching that God has given everyone **free will** to make choices about how they live out their lives.

The Christian understanding of God's nature is shown in the belief in the **Trinity**. Although God is One, Christians understand him through three main aspects: Father, Son and Holy Spirit.

God the Father

Christians believe in an eternal God who is the source of all life, present and active in creation. Many Christians express this belief in their weekly worship when they recite their creed: *'I believe in one God the Father Almighty, maker of heaven and earth, and of all things visible and invisible.'* (*Nicene Creed*)

As the creator and sustainer of life, God is understood as the father who loves and cares for his children. Just as a good father also needs to guide and punish when his children go astray, Christians believe that God is their judge and they see it as their duty to try and please him.

God the Son

When Jesus was born, many Jews of the time believed that he was the Messiah whose coming had been predicted. Christians today share this belief. Jesus was given the title 'Christ' which is from the Greek translation of Messiah, meaning the 'anointed one'. Christians believe that God became man in the form of Jesus. The word 'Incarnate' (made flesh) is used to describe this and although Jesus had human feelings, as God he was believed to have power over life. He demonstrated this in his miracles of healing, his power over nature and his Resurrection. Christians believe that Jesus showed the love of God by taking on the burden of the world's sins and sacrificing his life to atone or make amends for them. By doing this, humankind was reconciled with God and was given the promise of eternal life. According to this belief (the **Atonement**), Jesus brought salvation which is reflected in the title 'Saviour'.

God the Holy Spirit

Before Jesus finally left the Earth, he promised his disciples that his presence would always be with them to inspire, comfort and guide them. They first experienced this presence entering them at the feast of **Pentecost**. The immediate effect was dramatic and they were heard to 'speak in tongues'. This is known as **glossolalia** and is an expression of spontaneous joy which comes out as words that are unintelligible to those who witness it. From this time on their lives changed as they felt the power of the Holy Spirit guiding them. They went about preaching, healing and drawing people to them. Many became followers and through baptism and the laying of the disciples' hands upon them, the Holy Spirit was transmitted to them, too. Christians look upon the event at Pentecost as the birthday of the Christian Church and celebrate it six weeks after Easter on **Whit Sunday**.

The Holy Spirit, sometimes called the Holy Ghost or Paraclete, is often represented symbolically as a dove. It is believed to be the living force of God's power in the world.

Many Christians remind themselves of the three-fold nature of God by ending their prayers with the words, 'In the name of the Father, the Son and the Holy Spirit'.

Morality

The basis for morality among Christians comes from their knowledge and understanding of God, as revealed through:

- the Bible
- the teachings and example of Jesus
- the authority of the Church.

The Bible

The book of Genesis describes how Adam and Eve disobeyed God and were banished from the Garden of Eden. This is known as the **Fall** and many Christians believe that, as a result, sin came into the world and has been passed down and inherited by each generation ever since. This is known as **orginal sin**. Christians believe that although Jesus rescued them from sin, they still need to refer to the teachings of the Bible, their Church and their consciences to overcome the temptations to sin.

The law – the Ten Commandments (*Exodus 20*) give a framework for the way life should be conducted in family and social relationships.

The Prophets – spokespeople for God in different generations taught about justice and righteousness. Their words are recorded in the Old Testament.

The teachings and example of Jesus

Obeying the law

Jesus often quoted the Ten Commandments when reminding his listeners of the importance of moral behaviour. He too knew that living in society required obedience to society's rules, however, he taught that loyalty to God should come first. When he was asked to whom one should pay taxes, he replied: *'Pay the Emperor what belongs to the Emperor and pay God what belongs to God.'* (*Mark 12:17*)

Inner morality

Jesus was often criticized for breaking the laws, such as the law forbidding work on the Sabbath. He taught that laws were a framework for guidance but that there was a danger in thinking that a person only had to keep to the rules to consider themself good. This could lead to hypocrisy as true goodness came from within.

Love and compassion

When he was asked which were the most important of all the laws Jesus said that the first is to love God with all your being and the second (often referred to as the **Golden Rule**) is: *'Love your neighbour as you love yourself.'* (*Mark 12:31*)

Jesus taught that every action taken should be guided by these principles. In his Sermon on the Mount (*Matthew 5–7*) he said that love did not just involve family and friends but enemies too. This kind of love requires Christians to show compassion and forgiveness to those who have wronged them.

The authority of the Church

Church leaders and preachers teach Christian morality to their members and they also interpret Christian teaching for present day circumstances. Young people receive guidance through Sunday School and other groups.

In the Roman Catholic Church authority comes from the **Pope** in Rome whose ruling is circulated through documents known as **encyclicals**. The Anglican Church has a ruling body known as the **Synod**, with representatives from the **clergy** whose head in England is the Archbishop of Canterbury. The Free Churches are self-governing.

The sanctity of life

A medical team working to save a life

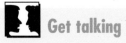 **Get talking**

- This unit is called 'The sanctity of life'. Looking at the photo, what do you think it means?

- In what ways do you think human life is special?

- What are the most precious things in your life?

The greatest gift

There are few people, whether they have a religious faith or not, who do not value the gift of life. The wonder of seeing a newborn child or the sadness at seeing the needless destruction of innocent creatures are feelings most of us share. It is true too, that we often curse life and think it treats us badly. Certainly those who are ill or have disabilities may feel this. However, the belief in the importance of preserving life is worldwide. The difference between those with religious faith and those without is a question of how they see its purpose.

Two entertainers give their views on the meaning of life:

> *Life is so precious and it scares me that people don't realize it until it is too late. God created a beautiful world and sometimes we get so busy that we forget to notice all these wonders, great and small.*
>
> **Britney Spears**

> *A cowslip in the hedgerow doesn't* mean *anything, neither does a sunrise over a tropical sea, or a thunderstorm. They are wonders of Nature … If I had to give a short answer it would be "Life is meaningless, but it is wonderful."*
>
> **Ronnie Barker**

Fact file

The word **sanctity** means purity or holiness. When it is used to describe life itself it expresses the idea of a preciousness worthy of the highest respect.

In the the first chapter of *Genesis* it says that God was the creator of all life and that human beings were made in his image. The taking of another's life is a sin against God and the sixth of the Ten Commandments says: *'Do not commit murder.' (Exodus 20:13)*

Christians believe that life is a precious gift from God and that each and every person is known to him. To them, the purpose of life is to love and serve God and to treat all people as being in the image of God and as they would want to be treated themselves. *'Love your neighbour as you love yourself.' (Mark 12:31)*

Jesus showed in his teaching and example that everyone should be valued. Christians believe that this understanding of sanctity should influence them in all the challenging decisions they have to make on life and death issues such as genetic engineering, embryo technology and abortion.

Recall and evaluate

1 Are the following from the Old or New Testament?

    a Creation story

    b Life of Moses

    c the Gospels

    d Ten Commandments   **(4)**

2 Is it as wrong to take an animal's life as it is a human's? Give reasons to support your answer.   **(6)**

Genetic engineering

Geneticists lay claim to 'God's creature'

Get talking

● What are the dangers in allowing scientists to experiment with life?

This photo shows a mouse genetically manipulated for scientific purposes. It produced a strong reaction from many people who felt that this experiment went beyond the accepted boundary of the right to interfere with life

Fact file

Genetic engineering is the process of changing the genetic make-up of living organisms. It is now widely used in research to find cures and relief for illnesses and disabilities.

Many Christians are not against this as they believe that the skills of science are gifts given by God and that to look for ways of relieving suffering is in keeping with Christian teaching. They point to the fact that Jesus cured sick and diseased people, showing it was part of God's purpose to overcome things that spoil creation. In Roman Catholic teaching this would be supported by their belief in the '**natural law**' (that which is in keeping with human nature).

However, Christians are not in favour of genetic engineering when they consider it is not done for right and moral reasons – such as to produce more 'perfect' examples of animals and vegetables which customers will want to buy. They are aware of the dangers of human interference with life which is a gift from God and should be respected. Many Churches are concerned with the possible misuse of scientific experiment and support the Human Fertilization and Embryology Authority which supervises work in the genetic sciences in hospitals and laboratories to make sure such work serves the common good.

Embryo technology

*I often wonder what they would reply
those couples with their children
in the street,
if I should say: 'What is it I can't buy
that you possess and got for free,
complete,
something that I'd give the world to own,
and with the world to give, still could
not own?'*

Roger Frith

Helping to overcome infertility

An embryo is the life formed when a sperm fertilizes an ovum (egg). It is estimated that approximately one in ten couples is unable to have children naturally and in many cases embryo technology is used to help overcome this problem (see page 96).

Methods used

When sperm is inserted into a woman using mechanical means it is known as artificial insemination.

AIH: artificial insemination by the husband.
AID: artificial insemination by a donor.
IVF: in-vitro fertilization, which takes place clinically, outside the womb. The sperm may be provided by the husband or by another man. (The first 'test tube baby' was born in 1978.)
Egg donation: an egg is donated by another woman.
Embryo donation: an embryo is donated by another man and woman.
Surrogate motherhood: pregnancy is undertaken by one woman to provide a baby for another woman.

As a result of the 1982 Warnock Report, *Human Fertilization and Embryology*, the present legal position can be summarized as follows:
● infertility is a valid reason for treatment
● the human embryo should be protected in law
● a limited amount of research on embryos is permitted 'up to the end of the 14th day of fertilization'
● a licensing authority must regulate procedures.

How Christians view infertility treatments

Christians believe that children are a blessing from God and most Churches accept the use of science to help childless couples, as long as a third party is not involved. AIH is the preferred method as the sanctity of marriage is still maintained. Other methods, which do not involve the husband, are thought by many Churches to be undesirable and lead to problems of identity for the children.

The Roman Catholic Church has an added concern about IVF. It believes that the success of fertilization using this method involves creating 'spare' embryos which are either thrown away or used for experimentation. As it is considered that life begins at conception, this in effect is the taking of life.

Recall and explain

1 Describe two different methods to help overcome infertility. **(4)**

2 Why do you think people might be concerned about the mouse experiment? In your answer you can refer to religious and non-religious reasons. **(6)**

Abortion

To him:
You said that you'd support me
It seems you've changed your mind?
You said you wouldn't leave me
– it's not just me you've left behind.
You said we'd stay together
You said we'd see it through
There's a child alive inside me
God, tell me what to do.

To her:
Can't you see I'm in a corner
It's not what we agreed.
It's surely not a baby
When it's only still a seed.
Just give me time to weigh things
Am I ready for a wife?
Can I live in peace while knowing
I've sacrificed a life?

 **Get talking**

- What sympathy do you have for the viewpoints of the boy and girl in the poems?
- In what way might the relationship between the couple change:

    a) if the girl has an abortion?   **b)** if she doesn't?

Life in the balance

'If children are to have rights then the most basic right must be to life itself.'

'Legal abortion means a woman doesn't suffer the horrors of old wives' remedies and back-street abortions.'

'An abortion is carried out every four minutes, day and night. This is creating a shortage of young people and an imbalance in the population.'

'My family won't have me back if they find out I'm pregnant.'

'How could I bear to bring into the world a child whose father is a violent rapist?'

'When I look at her now I'm filled with love and pride. To think I nearly decided to have her aborted!'

Abortion

Abortion is the premature removal from the womb of a foetus during pregnancy. If this happens naturally it is known as a spontaneous abortion, or **miscarriage**. Most abortions take place when the pregnancy is unwanted. They used to be carried out illegally. It is still illegal in some countries, while in China it has been used to help control the population. In China the state restricted a woman to having only one child in the 1980's. This policy was relaxed slightly in the 1990's.

As a result of the 1967 Abortion Act which was amended in 1990 by the Human Fertilization and Embryology Act, in England, Scotland and Wales a woman is legally allowed to have an abortion in certain circumstances.

Doctor

Not obliged to agree.

Must sign certificate with another doctor.

Cannot perform abortion after 24 weeks.

Woman

Can have abortion:
● if life is in danger
● if health would be affected
● if family would suffer.

Can go to private clinic if NHS permission is not given.

Man

Has no right to be consulted.

Cannot raise any objection.

Fact file

Christians believe that life is a gift from God. *'You created every part of me; you put me together in my mother's womb.'* (Psalm 139:13)

Although they are divided in their views about abortion, they all take the issue very seriously. The Roman Catholic Church is against to abortion under any circumstances, believing that life is known to God from the moment of conception.

Other Christian Churches are against abortion being used for social reasons or as a means of birth control but they accept that in some instances an abortion may be a preferred choice – such as in cases where the mother or child would suffer if the pregnancy continued.

In spite of differing views about abortion, Christians believe in a compassionate approach to the problem and agree on the importance of pastoral care for those faced with parenthood in difficult circumstances. This includes looking at alternatives such as adoption, and counselling for those who have undergone abortion.

Recall and explain

1 What is meant by the term 'abortion'? **(2)**

2 Why might some Christians consider abortion an example of absolute morality and others as an example of relative morality? (See page 11.) **(8)**

Attitudes to sex and family planning

THEY USED TO WANT TO GET INTO THE FOREIGN OFFICE – NOW, IT'S HEAVEN

JESUS SAVES

> *I kissed my first woman and smoked my first cigarette on the same day. I have never had time for tobacco since.*
>
> Arturo Toscanini, 1867-1957 (musician)

In a recent survey of Oxford and Cambridge students one third claimed to be virgins and one in eight said they would not have sex before marriage.

Changing views

The cartoonist's reaction to the student survey suggests the idea that those who refrain from sex must be religious. This reflects the view that many people have of the Christian Church, which is that it is against anything as pleasurable as sex. This is mainly because the way in which Christian teaching was interpreted in the past gave the impression that sex even within marriage was a necessity rather than something to be enjoyed. As the majority of people in the United Kingdom used to be Christian, this idea influenced the whole of society for many centuries. It was not until the sexual revolution of the 1960s that sex outside marriage came to be more widely accepted and there was a much more open attitude towards the whole subject. This change has led to confusion for many people. Church leaders have had to take up the challenge of giving a clear interpretation of what Christian teaching means in today's world.

Get talking

- **What are the pressures upon young people to have sexual relationships?**
- **What are the dangers?**

Fidelity

Christian teaching on marriage (see page 30) includes the belief that fidelity (faithfulness) is important. The seventh Commandment states: '*Do not commit adultery*' (*Exodus 20:14*). Jesus once said that it was even a sin to have adulterous or lustful thoughts (*Mathew 5:28*).

However, his attitude towards a woman about to be stoned for adultery was one of compassion for her. This has led many Christians to see the importance of tolerance and understanding of those who have given in to temptation.

Fact file 1

In the book of Genesis in the Bible it says that God created man and woman to be partners for each other and to have children. Christianity teaches that sexual intercourse should take place within marriage. Some Churches now accept that couples choose to live together (**cohabit**) for sound reasons and where there is strong commitment, they are not opposed to it. However, it is still believed to fall short of what God has intended.

Christians believe that casual sex or promiscuity encourages people to be viewed merely as objects. They believe that sexual intimacy should be a part of a strong loving relationship of mutual respect '...*the man who is guilty of sexual immorality sins against his own body. Don't you know that your body is the Temple of the Holy Spirit, who lives in you and who was given to you by God?*' *(1 Corinthians 6:18–19)*

Chastity

A response to modern sexual attitudes has come from Baptist churches in America who teach that **chastity** – the refraining from sexual intercourse and remaining a virgin – until marriage is a positive act which can be fulfilling in itself. 'Chastity Before Marriage' began in Nashville in 1992 and is now spreading world-wide. It is seen as a commitment to God and those wishing to become a part of it who are not virgins can re-commit themselves through prayer. As well as being in line with Christian teaching, its followers believe it is a way of helping to stop the spread of sexually-transmitted diseases. A ceremony has been introduced in which parents give children rings and children make vows which include:

Parent: Let this ring be a constant reminder to you to remain sexually pure.

Child: I make a commitment to you to be sexually pure from this day until marriage.

TRUE LOVE WAITS

Creative assignment

Imagine you are a Christian teenager and your boyfriend or girlfriend wants you to have sex. Write your reply to him or her in the form of a dialogue or letter.

Fact file 2

Some Christians choose to remain unmarried and refrain from sexual relationships on a permanent basis. This is known as **celibacy**. They remain chaste or pure because they believe that their calling to serve God requires them to do so. They feel they are better able to give their time and concentration to serving God without being distracted by sexual relationships. The apostle Paul was celibate and encouraged his followers to be the same. However, he accepted that this advice was not suitable for everyone. *'Now to the unmarried and the widows I say that it would be better for you to continue to live alone as I do. But if you cannot restrain your desires, go ahead and marry.' (1 Corinthians 7:8–9)*

Celibacy applies to those taking Holy Orders in the Roman Catholic Church. In other Churches, there is no such obligation and it is thought by many that being married helps a minister to have a better understanding of family problems.

Anyone can choose to be celibate and some Christians from both the Anglican and Roman Catholic Churches who take on the vows of celibacy are those who choose to leave their homes and take up a communal way of life. They will belong to a religious order of sisterhood or brotherhood and give their lives to God, either in prayer and devotion or in serving the community.

A nun gives her views on celibacy:

'I am aware that I have sacrificed the chance to have children, but I don't regret my vow of chastity.'

'Of course I am curious about sex and do sometimes imagine what it would be like with particular men I know. But for a Catholic, a sexual relationship binds you inextricably to that one person. As a Dominican sister I have committed myself to being there for everybody, for the rest of my life.'

Recall, explain and evaluate

1 What is the difference between celibacy and cohabitation? **(4)**

2 Explain why many priests decide to take a vow of celibacy. **(2)**

3 Do you think there is any point in having 'Chastity Before Marriage' ceremonies? In your answer you should consider more than one point of view. **(4)**

Family planning

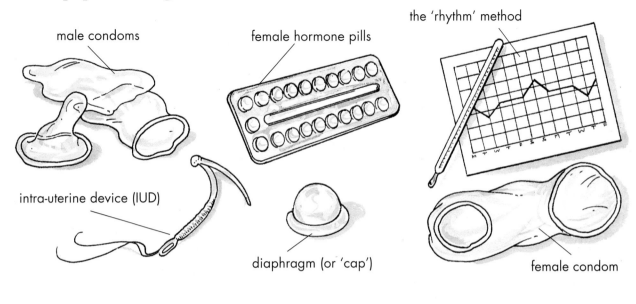

male condoms

female hormone pills

the 'rhythm' method

intra-uterine device (IUD)

diaphragm (or 'cap')

female condom

Fact file

There are differing views on family planning within Christianity. The majority of groups, including the Church of England and Methodists, agree with contraception providing that the methods used are acceptable to both partners. Although Bible teaching states that God said, *'Have many children' (Genesis 1:27),* a modern viewpoint is that this applied to a time when the population was small. In today's world where there is overcrowding and poverty, many Christians consider it is unfair to bring children into a life of deprivation. They believe that in family life, quality is more important than quantity. Methodists are among those who believe that responsible contraception helps a marriage by allowing more opportunity for relationships to develop.

The Roman Catholic Church believes that, in keeping with the natural law, the sexual act should reflect the total self-giving of two people in love, through marriage. When making decisions about a family, couples are encouraged to use the natural 'rhythm' method, when sexual intercourse only takes place during the infertile periods of a woman's cycle.

 Get talking

● Which of the methods of contraception in the illustration above do you think are considered to be natural forms of birth control?

 Recall and explain

1 Define the following words: contraception, natural law, love and lust? **(4)**

2 Explain why there are different views amongst Christians about the use of contraceptives. **(6)**

Homosexuality

Note: A bigot is someone who is intolerant of others.

 Get talking

- **What other kinds of bigotry have you come across in people's attitudes and actions?**

There is a growing willingness among many Churches to accept same-sex relationships.

Special friendships may develop into longer-lasting partnerships; the sharing and commitment helping to deepen the loving, joyful relationship … love is … the acceptance of all aspects of our nature, including … our sexuality. (The Recognition of Same-Sex Relationships, The Religious Society of Friends (Quakers))

Some Churches still teach that the expression of same-sex relationships with physical acts is wrong.

Whilst the Church sees a homosexual orientation as not being a sin, it does point out the difficulties which can arise. It reaffirms its teaching that to seek to express such an orientation in particular acts is always wrong. (The Roman Catholic Church)

Fact file

The few specific references in the Bible to homosexuality and lesbianism condemn it as being displeasing to God. '*No man is to have sexual relations with another man; God hates that.*' (Leviticus 18:22)

There is no direct teaching from Jesus about homosexuality in the Gospels. Some Christians are against homosexuality and lesbianism, believing that it is against the natural order created and intended by God. St Paul said: '*Even the women pervert the natural use of their sex by unnatural acts. In the same way the men give up natural sexual relations with women and burn with passions for each other.*' (Romans 1:26–7)

Other Christians believe that there can be stable same-sex relationships based on love and commitment but that promiscuity in all relationships should still be condemned. They believe that all people are equal in God's sight and should be shown love and compassion whatever their sexual orientation.

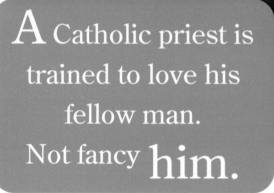

> # A Catholic priest is trained to love his fellow man. Not fancy **him.**

The film *Priest* tells the story of a priest and his inner conflict about his homosexuality

Changes in attitudes, which have led to an increasing number of gay people 'coming out' (announcing their homosexuality or lesbianism publicly), have encouraged some clergy to become open about their own sexuality. Many Churches now accept homosexual orientation among their clergy but believe that they should abstain from physical acts.

The 1991 Church of England report, 'Issues in Sexuality' states:

'God has endowed them with spiritual gifts, as he has other ministers, and we give thanks for all alike.'

Outrage

Outrage is a gay pressure group which supports the view that people in positions of authority should be honest about their sexuality.

Recall, explain and evaluate

1 What is meant by the term 'relationship'? **(2)**

2 Why do Christians have different views towards homosexuality? **(4)**

3 'It makes no difference to me if my vicar is gay, heterosexual or lesbian, just so long as *I know*.' Do you think churchgoers have a right to know their vicar's sexuality? Give reasons for your answers. **(4)**

✚ *Marriage*

Marriage still children's goal

In a recent poll, 82 per cent of children interviewed thought that they would get married. Although the number of people getting married is on the decline in the UK, it is still the most popular option for a relationship.

A couple at a Pentecostal church have their engagement blessed by the pastor

 **Get talking**

● Do the findings of the poll match your own views?

● What would you consider the most important qualities of a marriage partner?

Fact file 1

Christianity has always valued the institution of marriage as a gift from God.

'But in the beginning, at the time of creation, God made them male and female, as the scripture says. And for this reason, a man will leave his father and mother and unite with his wife, and the two will become one.' (Mark 10:6–8)

Many Christians, even those who are not regular worshippers, wish to marry in church as they feel it is important to make their solemn promises or vows in God's house.

The Roman Catholic, Orthodox and Anglican Churches regard marriage as a sacrament which is an outward sign of an inward blessing from God (see page 14). Through this blessing each partner becomes the channel of God's love to the other. Couples marrying in a Church of England service are reminded of this when the priest says: *'God is love, and those who live in love live in union with God: and God lives in union with them'* (1 John 4:16). Through the sacrament the couple become 'as one flesh'.

Preparation

Getting married is one of the most important milestones in a person's life. Very few people enter marriage without some kind of preparation. Unfortunately, it is easy to be more concerned with preparations for the day itself rather than the lifetime that follows, and millions of pounds are spent each year on outfits, flowers, stationery and photographers.

Purpose

A simple summary of the meaning and purpose of Christian marriage:

Procreation – men and women were created to have children.

Union – a loving partnership of living together.

Rearing children – channel for nurture and security.

Pattern for society – family unit of mutual support.

One flesh – sexual intimacy as an expression of love.

Sacred – blessed by God.

Endless – lifelong faithful relationship.

Fact file 2

The Christian Church believes it is important for couples to be prepared for their lifelong commitment and many Churches expect couples to attend a course of instruction prior to the day. This will include an explanation of the service they will be taking part in. They will be advised and challenged to think seriously about their future roles and commitment. Subjects such as communication, money and coping with conflict will be covered. There will often be leaflets and videos to support this preparation. People who have not been divorced are generally entitled to marry in the Church of England church in the parish where one of the couple lives. It is not usually possible for it to be elsewhere unless one or other is a worshipper at a particular church. The wedding can only be legal if either a Common Licence or an Archbishop's Licence has been obtained or if **banns** are read. These are announcements of the couple's intention to marry and must be read out in church on three consecutive Sundays during the three months prior to the wedding. This must take place in the parish(es) of residence as well as the church where the marriage is to take place.

Recall and explain

1 What is the difference between a marriage and a wedding? **(4)**

2 How do you think preparation classes might help couples plan for their marriage? **(6)**

Promises! promises!

I, N, take you, N,
to be my [husband/wife]
to have and to hold
from this day forward;
for better, for worse,
for richer, for poorer,
in sickness and in health,
to love and to cherish,
till death us do part,
according to God's holy law;
and this is my solemn vow.

The vows made by those marrying in the
Anglican Church

Fact file 3

The marriage service varies in different branches of Christianity but the making of vows is common to them all. These are spoken aloud and state the couple's beliefs about the purpose of marriage and their intention to commit themselves to each other for life. The promises are reinforced by the giving, receiving or exchange of rings. The ring's circular shape, which has no end, symbolizes the never-ending aspect of the marriage. In Orthodox Churches a crown is placed over the heads of the bride and groom by the priest who blesses them.

 **Get talking**

- Which of the vows do you think would be hardest to keep?

 Creative assignment

Make up a set of vows that reflect your views on marriage and which you think would be suitable in a wedding ceremony for today.

ASTON VILLA FOOTBALL CLUB

Brighton Pavilion

What do these two have in common?

The answer is that they are among the hundreds of different places that have received licences to host a civil wedding service. In April 1994 the law was changed to allow any venue to apply for such a licence. The law states that the premises must be dignified and should not take anything away from the solemnity of the marriage. This ruling reflects the fact that today's society is more **secular** (non-religious) and that the church is not an appropriate place for everyone to marry. Although there is the alternative of the register office, many feel that this can be very impersonal. Some Christians, too, prefer a different venue and do not think that it necessarily makes the vows any less valid. The practice of Christian weddings taking place elsewhere, such as in the family home, is common in America.

Recall and evaluate

1 What does the word 'vow' mean? **(1)**

2 State two Christian wedding vows. **(2)**

3 'If you've made promises in a place of worship then you must stick to them.' Do you agree? In your answer you should consider more than one point of view. **(7)**

Bride and groom during their nightclub wedding service

A couple made marital history by being the first pair to wed in a British night-club which was followed by a twelve-hour extravaganza of installation art, alternative music and live performances. The couple exchanged vows using microphones. The bride wore a swirling hooped and hologrammed dress of love hearts, the groom a medieval outfit. The couple's mothers appeared on stage and the four sang vows written by the newlyweds. An altar was provided and the bride's mother, a reverend, gave a blessing. Despite the modern nature of the occasion, the bride said the couple's motives were entirely traditional. 'A wedding signifies, to me, romance and love and a belief in commitment to a relationship.'

Divorce

For Sale
only three careful owners

Broken promises

● The United Kingdom has one of the highest divorce rates in the developed world.

● In recent years divorces in the UK have doubled and around 50 per cent of all marriages will now end in divorce.

● Every week thousands of children are told that their parents are splitting up.

Get talking

● Who are affected by a couple's decision to divorce?

● What can be done to help those involved in the situation?

Many reasons are given to explain the break-down of marriages but one factor is that divorce has become accepted by society in a way that it was not a generation and more ago.

The **1971** Divorce Reform Act allowed that a court of law could grant a divorce on grounds of

5 years

The **1984** Matrimonial and Family Proceedings Act allowed divorce after one year of marriage.

1 year

adultery, cruelty, desertion by one partner for at least two years, or mutual agreement by both partners after a separation of two years. A five-year separation was required if one partner did not want a divorce.

In **1995** Lord Mackay introduced a White Paper removing the need to prove 'fault' in a marriage, but compelling couples to spend a year in mediation and encouraging them to negotiate their own settlements, thus greatly reducing the role of lawyers.

Fact file

When Jesus was asked about divorce he replied: *'I tell you, then, that any man who divorces his wife for any cause other than her unfaithfulness, commits adultery if he marries some other woman.' (Matthew 19:9)*

The vows made when a couple get married in a church reflect and reinforce the Christian belief that marriage is a commitment for life. *'No human being then must separate what God has joined together.' (Mark 10:9)*

Christian Churches are united in this belief, although most of them accept the sad fact that a partnership can irretrievably break down and that, in such cases, divorce should take place. They take the view that if a marriage becomes destructive, such as when there is abuse, it is not in the best interests of those involved for it to continue.

The Roman Catholic Church is an exception to this and, even if a state divorce is granted, it would still consider the couple to be 'one flesh' until one partner dies. In very rare cases a Roman Catholic marriage can be **annulled**, for example if it had not been consummated (no sexual intimacy having taken place) or if one partner had been forced into marrying against his or her will. It is only in these exceptional cases that remarriage is permitted. Other Churches can allow remarriage, although some clergy are reluctant to carry it out.

Family rites help stepchildren

A family wedding ceremony, becoming popular in America, is being promoted to help children accept a parent's remarriage. After the newlyweds exchange rings, their children from previous marriages join them for a special service on the 'family' nature of remarriage. Each child is given a medal with three inter-locking circles to represent family love.

Children's rites: a couple use the family wedding ceremony which involves children of previous marriages

Bride back at church 20 years on – for divorce

The minister who conducted the service at the United Reformed Church in Sheffield said, 'As Christina was married in church, she felt she needed to have the ending of the marriage marked in church, too It is the first service of its kind I have performed, but it seems to have worked well. Mrs Houston wrote her own liturgy which concentrated on remembering the good things which came from the marriage.'

 Recall and explain

1 To not commit adultery is one of the Ten Commandments. State a further two commandments. **(2)**

2 Describe the Roman Catholic attitude to divorce. **(3)**

3 Explain the role a Church might play if a couple are considering a divorce. **(5)**

Home and family

> •I find it sad that religion no longer seems to play such an important part in family life; certainly not as much as it did when I was a child in Jamaica ... one of the first things my parents taught me was respect. I learned to respect my elders; I learned to respect other people; I learned to respect other people's possessions.•
>
> Linford Christie

Christian Research Association Survey

- On average, fathers spend 25 minutes per week (3½ minutes per day) in genuine conversation with their child or children.
- On average, mothers spend 38 minutes per week (5½ minutes per day) in genuine conversation with their child or children.
- On average, children spend 21 hours per week watching television.

 **Get talking**

- Why do we need families?
- What have you learned from your parents and grandparents about family life when they were young?
- What do you think is meant by 'genuine conversation' referred to in the chart?

What makes a family?

The family, in spite of changing patterns and structures over recent years, is still thought to be the best means of rearing children and helping to maintain a stable society. The basic family unit of two parents with children is called a **nuclear family**. In the past families were larger, with grandparents and sometimes other relatives living with or near each other as an **extended family** (see page 108).

Changing social patterns of the family

- People often move away and are less likely to have such close ties with the older generation.
- The use of contraception has led to smaller families.
- High divorce rates have led to a large number of one-parent families.
- The majority of women work outside the home.
- The fear of unemployment puts pressure on breadwinners to work extra long hours which can affect family life.

Fact file

Christianity teaches that the family is God's plan for the protection and nurturing of human beings. There are several references in the Old Testament which were later developed by Jesus showing God as a loving and forgiving Father, providing Christians with an ideal. This is best shown in the story of the Lost Son. When his father saw him returning in shame after a life of wastefulness *'his heart was filled with pity, and he ran, threw his arms round his son, and kissed him.' (Luke 15:20)*

The fifth Commandment given to Moses says that children should respect their parents *(Exodus 20:12)*. This is reinforced in the New Testament which also teaches that parents should respect children. *'Parents do not treat your children in such a way as to make them angry. Instead, bring them up with Christian discipline and instruction.' (Ephesians 6:4)*

Jesus himself was born into a family and when he was dying on the cross he asked his mother and friend John to look after each other as mother and son.

The charity **Methodist Homes** is an example of a Christian organization which aims to provide a caring environment for elderly people who are no longer in their family homes. They offer a range of day and residential facilities and services which allow each individual to be cared for with dignity and respect.

 Creative assignment

Make a list of the positive things you both *give* to and *receive* from family life. Think of an imaginative way of showing these points, e.g. collage, graph.

Listen to your father; without him you would not exist and when your mother is old, show her your appreciation. (Proverbs 23:22)

The family of the Church

When Jesus was asked who were his mother and brothers, he indicated everyone around him. He was not rejecting his immediate family but showing that his followers were all part of the larger family. Christians today look upon their Church fellowship in a similar way and see it as a community which supports and nurtures family values and Christian ideals.

New members welcomed

Infant baptism

Just as a new child is welcomed into the world by its family, so is a Christian child welcomed into the family of the Church. This is usually done through **baptism** which often takes place as part of a main service so that everyone in the community shares the celebration and gives support. The **font** containing the water for baptism is often near the entrance to the church to symbolize the child entering the family of the Church. In Anglican and Roman Catholic churches, **godparents** or **sponsors** are chosen to witness the baptism and they agree to take on special responsibilities for the Christian upbringing of the child. This can provide a positive support to the parents. In Baptist and United Reform churches baptism does not take place until a person is old enough to make a personal decision to express their faith. However, birth is celebrated with a service of **dedication** when all the church members will join in the giving of thanks. In Orthodox churches, the sacrament of **Chrismation** takes place immediately after the baptism. The priest will anoint the child with holy ointment, making the sign of the cross, reciting the words, 'The seal of the gift of the Holy Spirit.'

A person can join the family of the Church at any time and many adults are baptized when they become Christians.

Full family membership

Confirmation

In the Anglican Church, when young people are old enough to confirm the decision made on their behalf as babies to join the Church family, they attend classes which teach them about the Christian faith. They then take part in a **confirmation** service where they will receive the Holy Spirit (see page 16) through the 'laying on of hands' by a bishop. From this time on they are able to take a full part in worship and receive Holy Communion. In the Roman Catholic Church, a similar period of instruction is given leading up to the taking of **First Communion**.

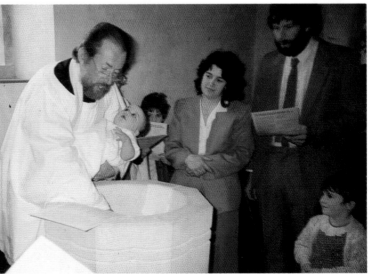

A new member is welcomed into the Christian family

Worship at home

For many Christians, it is part of family life to pray and read the Bible together. In Orthodox homes, there is often a shrine or corner set aside for worship where icons of saints are the focus of devotion. Christians who practice worship in the home, whatever their tradition, see it as a way of binding the family together and of nurturing the religious life of its member.

The Christian family in a secular society

Although worship in the home is still important, for some, society today is a largely secular (see page 33) one and many of the traditions which linked Christianity with the home have become less common. It is not many years ago that it was the practice in most households for family grace to be said before and after a meal, to thank God for the gift of food. Prayers at bedtime were as much a part of the routine as cleaning teeth. Sunday was a special day for being together and remembering God. Now that Sunday is not regarded in the same way by the nation as a whole, it can be difficult for Christians to keep to some of their traditions.

The pressures

- Shops opening seven days a week has made it difficult for Christian families to be together, as parents may be working.
- Sport and leisure opportunities are often considered to be a more exciting alternative to attending church and being with the family.
- Seeing non-Christian friends who are allowed freedom on Sunday can be difficult for Christian teenagers.
- Society is more permissive towards moral issues than many Christian parents would like. Young people are under pressure not to conform to what are often seen as old-fashioned ideals.

ON THE SEVENTH*
DAY THEY SHOPPED

*(N.B. Although the headline refers to the seventh day, for most Christians, Sunday is the *first* day of the week. The exception to this are the Seventh Day Adventists who observe Saturday as their day of worship.)

Recall and evaluate

1 How do Jesus' teachings and actions reflect the importance of the family in Christianity? **(5)**

2 Recently a vicar refused to baptize a baby because the parents did not normally attend church. Do you think this was right? Give reasons for your answer. **(5)**

The response

"Hold it, dear – I think the Vicar meant you to read it."

The Positive Parenting Pack is one of many resources to support Christian parents

Many Christian parents have accepted changes in society and adapted to them. They are often happier anyway with a less strict atmosphere towards Christian duty. They want their children to look upon Christianity as something to be enjoyed. Many Churches, too, are adapting to change and providing lively alternatives to traditional worship (see page 65). All Churches have support groups for families; for children this includes Sunday school and Youth groups, which are an important aspect of Christian nurture.

 Creative assignment

Design a leaflet for new members of a Christian Church, using relevant pictures and symbols.

Members of MAYC, part of their Church family

Members of MAYC (the Methodist Association of Youth Clubs) are given the opportunity to put the Christian values of caring for others into practice. Through the MAYC World Action Team they take up a major action focus each year. During one recent year their efforts were concentrated on homelessness. This project included:

● seeking advice from leading pressure groups
● intensive research on homelessness in members' own locality
● widely publicizing the results of their findings and raising public awareness
● taking part in an overnight 'sleep-out'.

'Treat the older women as mothers and the younger women as sisters, with all purity' *(1 Timothy 5:2)*

The following questions give you a chance to re-examine the issues raised in the preceding units. Remember to look at the number of marks for each question and to develop your answer accordingly.

a Name any *two* sources of moral authority a Christian might refer to before making a decision. **(2)**

b Describe the role the Church plays in supporting family life. **(6)**

c How might a Christian's behaviour be affected by their religious beliefs? In your answer you need to refer to *two* of the following: abortion, sex outside marriage, care of the elderly. **(7)**

d '"Love your neighbour as yourself " is not relevant in the twenty-first century – it's look after number one now.'

Do you agree? Give reasons for your answer, showing you have considered other points of view. **(5)**

Sexual discrimination

In recent years much has been done to highlight the fact that women have not been treated equally to men in society. Prejudice and discrimination (see page 58) on the grounds of gender is known as **sexism**. People who feel strongly about sexism against women are often called **feminists**. Feminism is a broad term which covers a range of beliefs and ways of regarding women's rights.

The Sex Discrimination Act passed in the UK in 1975 made it illegal for employers to discriminate on the grounds of gender.

Get talking

- What evidence have you come across of sexism against women?

- Are there jobs that you think are better done only by men or only by women?

Fact file

Christians believe that God created humanity, male and female in his own image. Although male characteristics are attached to God such as King and Father, in *Isaiah 66:12–13* it says, '*I will comfort you in Jerusalem, as a mother comforts her child*'. Jesus addressed God as Father, but he also taught: '*God is Spirit*'. (*John 4:24*)

Jesus lived in a male-dominated society and his twelve closest apostles were all men. However, he showed respect and regard for women. Two of his close friends were the sisters Martha and Mary and it was to their home that he escaped for refuge during the last days before his arrest. He showed compassion for a woman who had committed adultery, and openly criticized the men who were condemning her, for their hypocrisy. It was to women that he first appeared at the Resurrection. The apostle Paul later said, '*… there is no difference … between men and women; you are all one in union with Christ Jesus.*' (*Galatians 3:28*)

Throughout history women have played an important role in putting faith into action. Many have helped spread Christianity as missionaries, such as Gladys Aylward. Others have had great influence as social reformers, such as Florence Nightingale in nursing and Elizabeth Fry in prison reform.

Creative assignment

Design a panel for a stained glass window, tapestry or patchwork quilt which highlights the achievements of a Christian woman from the past or present.

Past …
Elizabeth Fry was a nineteenth century Quaker who showed great compassion for women in prison and successfully campaigned to improve conditions for them

Present …
Methodist women representatives at a UN Conference on Women in Beijing, China

The ordination of women

Dawn French, who played the title role in *The Vicar of Dibley*

Geraldine: Hello. I'm Geraldine. I believe you're expecting me.

Mr Horton: No, I'm expecting our new vicar. Unless of course you are the new vicar and they've landed us with a woman as some sort of joke!

Geraldine: *(Removes her coat to reveal her clerical dress.)* Oh dear!

Mr Horton: Oh my God!

Geraldine: You were expecting a bloke. Beard, Bible, bad breath and instead you get a babe with a bob-cut and a magnificent bosom.

(Enter Owen)

Mr Horton: Ah, Owen – this is Geraldine, she's the new vicar.

Owen: No she isn't – she's a woman.

Mr Horton: This is outrageous. I won't have my vicarage used like some laboratory animal to see if women vicars work. What is happening? Are we to have topless bathing on the rectory lawn during the summer … If Jesus wanted women to spread the Gospel he'd have appointed them. It's Matthew, Mark, Luke and John not Sharon, Tracy, Tara and Debbie. No, it won't do.

From the BBC comedy series *The Vicar of Dibley*.

Get talking

- Why do you think some people are against women becoming priests (ordination)?
- Do you think they are right?

Fact file

Women play an important role in the Christian Church. Although the majority of clergy are men, women are allowed to be ministers in many Churches including the Baptist, Methodist and United Reform Churches. They are not permitted to be priests in the Roman Catholic Church. For many years women in the Church of England have taken part in worship and administration as **readers** (people not ordained but with a license to conduct parts of the services) and **deacons** who assist with pastoral (caring) work, administration and helping conduct services. This has entitled them to perform baptisms and conduct weddings and funerals. However, until 11 November 1992 when the **Synod** (the Church of England Council) voted to ordain women as priests, they were not able to bless the bread and wine for Holy Communion, bless a congregation in God's name or absolve (pardon) people of their sins. The first **ordinations** in England took place in 1994. Both men and women Christians are divided about the decision that was made.

Woman's touch fills church's pews again

The arrival of women priests may be helping to stem the long-term decline in the numbers of people attending church. The Church of England's National Officer for Evangelism, Canon Robert Warren, says there is evidence that churches led by women priests are tending to attract new members – in contrast to many led by men, where congregations are static or in decline.

Since the ordination of women a number of Anglicans who disagree have become Roman Catholics.

A woman priest blesses the bread and wine at Communion

Forward in Faith was formed in 1992 following the Synod's decision to allow women to become priests. It believes that the ordination of women is against the historic teaching of the Church. The all-male priesthood goes back to the time of Jesus and this tradition should remain unbroken.

WATCH works for an inclusive church in which women take their place alongside men at every level. It also supports and monitors ordained and lay women as there are still those who do not agree with women being priests or taking leadership roles in the church. WATCH is campaigning for women to be consecrated as bishops.

Recall, explain and evaluate

1 State two ways in which women have been discriminated against. **(2)**

2 Explain the different attitudes held by Christians concerning the ordination of women. **(4)**

3 'If Jesus had wanted women to spread the Gospel he'd have appointed them.' Do you agree? Give reasons for your answers. **(4)**

✝ Work

The members of the three-girl group Destiny's Child are from Christian family backgrounds. When their lives as pop icons become pressurized and they feel isolated from normal life, they 'pull out their bibles and get that spiritual connection.'

According to Kelly, 'We have a big effect on people and we're introducing people to God that might not go to church and we reach people that may never read the Bible. That's very important to us.' They thank God for their success, saying, 'God is good … We are truly blessed.'

Get talking

- **Do you know what career you would like to take up when you leave school?**

- **What questions would you want to ask an employer?**

Some people are lucky enough to be in jobs or careers that are not only well paid but which are satisfying. Others would say that their work is a means to an end, to be endured rather than enjoyed. Even less fortunate are those who are not employed at all.

Church launches a fresh crusade over the jobless

David Sheppard, former Bishop of Liverpool, at the launch of a church inquiry into unemployment

Fact file

Jesus said: *'I have come in order that you might have life – life in all its fullness.'* (John 10:10)

Christians are taught that all life, whether at work or leisure, should be lived according to God's will. Work is considered to be positively good and not just a necessity. Christians believe that God has a purpose for each person. They think it is important for everyone to give great thought to choosing a career or job which best uses the talents and gifts which God has given them. Some kinds of work are called **vocations**. This comes from the Latin word **vocare**, meaning 'to call'. Christians often believe that they are called to follow a certain path, regardless of pay and working conditions. An example of this in the twentieth century was Mother Teresa who stood out as an example of a life dedicated to serving others.

Christians believe that work is every person's right and many leaders of Churches speak out against unemployment.

Morality in the workplace

Christians believe it is important to apply moral standards to work. This sometimes leads to challenges and decisions.

'MAKING A STAND FOR MY FAITH'

A CATHOLIC scientist has been sacked after he refused to analyse emissions from incinerators which might have been burning aborted babies.

Christianity teaches that workers should give of their best and not be lazy. Traditionally, hard work was seen as a duty and a virtue, particularly by Protestants, and so this attitude is often referred to as the '**Protestant work ethic**'. However, Christians also believe there should be time for leisure and rest. Many Christians are opposed to the changes in the law which now allows Sunday trading (see page 39). The campaign group, **Keep Sunday Special**, believes that no work should be done on Sundays, in keeping with the commandment: '*Observe the Sabbath and keep it holy. You have six days in which to do your work, but the seventh day is a day of rest dedicated to me.*' *(Exodus 20: 8–10)* (see page 39). The group is still active and concerned that even further changes might be made which interfere with people's essential time for recreation. These are their original REST principles showing the only acceptable activities on Sundays.

Recreation – becoming refreshed and revitalized.

Emergencies – visits to hospitals or sick relatives.

Social gatherings – cooking for family meals.

Travelling – visiting friends and relatives.

Speaking after collecting the award he said that he had always watched the BBC Sports Review of the Year since he was a boy, but the timing was unfortunate in that it clashed with church.

Jonathan Edwards, BBC Sports Personality of the Year, collecting his award.

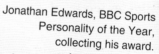

Recall, explain and evaluate

1 Give two examples of vocations. **(2)**

2 Explain why Sunday is a special day for many Christians. **(4)**

3 Jesus taught that money should be used responsibly. What do you think is meant in the advert above by 'Socially Responsible Investment'? **(4)**

Creative assignment

Make up a story in which a Christian is faced with a moral dilemma in the workplace. Show how he or she decides what to do. You could draw your story as a strip cartoon.

Wealth and poverty

The God letters

The Lord God says:
'Share your bread
with the hungry,
bring the homeless poor
into your house,
cover the naked.'

Dear Lord God
We have got
new carpets
so this will
not be possible.

(Steve Turner)

MARTHA AND I HAVEN'T CHANGED OUR BELIEF THAT CHRISTIANS SHOULD STICK TO THE NECESSITIES OF LIFE, WE JUST HAVE TO KEEP REDEFINING THE MEANING OF NECESSITY.

© Joel Kauffman

Get talking

- What do you consider are the necessities in life and what are luxuries?

- What material possessions would you find hardest to do without?

A material world

Britain is often described as being a materialistic society which values money and possessions more than things of deeper worth, such as justice and compassion. The word 'consumerism' has entered our language and millions of pounds are spent by advertisers persuading us to spend. The more we are caught up in such a culture the harder it can be to take on the challenge of making this a fair world.

Fact file 1

Christians believe that a person's value should be judged by their actions and not by money or possessions. Jesus taught that wealth encouraged greed and selfishness and did not lead to true happiness. A rich young ruler, wanting to follow Jesus, asked what he should do. When Jesus told him to sell his possessions and give the money to the poor the man was unable to do it and walked away sadly. Jesus told his onlookers: 'It is much harder for a rich person to enter the kingdom of God than for a camel to go through the eye of a needle.' (Luke 18:25)

The disciples of Jesus were encouraged not to carry possessions or money when travelling. After his death, they shared all that they had and sold what they did not need to feed the widows and poor. 'They would sell their property and possessions, and distribute the money among all, according to what each one needed.' (Acts 2:45)

Some young people find scratch cards hard to resist

'Other people are like the seeds sown among the thorn bushes. These are the ones who hear the message, but the worries about this life, the love for riches, and all the other kinds of desires crowd in and choke the message, and they don't bear fruit.' (Mark 4:18–19)

'Do not store up riches for yourselves here on earth, where moths and rust destroy, and robbers break in … Instead, store up riches for yourselves in Heaven … For your heart will always be where your riches are.' (Matthew 6:19–21)

A nation of gamblers?

Since its introduction in 1994 the National Lottery has been described by many as a 'national obsession'. Twice a week, millions of people will be found 'glued' to their television sets, waiting for the numbers to be drawn. All of them hope to win the jackpot, but the chance of this is only 14 million to 1. Other statistics reveal that the majority of people taking part are from the lower income range, they spend, on average, several pounds per week.

Recall and explain

1 What is meant by the term 'materialism'? **(1)**

2 Recall a story Jesus told about wealth. **(3)**

3 Explain what Jesus meant when he spoke of storing up riches in Heaven. **(2)**

4 How do you think Christians can store up riches in Heaven? **(4)**

Fact file 2

Many Christians are opposed to the National Lottery and some Churches have reacted strongly against it. Methodists, who have always spoken out on the dangers of gambling, are particularly concerned with the effect of the lottery on young people. They want to see stricter rules concerning the easy access to scratch cards and a limit of £500,000 on the lottery jackpot.

The Church of England is also concerned and is against receiving lottery money for its worship and pastoral work. The Churches as a whole believe that gambling can encourage greed and therefore goes against Christian teaching about the right attitude to wealth. They are aware that many charities are worse off since the introduction of the lottery, even though it is acknowledged that some have gained.

World poverty

 **Get talking**

There is a saying: 'Charity begins at home'.

- What are your views about this?
- Why are some people reluctant to give to charity for people in other countries?

In measuring the distribution of wealth, the world is usually divided into the **developed** and **developing** countries, often referred to as the First World and Third World. The developed countries, of which the UK is one, make up only 24 per cent of the world population but receive 83 per cent of the world's wealth. The poorest 20 per cent only receive 1 per cent of the wealth.

It is hard to grasp what statistics like these mean in real terms. Wealth is relative and there are many people living in difficult economic circumstances in Britain who would find it hard to believe that others would describe them as rich. Poverty has always existed but with modern means of communication we are made more aware of it through our televisions and newspapers. There is no single cause of Third World poverty; it can be the result of natural disasters, war, over-population and bad government. It cannot be denied that a large contributory factor is the greed of the rich countries. The unfairness of the situation has led many people to search their consciences.

The U2 song 'Where the streets have no name' was written after Bono's visit to Ethiopia.

I had no culture shock going to Ethiopia but I did coming back and I started to ask myself some real fundamental questions about the way I was living in the First World as opposed to the Third World. The people I left behind me had such a strong spirit and that really shone in my memory, whereas I came back to this big fat spoilt child of the West and I started to get confused, seeing our cities as wastelands. Even though we weren't physically impoverished I started to see that we're spiritually impoverished.

(Bono)

5,792,797,821

NOT ONE OF THEM IS FORGOTTEN BY GOD

Part of Tearfund's 'People Count' campaign to draw attention to the plight of the poor

Christian love in action

There are many responses to poverty from Christians, both on an individual basis and through groups such as Christian Aid, CAFOD and Tearfund.

Tearfund is a Christian organization which aims to lessen the suffering of people in need. It is active in over 80 countries, serving people of all races and religions. The areas of need it focuses upon are healthcare, water, agriculture, disaster relief, AIDS care and education. Christian pop star Cliff Richard has for many years been closely associated with its work, raising hundreds of thousands of pounds.

Tearfund believes that every person is special to God. Long-term projects help people to be independent and self-sufficient. It believes that in this way people are given dignity and self-respect.

Jesus said: '*I was hungry and you fed me, thirsty and you gave me a drink; I was a stranger and you received me in your homes, naked and you clothed me; I was sick and you took care of me ... Whenever you did this for one of the least important of these members of my family, you did it for me.*' (Matthew 25:35–40)

Creative assignment

Look up *Matthew 6:19–21* and using part or all of it (or one of the references used in this section) as the centre-piece, create a poster with words and symbols showing 'riches' that money cannot buy.

'You cannot serve both God and money'
(Mathew 6:24)

The Bank of England museum

 **Get talking**

● What do you learn from the words and photo above about attitudes to money.

Blessed are the
PEACEMAKERS

❛I love to queue at bureaus
To multiply my Euros,
Discarding the peseta and
the franc.
Oh keep me from the curse
of a very empty purse
My favourite place of worship
is the bank.❜

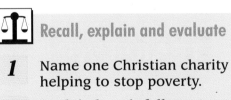

Christians all over the world see it as their duty to give to those in need. This is a collection envelope from a church in Sinapore

Fact file 3

It can be difficult for Christians in a materialistic society to live up to the ideals which Jesus set. The Christian Church is often criticized for not making a strong enough stand against poverty, and the wealth within some Churches is sometimes seen as a sharp contrast to the simple life led by the early Christians. *'Suppose there are brothers or sisters who need clothes and don't have enough to eat. What good is there in your saying to them, "God bless you! Keep warm and eat well!" if you don't give them the necessities of life? So it is with faith: if it is alone and includes no actions, then it is dead.' (James 2:15–17)*

Recall, explain and evaluate

1 Name one Christian charity helping to stop poverty. **(1)**

2 Explain how it follows Jesus' teaching on wealth and sharing. **(4)**

3 'If the Church cares so much about poverty, why doesn't it sell all its buildings and give the money to the poor?' Do you agree? Give reasons to show you have considered more than one point of view. **(5)**

The natural world

...WHEN WE'VE FINISHED WRECKING THIS ONE WE'LL JUST FIND ANOTHER!

WHOSE EARTH?

THE EARTH IS THE LORD'S PSALM 24:1

What is Green?

Concern for the environment has become a major issue in recent years and most people are aware that something is seriously wrong with the way the Earth is treated. We are often left feeling guilty about our lifestyle, knowing that so much of what we do causes damage. It can be tempting to ignore the threats and warnings in the belief that any contribution we make would be too small to have any effect. The problems are often difficult to understand because they are described in scientific jargon that we don't understand. Unless we are fishermen or farmers it is harder to be aware of the balance and rhythms of nature, when food comes from shops and warmth from the flick of a switch.

Get talking

- In what ways in our everyday modern living do we harm the environment?
- Which of these ways concerns you most?

Cracking the jargon!

Environment: the natural and social conditions of living.

Ecology: the study of life in relation to its environment.

Conservation: protection and care of natural resources.

Sustainability: ability to maintain life without damage to the

Biosphere: the Earth's surface and atmosphere.

Acid rain: rain that has a high concentration of pollutants.

Global warming: the effect on climate caused by the

Greenhouse effect: sunlight coming in, but the heat not escaping.

CFCs: (chlorofluorocarbons) used in aerosols, fridges etc.

Ozone layer: protective layer above the Earth, absorbing radiation.

Deforestation: stripping of trees from an area leading to

Soil erosion: removal of topsoil by wind and rain, upsetting the

Ecosystem: self-sufficient system in nature with cycle.

Fact file 1

Christians believe that the Earth and all of nature belong to God who created it. Humanity is part of that creation and has been given the role of **steward** or curator.

In the story of Adam and Eve in the book of Genesis it says that God provided a perfect environment for the first man and woman to use and enjoy. They were also given the responsibility of caring for it. *'Then the lord God placed the man in the Garden of Eden to cultivate it and guard it.' (Genesis 2:15)*

The story goes on to show how when they disobeyed God's instructions not to eat the fruit of the tree of knowledge, Adam and Eve were cast out of the garden. Christians often compare the story with what happens today when people abuse the resources given to them. The environment becomes spoiled and can no longer be enjoyed. The story serves as a reminder to Christians that it is their responsibility to care for the world.

Christian response

Much of the work done by Christian aid agencies such as Christian Aid, CAFOD and Tear Fund (see page 51) is concerned with drawing attention to the abuse of Creation. Working as they do in the poorest countries of the world, they see at first hand the human misery and destruction that results from the unjust way the Earth's resources are distributed.

Christian Aid
We believe in life before death

 CHRISTIAN ECOLOGY LINK

Christian Ecology Link

This was formed in 1998 and has support from many Churches. Its aim is to make people aware of the need to preserve the Earth's resources. It stimulates interest by running conferences and producing newsletters and publications.

Martyr for the environment

Chico Mendes was the founder of the Alliance of the People of the Forest. He was a Brazillian rubber tapper who taught that it is possible to generate income from the forest without destroying it. He introduced the idea of setting aside areas for collecting forest products such as rubber and Brazil nuts. He won fame and admiration around the world as leader of a non-violent campaign against deforestation by the cattle barons and plantation owners. He was murdered in 1988 at his home in front of his wife and family. His work still goes on (see page 67).

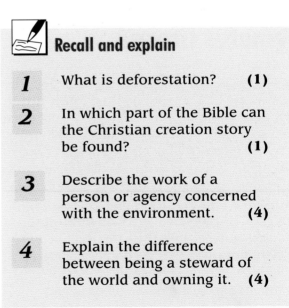

Recall and explain

1 What is deforestation? **(1)**

2 In which part of the Bible can the Christian creation story be found? **(1)**

3 Describe the work of a person or agency concerned with the environment. **(4)**

4 Explain the difference between being a steward of the world and owning it. **(4)**

Giving praise for the environment

Christians see creation as evidence that God's hand is at work in the continuous cycle and patterns of the seasons. They remind themselves of this in their weekly worship and at certain times throughout the year.

Supplication (asking through prayer)

The most important prayer that Christians use is the Lord's Prayer in which they show that their needs must not be taken for granted: *'Give us this day our daily bread'*.

There are certain days in the Church of England and Roman Catholic calendars which are called **Rogation days**. The word means supplication and it is the time for remembering that humans are dependent upon God's creation in their lives. Special prayers are used and some churches mark the Rogation with processions. In the past it was often a time for fasting.

… Bless all men in their daily work, and, as you have given us the knowledge to produce plenty, so give us the will to bring it within reach of all; through Jesus Christ our Lord.

(From a Rogation prayer, *The Alternative Service Book*)

Creed

Each week Christians reciting the Creed say: *'I believe in one God … Maker of heaven and earth and of all things visible and invisible'*.

Communion

At the Eucharist when bread and wine are taken, the minister says, *All things come from God'*.

Harvest

Each autumn Christians have a festival when they remember the abundance of Creation with a celebration of thanksgiving and praise for the good gifts of nature. Churches often use this time to remind themselves of those less fortunate by donating food or money. Americans have a similar celebration on Thanksgiving Day at the end of November.

Fasting

The period of Lent is the 40 days leading up to Easter when some Christians remember Jesus' temptations when he went without food. For them it is a time of fasting when Christians give up luxuries to remind themselves of the need to avoid greed. Many Churches have a Lenten Appeal when money saved from fasting is collected and distributed to hungry people.

Celebrating new life

At Easter, God's continuing involvement with humankind through the resurrection of Jesus is linked with spring, the season of renewal. Eggs are used as a reminder of the creation of new life.

Animals

'God said to Noah … I am now making my covenant with you … and with all living beings – all birds and all animals … as a sign of this everlasting covenant which I am making with you and with all living beings I am putting my bow in the clouds …
Whenever I cover the sky with clouds and the rainbow appears, I will remember my promise to you and all the animals …'
(Genesis 9:8–15)

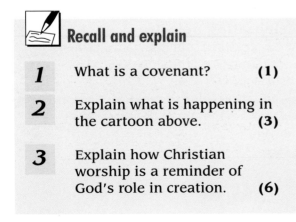

Recall and explain

1 What is a covenant? **(1)**

2 Explain what is happening in the cartoon above. **(3)**

3 Explain how Christian worship is a reminder of God's role in creation. **(6)**

Fact file 2

Animals are part of God's creation and Christians believe that the exploitation of them is against the will of God. Opinions are divided about how they should be treated. Although all Christians would agree that unnecessary cruelty goes against the belief in the sanctity of life, not everyone is against the use of animals for food or scientific experiment under humane conditions. Other Christians believe that animals should have the rights of humans and actively campaign to stop such things as experimentation, blood sport, fur trading and transportation of live animals.

Some Christians choose to be vegetarians in the belief that many methods used in meat production are inhumane and cruel. They are concerned, too, that one of the reasons for deforestation is to make room for cattle to be bred for meat and that the Earth's resources are being abused for gain and greed.

Most Christians are concerned to protect vanishing and endangered species and many have involved themselves in the creation of bird and animal sanctuaries. The sanctuary is the holiest part of many churches and is where people in the past would often go to escape danger.

The image of the caring, attitude towards animals is highlighted by Jesus' description of himself 'The Good Shepherd' *(John 10:11)*. Some priests and ministers are known as **pastors**, an old word for shepherd.

The words below were first used at a Harvest Festival celebration at Winchester Cathedral. They form a covenant (promise) made by Christians, to care for all living creatures.

Rainbow Covenant

Brothers and sisters in creation, we covenant this day with you and with all creation yet to be.

With every living creature and all that contains and sustains you.

With all that is on Earth and with the Earth itself.

With all that lives in the waters and with the waters themselves.

With all that flies in the skies and with the sky itself. We establish this covenant, that all our powers will be used to prevent your destruction.

We confess that it is our own kind who put you at risk of death.

We ask for your trust and as a symbol of our intention we mark our covenant with you by the rainbow.

This is the sign of the covenant between ourselves and every living thing that is found on Earth.

The Assisi Declarations

On 29 September 1986 Christian leaders joined leaders from the other five major world religions at the 25th anniversary of the World Wide Fund for Nature in Assisi to declare their promise for conservation. Assisi was chosen for this major event in honour of St Francis who lived there in the 13th century. He is sometimes referred to as the 'Green' saint for his preaching on conservation and for his love of all creatures, whom he describes as his 'brothers and sisters'.

Through the workings of his spirit, Christ's tree extends its roots to the whole cosmos … Only the sinful failure to abide in God's love and to live according to his wisdom can blind men and women to the harmonious beauty of all God's creatures …

Father Serrini

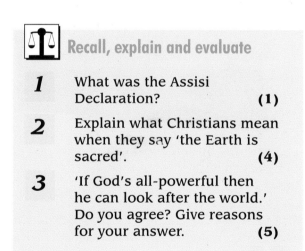

Recall, explain and evaluate

1 What was the Assisi Declaration? **(1)**

2 Explain what Christians mean when they say 'the Earth is sacred'. **(4)**

3 'If God's all-powerful then he can look after the world.' Do you agree? Give reasons for your answer. **(5)**

Creative assignment

Make up a playlet about a group of young people going out for a meal. The group should include two Christians, one of whom is a vegetarian.

Prejudice and discrimination

Stephen Lawrence's parents, at his funeral in 1993

On 22 April 1993, Stephen Lawrence was killed in a racist attack. Here is part of a testimony from three of his friends who are Christians.

'We cannot begin to express the feelings that we have experienced from that day onwards, both individually and as a group. The events of that day have affected all our lives. Things that were once so important now seem trivial in comparison. How can we concentrate on what would normally be the more important aspects of our lives, like education and exams, when one of our friends has just been murdered because of the colour of his skin ... Is it really only the few who commit the act of murder who are at fault? It is us who built the world we live in ... This is what we have done with God's free will.'

(From 'Colour Me Blind', a cassette tape made and sold by Stephen's friends, which gives the Christian view of racism. The proceeds go to raise money for poor people in South Africa.)

 Get talking

- In what way do Stephen's friends think it is everybody's fault?
- Do you agree with them?

One race – the human race

Prejudice means **pre-judgement**, taking a dislike to someone for no good reason. To take action as a result of it is known as **discrimination**. Prejudice can take many forms such as discrimination on the basis of sex, age or disability. To discriminate against people because of their race or colour is known as **racism**.

Britain is a multi-racial society with a wide diversity of ethnic groups. Many people in these groups find themselves on the receiving end of prejudice and discrimination.

Fact file

Christian Churches are against prejudice and discrimination based on the belief that everyone is created by God and equal in his sight. *'From one human being he created all races on Earth and made them live throughout the whole Earth.' (Acts 17:26)*

The many laws which Moses received from God gave guidance for people to live in harmony with each other and create a just society. *'Do not deprive foreigners and orphans of their right.' (Deuteronomy 24:17)*

Jesus' own example and teaching supported beliefs in equality, the best example being his parable of the Good Samaritan. The Samaritans were a mixed race and suffered much discrimination. Jesus chose one of them to be the hero of his story in order to show the true meaning of the word 'neighbour'. When the listeners were asked to identify the true neighbour, Jesus replied, *'You go then, and do the same.' (Luke 10:37)* The apostle Paul reinforced these views in his teaching to the early Christians: *'There is no longer any distinction between Gentiles and Jews … Christ is all, Christ is in all.' (Colossians 3:11)*

Trevor Huddleston – Campaigner for equality

Trevor Huddleston was born in Bedford, England in 1913. He became ordained as a Church of England priest and in 1943 was sent to work as a parish priest in Sophiatown, near Johannesburg, South Africa. He lived in a black township and was appalled by the **apartheid** system which was a total separation of white and black people. He saw it as contrary to the will of God and the teaching of Jesus to love one's neighbour as oneself. He became President of the Anti-Apartheid Movement and campaigned for non-violent protest, urging other countries to boycott cultural and sporting links with South Africa until apartheid came to an end. He died in 1998.

Bishop Trevor Huddleston on the day of the first South African elections after the end of apartheid

Recall and explain

1	What was the apartheid system in South Africa?	**(2)**
2	Who do you think Jesus meant when he used the word 'neighbour'?	**(2)**
3	Why are people prejudiced? You should refer to three reasons.	**(6)**

Christian responses to discrimination

In the past ...

One of the leading examples of a person who campaigned against racial discrimination was Martin Luther King. For over ten years he led the black people of America in their struggle for civil rights. He was a pacifist and used non-violent means of protest following the teaching of Jesus about non-retaliation.

'Bless those who curse you, and pray for those who ill-treat you.' (Luke 6:28)

He was assassinated on 4 April 1964 at the age of 39.

In the present ...

Today the Churches are responding in a variety of ways, both jointly and individually, to combat discrimination.

- The Church of England's Race and Community Relations Committee addresses such issues as the operation of nationality and immigration laws, the position of black and Asian people in the prison system and unemployment among black and Asian people.

- CARJ (the Catholic Association for Racial Justice) actively campaigns against racism.

Asian bishop warns of divided society

Dr Nazir Ali, Bishop of Rochester, Britain's first Asian bishop. He is known for his strong views on justice and equality.

Recall and evaluate

1 Describe how one Christian has campaigned against racism. **(5)**

2 'Racism will only stop when racists are put into prison.' Do you agree? In your answer show that you have considered more than one point of view. **(5)**

Archbishop Desmond Tutu

"I am puzzled about which Bible people are reading when they suggest religion and politics don't mix."

Archbishop Desmond Tutu was born in Klerkdorp, near Johannesburg on 7 October 1931. He grew up with first-hand experience of apartheid and it led him to decide that the best way in which he could serve his people was to become a priest. He rose to prominence and was constantly active in highlighting the evils of injustice. During the bitter struggles it was his Christian belief in justice and equality which drove him.

In his sermons and speeches he used examples from the Bible to show that God was against the unfair way leaders and governments treated the people. He pointed out that God showed he was on the side of the oppressed when he rescued the slaves from Egypt and that the Old Testament prophets spoke out against injustice. He was criticized by the South African government for meddling with politics but he refused to keep quiet, saying that apartheid was against the teachings of Christianity.

"If it were not for faith, I am certain lots of us would have been hate-filled and bitter … But to speak of God, you must speak of your neighbour … He does not tolerate a relationship with himself that excludes your neighbour."

He campaigned in his own country and travelled abroad to persuade other governments to become involved in the struggle for equality. As a result, his passport was taken away on several occasions. He chose to use non-violent means of persuasion, including protest marches and collecting petitions. Prayer has always been important to him, and a source of strength.

"Usually I get up at 4 a.m. It's quiet and peaceful at that time, which I need to collect myself. It's a time when I try to engage with God. It's meditation. I try to centre my self on God so that he influences the rest of the day."

In 1984 Archbishop Desmond Tutu was awarded the Nobel Peace Prize for his work.

He played a major part in bringing Apartheid to an end and on Election Day, 27 April 1994, he introduced the new democratically-elected president Mandela. He said, 'We of many cultures and races are become one nation. We are the Rainbow People of God.'

Since retiring as an archbishop, he has continued to be active in bringing about justice and reconciliation.

Creative assignment

Either write a poem about prejudice

Or write a paragraph suitable to go in the school prospectus for parents and new pupils entitled 'Racial equality at our school – what we believe and why'.

Liberation theology

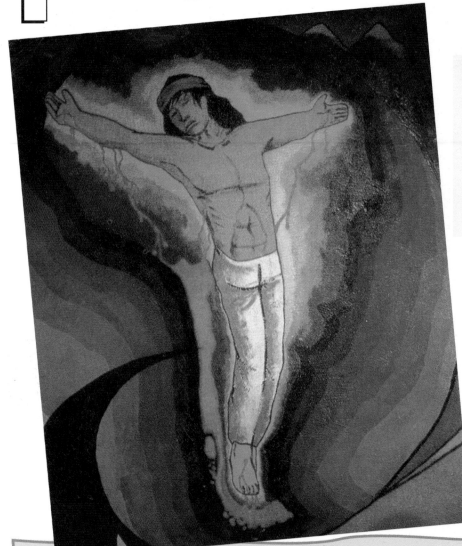

'Jesus the Freedom Fighter'

 **Get talking**

- In what way is the picture different from other pictures of Jesus you have seen?

- What sort of freedoms do people 'fight' for?

Fact file 1

Liberation theology is an expression of Christian faith in which followers believe that the teaching of Jesus requires action against the misuse of power and social injustice. Jesus is often depicted as a freedom fighter, as shown in the picture. *'He has sent me to proclaim liberty to the captives … to set free the oppressed.'* (Luke 4:18)

It is not a separate Church but a movement from within it. Its followers are found in both Protestant and Roman Catholic Churches mainly in Latin America, but also in Asia and South Africa.

Latin America has a big division between the rich and the poor. Many priests live among the poor, concentrating their work on giving practical as well as spiritual help. In countries where there is corrupt power, oppression and violation of human rights, many Christian leaders have suffered torture, imprisonment and death in the fight for freedom.

Oscar Romero

Let my blood be a seed of freedom, and a sign that hope will soon be a reality ...

Oscar Romero was born in 1917 and became Archbishop of El Salvador in 1977. He was a quiet man of prayer when he took up his post and his meekness encouraged the authorities to take advantage and step up their reign of terror against the Church. Priests were tortured and murdered and it was when he witnessed at first hand the murder of one particular priest that he began to change his thinking. From then on he gave up the idea of seeing his role as being on the side of the law. When public meetings were forbidden, he disobeyed and organized public demonstrations to protest against the wrongs that were taking place.

He encouraged new ways of worship (**liturgy**) to suit the needs of the oppressed people, giving them a means of expressing their feelings to God about the situation they were in. This drew a large response, which brought great risks both to himself and to his followers. Houses were searched and if a Bible was found the owners were beaten and tortured.

He had come to believe that it was not only wrong to ill-treat the poor but, as a Christian, it was equally wrong to keep silent. His inspiration came from the example of Jesus who had also bravely stood up for those who were being wronged. He knew, too, that this had cost Jesus his life. When asked if he himself was afraid of death, he said that his Christian belief in the Resurrection gave him courage to face it. He believed that if his death helped to bring justice nearer and make others brave, then it would not be in vain. *If I am killed, I will rise again in the people of El Salvador.*

In what was to be his last sermon, he directed his words to soldiers who had carried out an evil attack upon defenceless women and their families. He spoke to them about listening to their consciences and told them that even if they were commanded to do evil things, they should refuse to obey. Only the law of God to treat others as neighbours, should be followed.

Archbishop Romero was shot dead on 24 March 1980 as he celebrated Mass in a small hospital chapel. He is greatly revered by the people of Latin America as a great martyr who gave his life in the cause of freedom and justice.

Members of a church in Salvador designed this cross in memory of primary school teacher Maria Cristina Gomez who was tortured and murdered in 1989 for her leadership in the struggle for justice

Creative assignment

Using the symbol of the cross, together with modern images, design a poster or collage about justice or freedom.

Changing worship

Bar chart (millions) showing 1980 and 2000 attendance:

Denomination	1980	2000
Anglican	1·0	0·8
Roman Catholic	1·7	0·95
Baptist	0·25	0·2
Methodist	0·45	0·3

0 0·2 0·4 0·6 0·8 1·0 1·2 1·4 1·6 1·8 millions

1980

2000

How do you feel about attending church?

Bar chart of statements:

- Family wouldn't approve — 2.5%
- Too modern and trendy — 7.5%
- No desire to return — 12.5%
- Too old fashioned — 17.5%
- Work gets in the way — 17.5%
- Too dull and boring — 22.5%
- Not relevant to everyday life — 27.5%
- Sometimes wish I could go back — 35%
- Life is too busy — 37.5%

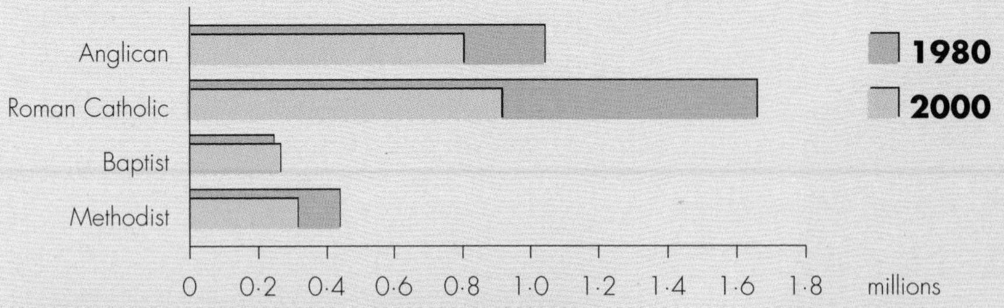

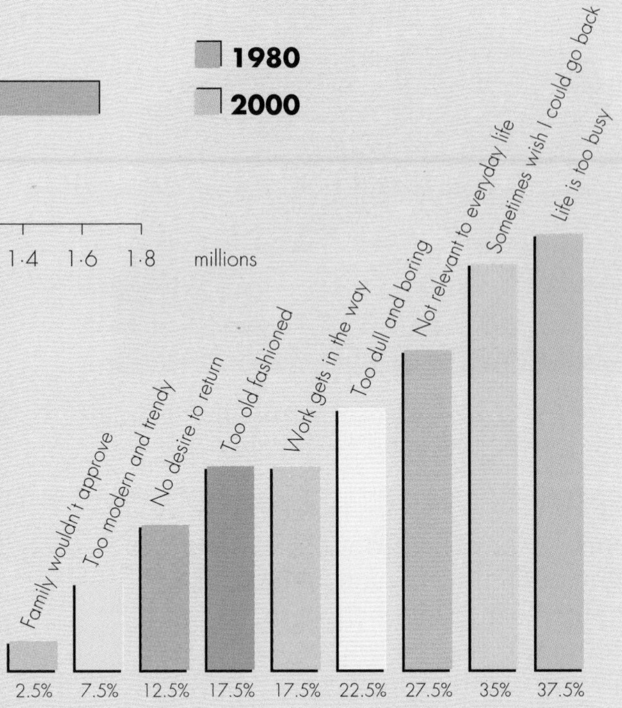

Note: those interviewed could select more than one statement.

Brand awareness

The giant M symbol of McDonalds' and the Shell symbol are more widely known than the Christian cross, global research for the International Olympic Committee has found.

Get talking

- What are your views about church services?
- How have your views been formed?

Downward trend

There has been a sharp decrease in church attendance in the Anglican, Methodist and Roman Catholic churches over recent years. In the period from 1980–2000, numbers dropped, as shown in the graph above.

Fact file

The very last instruction Jesus gave to his disciples was to spread the word. *'Go, then, to all peoples everywhere and make them my disciples: baptize them in the name of the Father, the Son and the Holy Spirit.'* (Matthew 28:19)

The word disciple means a follower of a teacher. Jesus had twelve special disciples who became his followers and whom he prepared and trained to continue his work. They were also known as **apostles** meaning messengers or those who are sent out to preach. Another translation of this is **evangelists**. The evangelical Churches today take their name from this and they see it as their mission as Christians to try to draw people into the Church. Many who come to Christianity this way undergo a conversion where they testify to the power of the Holy Spirit coming into their lives. They are sometimes called **born-again Christians**.

How is the church adapting?

St Gargoyle's

Miss Jones tried to enliven the litany* with a Mexican wave

*A form of prayer.

Churches are finding a number of ways to bring fresh and modern approaches to their styles of worship.

Soul Survivor

This is one of the many responses to young people leaving the Church. It compromises a festival of worship and music in contemporary style, aimed particularly at teenagers. Soul Survivor has attracted a wide following and its pattern of worship has provided an inspiration for youth services, which now take place in many Anglican churches around the country.

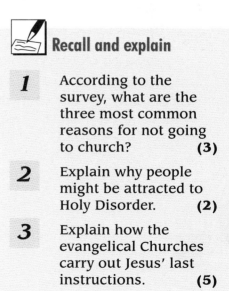

Recall and explain

1 According to the survey, what are the three most common reasons for not going to church? **(3)**

2 Explain why people might be attracted to Holy Disorder. **(2)**

3 Explain how the evangelical Churches carry out Jesus' last instructions. **(5)**

Church planting

HMM... I WONDER... ARE WE GETTING A LITTLE CARRIED AWAY WITH PEOPLE GROUP CHURCH PLANTING, FIONA?...

Upward trend

Despite an overall decline in churchgoing, some churches, such as the Baptists and Pentecostals, are seeing an increase in membership. Many new churches are springing up, mainly in smaller groups, often referred to as **House Churches**.

Church planting is the term used to describe the setting up of Churches that relate to the communities and cultures that they serve. Key figures in this movement see it as their role to reach out and meet the needs of different ethnic groups and economic classes of all kinds. They believe that Jesus came into a particular culture and time and related to it. The aim of Church planting is to do the same.

Alpha

One way in which people come to know about and become members of churches is through a popular fifteen-part introduction to Christianity called **The Alpha Course**. This movement, founded and based at Holy Trinity, Brompton in London, has spread throughout many countries of the world. Groups of volunteer Christians are trained to run the courses, which are held in homes and halls.

In addition to instruction, food is shared and those attending are able to relax in an informal atmosphere that aims to make them feel welcome and at ease.

Creative assignment

Write an assembly, on a moral topic, which is aimed at appealing to teenagers today.

✝ *Re-examine*

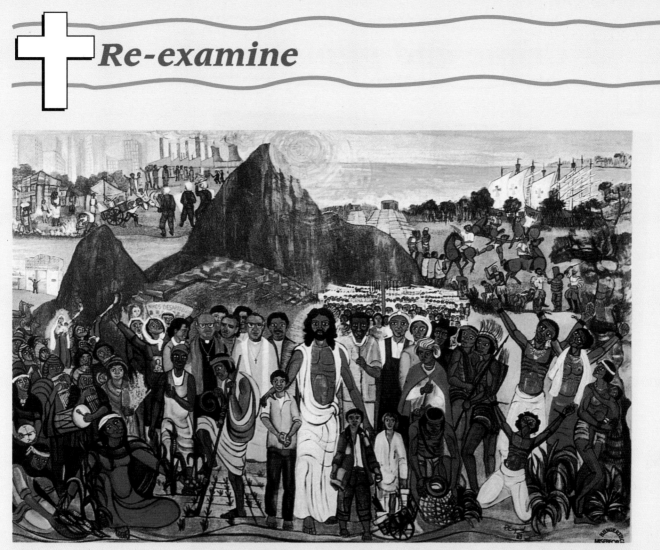

This lenten cloth, which Christians reflect upon during Lent, portrays representatives of the Latin American people and their Church. The risen Christ is in the middle surrounded by street children, bishops, farm labourers, nuns, women and children and martyrs such as Bishop Romero and Chico Mendes. The background depicts some examples of human rights abuses

The following questions give you a chance to re-examine the issues raised in the preceding units. Remember to look at the number of marks for each question and to develop your answer accordingly.

a What is the difference between absolute and relative morality? **(2)**

b Describe Jesus' teachings concerning responsibility towards humankind or the environment. **(6)**

c Explain how *two* of the people in the lenten cloth have put these teachings into practice. **(7)**

d 'I think religious people spend their time in prayer and worship – not in speaking out against social injustices.'

Do you agree? You need to refer to a range of references in support of your argument. **(5)**

Crime and punishment

The Bible is read to a prisoner on Death Row

 **Get talking**

● What kinds of crime do you see reported most often in newspapers and on television?

● What useful role do you think a Church leader can play by visiting prisoners?

starts with small offences which, if allowed to go unpunished, become habit-forming. There is no one answer as to why some people turn to crime. Factors such as poverty and unemployment are thought by many to play a part. Another reason put forward is that there is not enough moral education given to young people, or a high enough standard set for them to follow.

What is wrong?

A **crime** is an action considered to be wrong and punishable by law. A **sin** is an act of disobedience which goes against the will of God.

People commit wrongs for a variety of reasons. It is generally accepted that crime

Prisoners of conscience

Some people are imprisoned not for crimes they have committed but because they are victims of a government or system that denies freedom of belief or expression (see pages 62 and 79).

Reasons for punishment

- **Protection:** society needs to be protected from criminals.
- **Retribution:** many people believe that victims have the right to make criminals pay for the harm they have done.
- **Deterrence:** it is hoped that if people are punished they will think twice about repeating their crime. It might also deter others from following the same path.
- **Reparation:** it is thought that criminals should have the right to pay for what they have done so that they can have a 'clean slate' and be cleared from guilt.
- **Reform:** punishment should be positive and constructive so that criminals have the opportunity of learning to change for the better and making a useful contribution to society.

Forms of punishment

For less serious crimes offenders may be given community service, suspended sentences or fines. More serious crimes are usually punished by imprisonment.

Capital punishment

Although the death penalty can be legally carried out in some countries it was abolished in Britain in 1970. There are still many people, Christians among them, who believe that it should be brought back for the most serious cases of premeditated murder, such as terrorism. All Christians believe that all human life is sacred and only God can give and take life (see page 19). Their view is that everyone should have the chance to repent and make a fresh start.

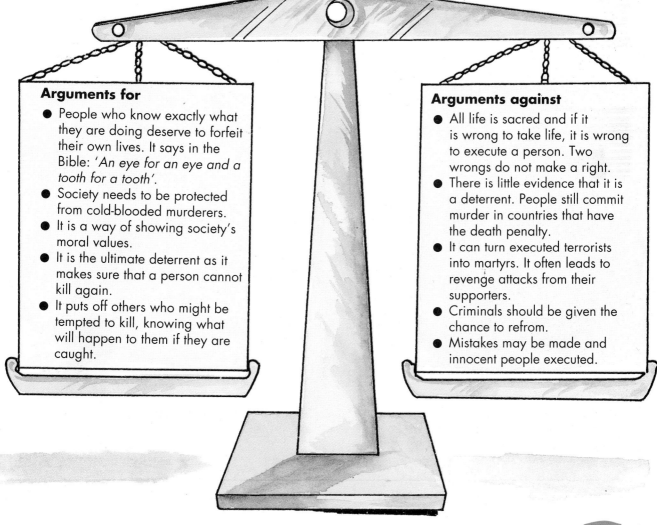

Arguments for
- People who know exactly what they are doing deserve to forfeit their own lives. It says in the Bible: 'An eye for an eye and a tooth for a tooth'.
- Society needs to be protected from cold-blooded murderers.
- It is a way of showing society's moral values.
- It is the ultimate deterrent as it makes sure that a person cannot kill again.
- It puts off others who might be tempted to kill, knowing what will happen to them if they are caught.

Arguments against
- All life is sacred and if it is wrong to take life, it is wrong to execute a person. Two wrongs do not make a right.
- There is little evidence that it is a deterrent. People still commit murder in countries that have the death penalty.
- It can turn executed terrorists into martyrs. It often leads to revenge attacks from their supporters.
- Criminals should be given the chance to refrom.
- Mistakes may be made and innocent people executed.

Some of Jesus' sayings about attitudes to crime and punishment!

'Why then do you look at the speck in your brother's eye, and pay no attention to the log in your own?' (Matthew 7:3)

'If someone slaps you on the right cheek let him slap your left cheek too.' (Matthew 5:39)

'Whichever one of you has committed no sin may throw the first stone at her.' (John 8:7)

Get talking

- **What is gained**
  - a) **by a person who forgives,**
  - b) **by a person who is forgiven?**

Fact file

Jesus was more concerned with people's inward honesty and morality than with outward shows of being good. He taught that, although keeping the law was important, it was what people were like inside that mattered. He said that criminal thoughts were as wrong as the deeds themselves. He was very critical of those who were quick to judge others' crimes while ignoring their own.

'Do not judge others, so that God will not judge you, for God will judge you in the same way as you judge others.' (Matthew 7:1)

Jesus was often criticized for mixing with people who were thought of as sinners, such as cheats and prostitutes. He took the view that it was important to God that people changed their ways and that he had come to help them do this. *'I have not come to call respectable people, but outcasts.'* (Mark 2:17)

Christian views on crime and punishment are greatly influenced by Jesus' teaching about forgiveness. Jesus told several stories to show that God not only forgave sinners but that he was happy when a person was reconciled to him. In one story Jesus told of a caring shepherd who had a hundred sheep but who did not rest until the missing one was found *(Luke 15:4–7)*. He compared the joy of the shepherd with the joy in heaven over one sinner who repents.

Jesus also showed what he expected people to do by his own example. When he was dying on the cross he asked God to forgive his murderers.

Reformers

Throughout history there have been people who have followed Jesus' teaching that people are worth helping, *whatever* they have done wrong. The work of such people has had far-reaching effects on society. Many of the reforms that have been made to the prison system were carried out by Christians such as Elizabeth Fry (see page 43), and the founders of the Howard League for Penal Reform..

The Salvation Army has always concerned itself with social justice and reform. It has provided support for such groups as prostitutes, alcoholics and ex-prisoners. Homelessness can sometimes lead to crime and the Salvation Army plays an important part in helping to prevent this by providing hostel accommodation which is offered in a non-judgemental way to any who seek it. It also helps to overcome homelessness in its work of locating missing persons. It helps re-unite people with their families if this is requested.

Forgiveness

Jill Saward was the victim of rape attack when she was violently assaulted in her vicarage home. Here are some of her words about her attackers.

❛*All I can do is go on praying that they will be healed, not just physically, but from all the things in the past that have led them to act in the way that they did … I had a dream back in the summer that I was asked to help with the rehabilitation of one of them. My first reaction was, 'No, I couldn't handle it.' but when I was thinking about it afterwards I realized that they could repent and turn round …*

Creative assignment

Write down the thoughts of a teenager who has done something wrong. You can write it as a diary entry, a prayer or a poem.

All this has taught me in a special way that no one is beyond the scope of God's love.❜

Lord Longford is a Christian who, because of his many years of campaigning for the release of Moors murderer Myra Hindley, was asked if he would be visiting the murderer Rosemary West. He replied, ❛*I'll go if I am asked and I imagine Rose West knows that by now. No one is irredeemable. You must hate the sin and love the sinner.*❜

Rosemary West

Penitence

Christians are taught that being sorry for their sins and asking for God's forgiveness are an important part of life. In reciting the Lord's Prayer they say: '*Forgive us our sins as we forgive those who sin against us*'. Admitting sin and asking God's forgiveness through prayers of confession are also part of many Churches services, including the Eucharist.

Recall, explain and evaluate

1   State any two of the commandments connected with crime. **(2)**

2   Explain the Christian attitude to forgiveness. **(2)**

3   How do you think Jill Saward's faith has helped her? **(2)**

4   'If we are to reduce crime then capital punishment must be reintroduced.' Do you agree? In your answer refer to other points of view. **(4)**

Conflict and peace

Headteacher Philip Lawrence was stabbed to death outside his school when dealing with a conflict involving pupils.

•*Violence is not a knife in the hand. It grows, like a poison tree, inside people who, unlike yourselves, have not learned to value other human beings.*•

(Frances Lawrence, widow of Philip Lawrence, to the pupils of his school.)

Relationships

Conflict exists at every level in life. We meet it from an early age in our personal and family relationships as well as in the wider world. Jesus taught that love was the basis for all human relationships and he was clear about how we should treat each other. There is no perfect translation in English for **'agape'** (the Greek word that is used to describe Christian love) but it involves regarding others as being formed in the image of God and treating them as one would want to be treated oneself.

Get talking

● What are the things that cause conflict among

a) friends and **b)** families? How are they usually solved?

Fact file 1

From what Jesus said and did it is clear that he did not believe in retaliation as a means of solving problems.

'Love your enemies and pray for those who persecute you.' (Matthew 5:44)

Although Jesus was not afraid of speaking out strongly against the wrongs of his day, it appears he adopted a non-violent approach. This can be seen even in times of extreme distress, such as during his arrest in the Garden of Gethsemane when he stopped his disciples from using force to defend him *(Matthew 26:51–52)*.

The only known occasion when he reacted violently was when he overthrew the money tables of merchants who had turned the holy Temple into a market place *(Matthew 21:12–13)*. Christians believe that this is an example of 'righteous anger', which is sometimes necessary in order to put something right. It is seen as different from letting personal anger or annoyance lead to loss of self-control which hurts others. At times of great conflict in his life Jesus used prayer to help him. Christians often follow this example.

War

Old testament God is depicted as both warrior and defender of his people:

'The Lord is a warrior; the Lord is his name.' (Exodus 15:3)

'He keeps your borders safe and satisfies you with the finest wheat.' (Psalm 147:14)

New Testament When Jesus came he taught:

Do not take revenge on someone who wrongs you. If anyone slaps you on the right cheek, let him slap your left cheek too. (Matthew 5:39)

1st century During its early years Christianity followed this teaching and rejected the idea of war.

IN THIS SIGN CONQUER

4th century In 312 CE, the Roman Emperor Constantine converted to Christianity and had a vision of the cross as a military symbol.

11th century Expeditions known as the **Crusades** took place to reclaim the Holy Land from the Muslims.

As time went on wars were fought for supposed religious ends (**Holy Wars**) with heretics and infidels (unbelievers) as the victims.

SO THAT'S WHAT CHRISTIANITY IS ABOUT

13th century Thomas Aquinas drew up the Just War principle, stating these conditions for war:

- It must be started by a properly constituted authority.
- There must be a good (just) cause and right intention.
- It must be the last resort.
- No more force than necessary should be used and civilians should be protected.

IN THE NAME OF THE LORD I DECLARE WAR TO ROOT OUT ALL EVIL

SHOULDN'T I TURN THE OTHER CHEEK?

DIDN'T JESUS LOVE HIS ENEMIES?

BUT WHAT ABOUT 'THOU SHALT NOT KILL'?

20th century Christians from all Churches are opposed to war, although many support it as a last resort in defence of their own or another's country against the attack of an aggressor, and only after all non-violent means of solving the conflict have failed. They believe this is in line with Christian teaching on loving one's neighbour and laying down a life for a friend (*John 15:13*). Others, including the Religious Society of Friends (Quakers) are totally against war under any circumstances.

Recall, explain and evaluate

1. What is the Just War principle? **(4)**

2. Explain why Christians sometimes feel it is necessary to fight. **(6)**

Nuclear warfare

With modern chemical and nuclear warfare, it is impossible to limit the damage to civilians. This has led many Christians to believe that there can be no such thing as a just war. Others believe that nuclear weapons are justified as a deterrent.

Bruce Kent

Bruce Kent, a Catholic, gave up his priesthood to concentrate on working for The Campaign for Nuclear Disarmament (CND). He believed that it was against Christian teaching on the sanctity of life either to use, or threaten to use, weapons of mass destruction. He became CND's General Secretary, campaigning through protest marches and other non-violent means.

In 1995, the Church of England supported **ecumenical** (see page 75) action in favour of extending the Non-Proliferation Treaty (an agreement to halt further production of nuclear weapons).

The arms trade

Christians are concerned with the morality of selling arms, especially to poor nations who cannot afford enough food, healthcare and education. Profits from arms sales exceed the amount given in aid.

The assembly remains concerned over the continuing excessive dependence of the British manufacturing industry on the arms trade …

(United Reform Church)

Fact file 2 – Peace

In spite of the many military references in the Old Testament, peace is seen as a developing theme. The laws of Moses provided a basis for national peace. Later the prophets taught of an international peace when they foretold the coming of a Messiah who would be the 'Prince of Peace' and who would herald an age when wars would come to an end. '*He will settle disputes among great nations. They will hammer their swords into ploughs and their spears into pruning knives. Nations will never again go to war, never prepare for battle again.*' (Isaiah 2:4–5)

Christians believe Jesus was the fulfilment of that prophecy and they celebrate this at Christmas in their services and carols as they remember the message of the angels: '*Glory to God in the highest heaven, and peace on Earth to those with whom he is pleased.*' (Luke 2:14)

In his teaching in the Sermon of the Mount Jesus said: '*Happy are those who work for peace; God will call them his children.*' (Matthew 5:9)

Before leaving them, Jesus gave his disciples the gift of peace. *'Peace is what I leave with you' (John 14:27).* This is an individual peace and Christians believe that it is only possible to love others when one is at peace with oneself.

Aspects of peace

Pacifism: many Christians, including the Religious Society of Friends (Quakers), believe that all warfare is wrong.

'… there is something of God – the seed of the Spirit – in all people. Quakers believe that more can be accomplished by appealing to this capacity for love and goodness, in ourselves and in others, than can be hoped for by threatening punishment or retaliation if people behave badly.'
(Quaker Peace Testimony)

Eucharist: at the service, inner peace is asked for in prayer.

'Christ is our peace. He has reconciled us to God in one body by the cross. We meet and share his peace.'
(The Church of England *Alternative Service Book*)

In many church services it is common practice for Christians to offer a sign of peace to one another by exchanging a kiss or joining hands.

Action: peace is not just the absence of war but has to be worked for. *'… strive for peace with all your heart' (Psalm 34:14).* Many Christians are active in promoting peace.

Conscientious objectors: during World Wars I and II many Christians, along with other pacifists, refused to go to war. In order to be exempt from fighting they had to prove their beliefs were genuine. They were often branded as traitors and cowards.

Ecumenism: this includes active steps to help bring reconciliation between groups who have been divided. During the years of conflict between Protestants and Roman Catholics in Ireland, the Christian community of **Corrymeela** has provided a base for both sides to come together. Its name means 'Hill of Harmony'.

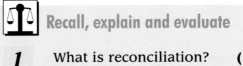

One of the many Christian groups working for peace

Recall, explain and evaluate

1   What is reconciliation?   **(1)**

2   Explain why some Christians believe a nuclear war could never be considered a 'just war'.   **(5)**

3   'Violence only ever leads to more violence.' Do you agree? Give reasons for your answer showing you have considered other points of view.   **(4)**

Creative assignment

Either design a poster with the caption 'Co-operation is better than conflict'

Or write a letter from a TV reporter working in a war zone to one of his or her family back at home in Britain.

Suffering and evil

Roy Castle, the popular entertainer who died in 1994, describes what happened on learning that he had terminal cancer.

‘*That five miles' drive home was the loneliest time I have ever experienced. I was numb and had to concentrate very deliberately on my driving. Humming, clattering wheels were ringing inside my head as past memories and future doubts thundered and flashed. Arriving home ... Fiona's eyes welled but she didn't blub as she made a cuppa ... Nothing was said. We just embraced and sobbed. The sluice gates were opened and we just held on to each other with all the love and tenderness we had built up over our thirty years together ... We are both strong Christians with a total trust in God, but this was stretching our faith somewhat! Fiona told me that whilst I was doing a voice-over she was praying and asking delicately, "What's happening, Lord?" She became aware of this message, "Just stand back and see what I am going to do through this." She was very convinced and I promise you Fiona is not a person to clutch at straws or hallucinate.*’

Roy and Fiona Castle

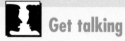 **Get talking**

Roy Castle died of lung cancer thought to have been caused through the smoke of other people's cigarettes (passive smoking).

● **What other kinds of suffering are caused through the actions of others?**

Why?

The question 'Why?' is so often associated with suffering.

Why me? – we ask when we are faced with suffering which seems to be undeserved.

Why them? – we ask when we see graphic pictures in newspapers and on our television screens of children suffering.

Why him or her? – we ask when someone who has lived a good life is struck down with a debilitating disease.

Why does God allow it? – we may ask when devastation from an earthquake leaves a trail of broken lives.

Why do some people seem to be born evil? – we ask when we read of cruel murderers.

The causes of suffering can be divided into two kinds:

natural evil – when disasters occur as a result of the normal pattern of nature being distorted, e.g. floods or hurricanes, and

human-made evil – when pain is inflicted by selfish or cruel actions, e.g. war or murder.

Some kinds of suffering do not fit neatly into one category and can sometimes be a mixture of the two. For instance, a drought may be a natural disaster but it could be the long-term result of thoughtless deforestation carried out by humans for personal gain. In the 1960's, a number of children were born with serious deformities. At first this looked like a natural accident of birth until it was realized that the Thalidomide drug their mothers had taken to help them during difficult pregnancies, had not been thoroughly tested and was the cause of the malformations.

There is, of course, no easy answer to the problem of evil and suffering. Everyone has to come to terms with the fact that it is part of all human experience. For some religious people, suffering can severely test their faith. Others find it is their faith which is the very thing that makes sense of it and which will help them endure it.

Rwanda – coming to terms with the consequences of war

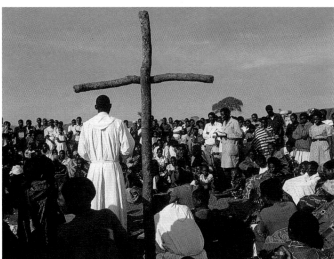

Fact file 1

Christians believe that God gave people free will to love and serve him. When this freedom is abused, it results in suffering. The story of Adam and Eve in Genesis tells how God gave them a perfect environment in the Garden of Eden but how through their disobedience they brought evil into the world. They were cast out from the garden and promised pain and suffering which would affect both themselves and future generations. This is known as 'The Fall'. Many Christians do not regard the story as historically true but view it as a myth. They see it as a powerful metaphor for what happens when people turn away from God. By humankind abusing freedom and ignoring God's plan for human behaviour, suffering is brought into the world. Just as the harmony of the Garden of Eden was spoilt, so too rejection of God's will means that the world is no longer as he intended it.

Some Christians believe in a supernatural evil force known as the devil (Satan) over which humans have little or no control (*Ephesians 6:10–13*).

Recall and explain

1 What types of suffering do you think the people in the photo have experienced? **(2)**

2 What is meant by the term 'The Fall'? **(2)**

3 From the extract by Roy Castle, explain how Fiona sees God as 'immanent' (see page 7) and 'personal'. **(6)**

Sportswoman Diane Modahl suffered greatly when she was suspected of using drugs. When she was near to despair she found that the words of *Footprints* gave her strength to cope with her suffering.

•*When I read this poem it hit me like a bolt. In my deepest hours of despair, Jesus had actually been carrying me and supporting me. I felt such a strong conviction that gave me so much comfort.*•

 **Get talking**

● **What are some of the ways that people without a religious faith seek relief from suffering?**

Fact file 2

Christians believe that God is compassionate and understands the suffering of his people. In becoming a person in the form of Jesus, he became involved with it. The evil brought into the world through sin was believed to deserve the punishment of death. Through Jesus, God took on that punishment and suffered death on the cross. In this way, the price for sin was paid and Christians believe that by the victory over death shown in the resurrection, evil can be conquered and hope given for eternal life (see page 16). This is one of the key beliefs of Christianity and is marked in its most important festival of Easter. The words of one of the songs sung at this time state:

•*There was no other good enough to pay the price of sin.*
He only could unlock the gates of Heaven and let us in.•

One night a man had a dream.
He dreamed he was walking
along a beach with the Lord.
Across the sky flashed scenes from his life.
For each scene,
he noticed two sets of footprints in the sand;
one belonging to him,
and the other to the Lord.

When the last scene of his life flashed before him,
he looked back at the footprints in the sand.
He noticed that many times
along the path of his life
there was only one set of footprints.
He also noticed
that it happened at the very lowest and saddest times in his life.

This really bothered him
and he questioned the Lord about it.
'Lord, you said that once I decided to follow you,
you'd walk with me all the way.
But I have noticed
that during the most troublesome times in my life,
there is only one set of footprints.
I don't understand
why when I needed you most
you would leave me.'

The Lord replied,
'My precious, precious child,
I love you and
I would never leave you.
During your times of trial and suffering,
when you see only one set of footprints,
it was then
that I carried you.'

The solemnity of Jesus' suffering, which is called the **Passion**, is reflected in the way Easter is celebrated. The 40 days leading up to Easter are called **Lent**. At this time Christians remember the temptations of Jesus. Traditionally it is a time of fasting and concentrating on God's forgiveness. In many churches brightly coloured banners and flowers are removed until Easter Sunday, the day when the Resurrection of Jesus is celebrated. The week leading into it is called **Holy Week** and in Roman Catholic and some Church of England churches Christians pray in front of the **Stations of the Cross**. These are pictures or statues showing the fourteen different stages of Jesus' journey to the cross and his crucifixion. On Good Friday, many Christians attend long services to mark the time of the crucifixion and processions often take place, when a cross is carried.

The story of Jesus' Passion is told in great detail in the final chapters of all the Gospels. His death on the cross was a slow and painful one and was the punishment used by the Romans for crimes against the State. It has become the symbol of Christianity and a metaphor for suffering. When people talk about a painful task they often describe it as 'the cross' they have to bear.

Dr Sheila Cassidy has spent many years of her life being close to suffering. She was on the receiving end of it in Chile when she was tortured and imprisoned for giving medical treatment to a wounded revolutionary. Since her return to England she has devoted her skills to hospice work (see page 86)

where she meets suffering all the time. Amid the pain and despair, she finds that there are those who are made stronger by their experiences. Suffering can bring out the qualities of compassion in the people who are caring for them. She is a Christian and, although she has no answer to the 'Why?' questions, she believes that God is still involved in every person's life. She writes:

> *I believe that God*
> *has the whole world in his hands.*
> *He is not a bystander*
> *at the pain of the world.*
> *He does not stand*
> *like Peter,*
> *wringing his hands*
> *in the shadows,*
> *but is there*
> *in the dock,*
> *on the rack,*
> *high on the gallows tree.*
> *He is in the pain*
> *of the lunatic,*
> *the tortured,*
> *those wracked by grief.*
> *His is the blood*
> *that flows in the gutter,*
> *His are the veins burned by heroin,*
> *his the lungs choked by AIDS.*
> *His is the heart*
> *broken by suffering,*
> *his the despair*
> *of the mute,*
> *the oppressed,*
> *the man with the gun to his head.*

Recall, explain and evaluate

1 Explain how Christians should respond when they see people suffering. **(2)**

2 Do you think having a belief in God helps people cope with suffering in their lives? Your answer should include evidence from personal research. **(8)**

Creative assignment

Either design a modern 'Station of the Cross' using modern symbols connected with suffering

Or write a poem about an evil of today that you feel strongly about.

Euthanasia

Pontius' Puddle

© Joel Kauffman

CONTROL OVER DYING MUST REST IN THE HANDS OF THE PATIENT!

NO, THE DOCTOR.

THE FAMILY.

THE COURTS.

IT'S NOT EASY BEING GOD. THEY USED TO BLAME ME FOR DEATH-- NOW THEY WANT TO BE IN CHARGE!

> **'More than 90 per cent of pensioners back voluntary euthanasia.'**

 **Get talking**

- What are the possible dangers of making euthanasia (mercy killing) lawful?

- What are your own views about it?

> **'A civilization's worth is best gauged by the determination with which it protects its most vulnerable members.'**

The right to die?

The term **euthanasia**, referred to as mercy killing, means 'easy death'. It describes bringing about or speeding up the death of a person, with or without consent, in order to relieve their suffering. It is illegal in Britain, but there have been attempts to change the law to make it legal. With advanced technology it is possible to keep people alive for longer which, in spite of the advantages, does not always give them a better quality of life or allow them to keep their dignity. The medical profession as a whole has been against the legalizing of euthanasia, aware of the responsibility it will put upon them. Doctors take the Hippocratic Oath to preserve life at all costs.

There are two kinds of euthanasia:
- **voluntary euthanasia** – where the person has expressed a wish to be allowed to die. This is sometimes referred to as assisted suicide.
- **involuntary euthanasia** – where the person is unable to make a decision but where it is the considered opinion of family and doctors that it would be in the patient's best interests to be allowed to die.

A move has been made towards voluntary euthanasia by permission being granted to withdraw medical treatment in certain cases. An example was Hillsborough victim Tony Bland, whose parents won a court case to have his life-support machine switched off after doctors decided it was unlikely he would ever regain consciousness.

Fact file 1

Christian views on euthanasia are based on the belief in the sanctity of life, which comes from the teaching that all people were made in the image of God and that it is for him only to give and take life. In his *Evangelium Vitae* of 1995 to Roman Catholics, Pope John Paul II described euthanasia as 'a grave violation of the law of God'.

Christians are concerned to protect people who feel they may be a burden on others and who may be under pressure to seek a speeding up of their own death. They also see problems in trying to make legal something which could lead to abuse by unscrupulous or unfeeling people. They are aware, too, of the weight of responsibility upon doctors. Many Christians believe that the role of the hospice with its caring approach is preferable to euthanasia. In Christian teaching there is thought to be a difference between allowing death to occur when further treatments are judged to be futile, and a deliberately caused death. Many Christians do not believe it is always right to use modern technology to prolong life at all costs.

The Hospice Movement

A preferred alternative to euthanasia for many people are hospices which are residential homes for the terminally ill (see page 86). The first hospice was founded by Dame Cicely Saunders. The Hospice Movement developed from the concern of Christians that people should be allowed to die with dignity. Hospice care concentrates on controlling pain and giving support to the emotional and spiritual needs of the patients. It is believed that deliberately to kill dying people is to reject them.

The Voluntary Euthanasia Society

This society takes the view that people should have the right to make their own decision about their own death. Members of the society carry a medical emergency card which, in the event of a serious accident, requests that they are not resuscitated nor that their life is artificially prolonged. They also recommend writing a 'Living Will' in which it can be stated that under certain conditions (such as senility and severe incapacity from which, in the opinion of two independent doctors, there is no prospect of recovery), their lives will not be sustained.

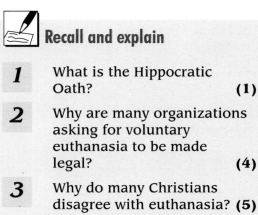

MEDICAL EMERGENCY CARD
supplied by
VOLUNTARY EUTHANASIA SOCIETY
13 Prince of Wales Terrace London W8 5PG 0171 937 7770

My Full name is

If there is no reasonable prospect of recovery I do NOT wish to be resuscitated or my life to be artificially prolonged
My Advance Directive is lodged with

Medical Information eg. blood group

2. After my death my organs may be used for medical purposes
3. Next of Kin

Signature   Date

Recall and explain

1 What is the Hippocratic Oath? **(1)**

2 Why are many organizations asking for voluntary euthanasia to be made legal? **(4)**

3 Why do many Christians disagree with euthanasia? **(5)**

Suicide

Kurt Cobain, lead singer of Nirvana, killed himself in 1994 at the age of 27. Here is an extract from the note he left behind.

There's good in all of us, and I simply love people too much. So much that it makes me feel just too sad. Sad, little sensitive, unappreciated, Pisces, Jesus man.
I had a good marriage, and for that I'm grateful ... Thank you all from the pit of my burning, nauseous stomach for your letters and concerns during the last years. I'm too much of an erratic, moody person, and I don't have the passion any more ... remember it's better to burn out than fade away ... Love, peace and empathy, Kurt Cobain.

 **Get talking**

- Why do you think people who are envied for their wealth and fame are unhappy enough to kill themselves? What things are missing in their lives?

- Apart from the grief all people feel at losing a loved one, what other feelings do you think accompany a suicide bereavement?

The Samaritans

In 1936 a young priest named Chad Varah was deeply affected by having to bury a fourteen-year-old girl who had committed suicide. As a result of this he later founded the worldwide organization known as the Samaritans to give support to depressed and suicidal people. It has no religious link but many Christians share the view of its founder who followed the teaching of Jesus' story of the good Samaritan by showing compassion to those driven to take their own lives.

Fact file 2

Christianity teaches that it is God who determines life and death. *'None of us lives for himself only and none of us dies for himself only.' (Romans 14:7)*

In the past, suicide was considered a great sin and the Church of England refused to bury those who had taken their own life.

Christian views have become more compassionate in recent times and it is believed that everything should be done to give love and support to those driven to attempt suicide. Many would see it as part of their mission of 'saving souls' to bring people back to a loving relationship with God. When the apostle Paul was in prison, and an earthquake destroyed the building, his jailer prepared to kill himself rather than face punishment from the authorities for allowing his prisoner to go free. Paul stopped him and the jailer later became converted to Christianity and was baptized.

Recall and evaluate

1   Describe the kinds of help the Samaritans might give to someone who is seeking help.   **(5)**

2   Why would a Christian consider it wrong to take their own life?   **(5)**

Death and beyond

What is dying?

*A ship sails and I stand watching till she fades on the horizon,
and someone at my side says, 'She is gone.'
Gone where? Gone from my sight, that is all.
She is just as large as when I saw her.
The diminished size and total loss of sight is in me, not her, and
just at the moment when someone at my side says, 'She is gone'
there are others who are watching her coming, and other voices
take up a glad shout. 'There she comes!' … and that is dying …*

(Bishop Brent)

Get talking

- When people are suffering bereavement, they experience many different emotions. What are they?

- What is being expressed about death in the words above?

The great taboo

In many Western countries such as Britain, death is a subject people often prefer not to talk about. Considering that death is a fact of life common to us all, this may seem surprising. One reason could be to do with the fact that society is more secular than it was and that fewer people believe there is anything to look forward to after death. This can make the fears, pain and loneliness of having to face death or bereavement more difficult. Perhaps this is why those who are not religious still turn to the Church to support them at such times. The ceremonies and customs associated with death can help people at a time when normal feelings are turned upside-down.

DEAD CENTRE

For funerals with a friendly face, a French company has introduced one-stop shopping for the hereafter; its supermarkets sell everything from floral displays to coffins. It aims to dispel the forbidding image of conventional undertakers, allowing the bereaved to take a trolley and browse the aisles, assisted by specially trained assistants and bereavement counsellors. Although Britain has not followed this trend, some places, such as the Funeral Centre, in Catford, London, do have their extensive range of items on display for customers to look at and select from. This is in addition to providing all the same services as other more conventional undertakers.

Fact file 3

Christians believe that God created each individual to be able to have a personal relationship with him which begins in this life but which is only fully realized in the next.

In the early centuries of Christianity, it was thought that the body itself would be resurrected after death. Most Christians now believe that only the invisible part of a person, the **soul** (inner self), lives on. For this reason cremation is now an accepted practice by many Christians as an alternative to burial for the disposal of a person's earthly remains.

Seventh Day Adventists do not believe that the soul separates from the body at death. They believe that the whole person dies and remains 'in sleep' until the Day of Judgement.

We have entrusted our brother N to God's merciful keeping, and we now commit his body to the ground (or to be cremated): *[earth to earth, ashes to ashes, dust to dust:] in sure and certain hope of the resurrection to eternal life through our Lord Jesus Christ, who died, was buried, and rose again for us. To him be glory for ever and ever.

* The words in square brackets may be ommitted.

The funeral

A funeral can take place at a church or crematorium and will be conducted by a minister of the Church. For some people, such as sailors, it can take place at sea and in the Book of Common Prayer there is a special prayer for this, beginning,

•*We commit his body to the deep …* •

The service can be simple with prayers, hymns and a short address, or longer with Holy Communion. This is called a **Requiem Mass** in the Roman Catholic Church. The Church recognizes the sensitivity of the occasion for grieving families, who are helped and advised about personal choices of music and words to be used.

In some traditions the coffin of the deceased person is left open and the body lies 'in state' for mourners to pay their respects (see page 88).

The burial

The final giving up of the body to be cremated or buried is called the **committal**, as Christians believe that the dead person is being committed into God's safe keeping. This will be accompanied by prayers.

In the case of a burial, this takes place at the graveside and afterwards mourners often sprinkle earth on or into the grave. It is usual for flowers to be placed with the coffin at the cremation or burial, with personal messages accompanying them. Many families now ask that other mourners donate money to an appropriate charity instead of buying floral tributes.

Words taken from the Church of England *Alternative Service Book* which are spoken at the funeral service

Respect and remembrance

The Christian view of the sanctity of life is reflected in the customs and rituals that are used when a person's earthly life comes to an end. These vary in different churches, although some are common to all.

Before death

In Anglican and Roman Catholic traditions anointing the sick is a ceremonial action which can be requested for very ill people. When it is performed on a dying person it is often referred to as the **last rites**. It involves rubbing oil on the person's forehead, and in the Roman Catholic tradition, the feet and hands too. It symbolizes the healing of the mind and strengthening of spirit and is accompanied by special prayers.

At death

Candles are often placed near the coffin as a symbol of hope for the future life and a reminder of the 'Light of Christ' who is the means of **redemption** (freedom brought about by his death). In Roman Catholic services incense, with its smoke rising upwards as a symbol of prayer, is sprinkled over the coffin.

After death

The place of burial is usually marked with a stone, often in the shape of a cross as a reminder of Jesus's death and resurrection. Some churches have a memorial garden where the ashes of cremated people are placed with plaques, often with Christian symbols and words.

In many towns and villages there is a stone memorial cross to commemorate those who have died in the two World Wars. Special services of remembrance are often held around these each year.

All Souls' Day

In addition to weekly **intercessions** (prayers on behalf of others), 2 November, the day after All Saints' Day, is marked on the Christian calendar as a time for remembering the souls of the departed.

In many Roman Catholic churches, people light candles regularly in memory of a dead friend or relative.

A wreath laid in remembrance of those who died in war

Candles being lit in memory of the dead

 Recall and evaluate

1 Describe what happens at a Christian funeral. **(5)**

2 'The money spent on funerals would be better spent on the living.' Do you agree? In your answer you should refer to a range of arguments. **(5)**

Helping the bereaved

The Church plays an important role in helping people who are dying or bereaved. Hilary is an ordained priest who works as a hospice chaplain.

Hilary

Ann: Would you like to tell me something about a typical day?

Hilary: Well, the first thing I do when I arrive at the office is to check for messages. For instance, there might be a note about the relatives of someone who has just died. They may want to talk about music and readings for the funeral.

Ann: Do people know what they want or do you give them ideas?

Hilary: Some do but they often value suggestions. I have a book that contains all sorts of readings, which I let them look at. The set passages from the services book also help, such as Jesus' words from John chapter 14: *'There are many rooms in my father's house ... I am going now to prepare a place for you'.*

Ann: So what's next?

Hilary: I look at the notes about new patients to see if there are any spiritual needs listed. For instance, there may be a Roman Catholic wanting the Sacrament of Reconciliation – what people traditionally called Confession – in which case I'll contact the Roman Catholic priest. Then I look to see who needs visiting.

Ann: This must be the most difficult bit. What sort of things do people want to talk about and how do you help them?

Hilary: There are no pat answers to some of their questions. I tell them that I believe that life is ongoing and I do try to take away fear. The picture language of hell and judgement is quite unhelpful. If they are worried by feelings of guilt I try instead to encourage them to talk through what they're sad and sorry about. I stress that forgiveness is free. I remind them of Jesus on the cross forgiving the dying thief. Or I remind them of the loving father who forgave the Lost Son. If they want, I read to them. The Psalms can be a comfort, or the Easter story with its stress on suffering and resurrection.

Ann: What about the grieving relatives? What do they ask you?

Hilary: Some want to know, 'Why her? She doesn't deserve it.' I try to explain that God doesn't specially select illnesses for individuals. There are natural laws that govern things. I don't pretend I have answers but I tell them I believe God is involved and cares. I take Holy Communion to those who feel the need for it.

We have a Quiet Room and once a month I hold a special service of thanks and remembrance. I try to create a peaceful environment, with a candle and a symbol of a butterfly. People can just stay quiet or talk about what they want to remember about someone. It seems to help.

Ann: Why a butterfly?

Hilary: For me it's a symbol of resurrection, of life changing and continuing. Thinking of a caterpillar changing to a butterfly can help people understand death as a new beginning – the person's life changing, but continuing.

Recall and explain

1 What do you think the role of the priest would be in helping the bereaved? **(4)**

2 What sort of qualities would the priest need to have to support the bereaved? **(3)**

3 Why do you think many Christians turn to the Church for support when they have been bereaved? **(3)**

What is heaven?

❛*I'm a Roman Catholic and have a strong belief … My sister died in the Marchioness tragedy … My opinion is that I will get to see her again – one day.*❜

Lawrence Dallaglio, England rugby player

❛*I don't think we have too far to travel. In a sense we are already there. After all, this is God's world – I believe he is in charge and all that is missing is the formula … If God's will was being done then there would be no difference between Earth and heaven.*❜

Archbishop Desmond Tutu

People's ideas about heaven are often a confused mixture of what they have been taught and what they would like it to be. Because we live at a certain time and place, it is too difficult for us to grasp a dimension of life that is beyond these things. Before the scientific discoveries that showed the movement of the planets, it was understandable for people to assume that their creator lived beyond the clouds. Today, some people find that the nearest they can come to an understanding of heaven is to compare it with the wonderful moments in life when time seems to stand still. They believe that these moments provide a glimpse or a clue of what might be to come.

A modern understanding of hell is that the view of it in the Bible as a place of torture is picture-language (metaphor) rather than a straightforward description. On Earth people experience pain and the feeling of being cut off when they have hurt someone they love. Hell can be thought of as the misery people will feel when faced with their shortcomings in the presence of God's purity. This hell will be a punishment in itself.

Church Elders pour cold water on hellfire and damnation

Andrew Brown
Religious Affairs Correspondent

Traditional doctrines of hellfire and eternal torment are "appalling theologies which made God into a sadistic monster and left searing psychological scars on many", according to the Church of England's Doctrine Commission.

The commision's latest report, *The Mystery of Salvation*, maintains "Annihilation might be a truer picture of damnation than any of the traditional images of the hell of eternal torment …"

The report rejects literal understandings of the Second Coming expressed in such biblical passages as: "He is coming with the clouds every eye will see him"; and: "This Jesus, who has been taken up from you into heaven, will come in the same way as you saw him go into heaven." The passages, it says "are not intended to provide literal depictions of the event, as though Jesus were a space traveller returning to earth".

Fact file 4

Many Christians believe that at some time in the future, Jesus Christ will return on the Day of Judgement and end the present world order. Those who have been redeemed (saved) will enter into the resurrection – life in heaven. Early Christians thought that the 'Second Coming' (**Parousia**), would happen soon, so death was looked upon as joyous, full of hope of resurrection to eternal life. In later times, when faith was less strong, white clothes and joyful songs were replaced by fears of punishment in hell and the wearing of black. It was believed that the soul of the dead person would enter a stage of preparation before entering heaven. This was called **purgatory**, where the soul was cleansed of all sins. It was the duty of the living to offer prayers to help shorten the time spent in this state.

The Roman Catholic Church still believes in the idea of purgatory but less emphasis is put on it now as can be seen in a prayer spoken at the funeral service (requiem): '*... the sadness of death gives way to the bright promise of immortality.*'

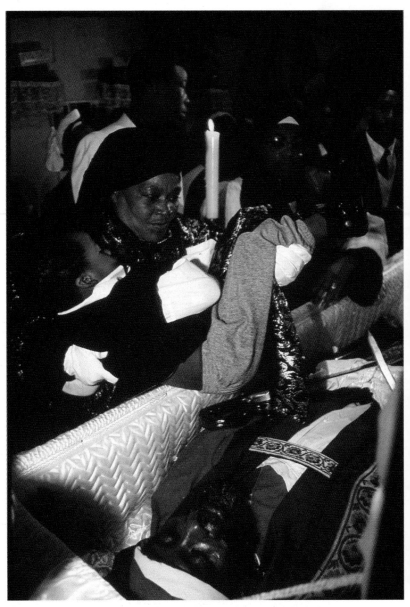

Mourners at a spiritual Baptist church pay their respects and each child member of the church is lifted across the body. The song 'Swing low, sweet chariot, coming for to carry me home' is sung as a reminder of the journey to eternal life

 Creative assignment

Either write a letter of sympathy to a friend who has just lost a close member of their family

Or do a piece of creative writing entitled 'My dream of an ideal world'.

✝ Re-examine

A Croatian soldier at prayer following the bloody battle for the Serb-held region of Krajina. Hundreds of thousands of refugees fled to Serbia

The following questions give you a chance to re-examine the issues raised in the preceding units. Remember to look at the number of marks for each question and to develop your answer accordingly.

a Describe *two* ways in which Christians might feel they have experienced God? **(4)**

b Describe what is meant by forgiveness and atonement in Christianity. **(4)**

c Explain why the Resurrection is of such importance to Christians today. **(7)**

d 'If there *was* a God then he wouldn't allow so much suffering in the world.'

Do you agree? Give a range of reasons to support your answer. **(5)**

Introduction

Muslims

The word **Islam** means the peace which comes from a willing obedience to **Allah** (God). The followers of Islam are called **Muslims** and the world-wide community of Muslims is known as the **ummah**. Islam has the second biggest following of any religion, next to Christianity. The largest groups of Muslims live in the countries of the Middle East, North Africa and in Pakistan.

The Arabs are descended from **Ibrahim** (Abraham), through his son **Ismail** (Ishmael). Muslims are divided into broad groups, the major differences between them being over the succession of the Prophet **Muhammad**. The largest group, which makes up about 90 per cent, are the **Sunni** Muslims. Many Sunnis believe that the **khalifahs** (successors of Muhammad) should be from Muhammad's own tribe and that the **imam**, the person who leads prayer, is an ordinary man chosen by the community. The **Shi'ite** Muslims believe that in every generation an imam from Muhammad's descendants is divinely appointed, with special powers.

In any world-wide community there is always a variety of ways in which a religion is practised. This is true, too, of Islam, although differences are often the result of cultural influences rather than religious ones.

Muhammad

Muhammad was born in **Makkah** (Mecca), which was the centre for trade and worship in Arabia, in 571 CE. He was orphaned when young and brought up by his grandfather and later his uncle from whom he learned to be a trader. When he was 25 he married a wealthy widow, **Khadijah**. Muhammad was concerned about the dishonest dealings of his people and how they worshipped idols. He began to spend periods of time alone in the mountains. During one of these stays he received a revelation from Allah.

It came to him through the angel **Jibril** (Gabriel) and was the first of many over several years. The words that came to him were dictated to scribes and they form the **Qu'ran**, the holy book of the Muslims.

Muslims revere the prophets for their teachings, but they regard Muhammad as the **seal**, as he was the last prophet and the one to whom Allah gave his final revelation. Muhammad, who is often referred to by his title **The Prophet**, began preaching the new faith in Makkah, where it was rejected. In 622 CE Muhammad went to **Madinah** where many people began to listen to his teaching. Muhammad's journey to Madinah is known as the **hijrah**. This marks the creation of the first Islamic state and the Islamic calendar begins from this event. When saying the name of Muhammad many Muslims add the words 'Peace be upon him'; when writing it they shorten it to PBUH. But although Muhammad is greatly revered, he is not worshipped. This is for Allah alone.

The Qur'an and the holy writings

The Qur'an is sacred to Muslims. They believe its words come from Allah and this is reflected in the way the Qur'an is used and treated. It is always read in Arabic so that it remains true and cannot be changed in translation. Whatever their first language, many Muslim children learn to read parts of the Qur'an in Arabic. Some people learn the whole of it as an act of devotion. Such a person is known as a **hafiz**.

To show respect, the Qur'an is handled with care, and ritual washing, **wudu**, takes place before touching it. It is usually kept in a cloth to protect it and is kept on a high shelf with nothing above it.

The Qur'an is divided into 114 **surahs** or chapters, and it contains everything needed for Muslims to learn about Allah's will and how to conduct every aspect of their daily lives.

In addition to the Qur'an, many of Muhammad's actions, **Sunnah**, and his sayings, the **Hadith**, are contained in writings which, together with the Qur'an, form the basis of the **Shariah**, the Islamic law.

The Pillars of Islam

There are five basic duties in Islam; known as the Pillars of Islam.

1   Shahadah – This is the Muslim declaration of faith which states, 'There is no God except Allah, Muhammad is the messenger of Allah.' These words are spoken many times throughout a Muslim's life. They will be whispered into the ear of a new baby and by a dying person. They are all that needs to be said when someone converts to Islam.

2   Salah – Muslims are required to pray five times a day – before sunrise, midday, mid-afternoon, early evening and late evening. Salah can be performed at any clean place although many Muslims go to the **masjid** (mosque) for this. Preparation for prayer includes wudu, the ritual washing of hands, face and feet. The prayers are spoken aloud and each is accompanied by a series of movements called a **rak'ah**. A prayer mat may be used and placed so that, when praying, Muslims will be facing the direction of Makkah. Friday is a special day in Islam and the noon prayer on this day, the **jumu'ah**, is performed at the masjid. The most distinguishing feature of the jumu'ah prayer is the **khutbah** or sermon.

In addition to the set salah, Muslims are expected to offer **du'a**, private prayers for which there is no set pattern.

3   Zakah – Muslims are expected to give 2.5 per cent of their annual savings in charity to the poor and others in need. The giving is seen as an act of worship.

4   Sawm – The Muslim month of **Ramadan** is when Muslims are expected to fast each day between dawn and sunset. During this time all food, drink and sexual relations are forbidden. Young children do not have to fast. Other groups such as the sick, elderly or pregnant may break their fast if their individual circumstances require it. The fast commemorates when Muhammad first heard the words of Allah and it reminds Muslims of those less fortunate than themselves.

5   Hajj – Each Muslim is expected to make a pilgrimage to Makkah at least once in their lifetime, if wealth and health permit.

Festivals

There are two main festivals in Islam. **Id-ul-Fitr** is a celebration of the end of Ramadan and **Id-ul-Adha** is a celebration of sacrifice which commemorates Ibrahim's willingness to sacrifice his son Ismail for Allah. Both occasions are marked by visits to the masjid for prayer and the giving of food or money to the poor.

The nature of Allah

Muslims believe in one supreme God and their whole lives are dedicated to worshipping him. Faith in him involves five important beliefs known as the **Five Articles of Faith**. They are:

- belief in Allah
- belief in his angels
- belief in his books
- belief in his messengers
- belief in life after death.

Unity of Allah

In Islam the belief in the unity or oneness of Allah is called **Tawhid**. The first Pillar – the shahadah – is a declaration of this belief and will be spoken many times during a Muslim's life.

Supremacy of Allah

The beauty and harmony that can be seen in creation shows Allah's power. Like Jews and Christians, Muslims believe that the one supreme God is transcendent and omniscient (see page 7).

Consciousness of Allah

Muslims are taught that they should be aware of Allah at every moment. This consciousness of him is called **taqwa** and their obedience to it is shown in many practices, particularly in the second duty or Pillar, salah. By praying on five occasions each day, at times which span all their waking hours, they are constantly reminded of him. The words which open every surah of the Qur'an: '*In the name of Allah – All Gracious, All Merciful*', are often spoken by Muslims before eating or beginning any action. Remembering Allah through the devotions of prayer and reciting from the Qur'an is known as **dhikr**.

Messengers of Allah

As Allah is so beyond human understanding, awareness and knowledge of him has been given to Muslims by means of specially chosen messengers. In Islam it is believed that throughout history there has been a line of communication through prophets known as the **rasul**, sent by Allah to teach people how to live. They each had an important part to play in revealing the nature of Allah. The last and most important one was Muhammad.

Worship of Allah

Muslims believe that Allah has 99 attributes or names, and they often recite these names using a string of 99 beads called a **subhah**. The Qur'an is thought to contain the true words of Allah. The art of writing them in the letters of the Arabic language is called **calligraphy** and, for many, learning to do this is an act of worship in itself.

Muslims believe that Allah is too great to be represented in the human mind, which is one reason why there are no pictures or statues in the masjid or mosque. Only aspects of his creation such as plants and flowers or patterns may be used.

The word masjid means a place of prostration. It is where Muslims, in removing their shoes and bowing low in prayer, remind themselves of the greatness of Allah. Indeed, any act of worship with the intention of obeying Allah is known as **ibadah**.

Morality

Islam is all-embracing, linking the religious, social and political ways of life into one. Muslims believe that all humans are born in the natural state of **fitrah** (free from sin) and with free will to react to the tests and temptations which will occur in life. It is taught that a jinn, one of Allah's created beings, called **Shaytan** (Satan) disobeyed him and was banished. In revenge he tries to destroy humans by turning them from Allah and tempting them to do wrong. In Islam, the duties Muslims are required to perform, such as frequent prayer and reading the Qur'an, strengthen their discipline and help them to resist evil and lead moral lives. The general conduct which affects attitudes and ethics is known as **akhlaq**.

Sources of authority

The guide for the whole of life is contained in the Qur'an which teaches the duties and moral responsibilities that are expected of Muslims. As well as the five Pillars of Islam, it includes the requirements concerning dietary laws, marriage, divorce and all aspects of human relationships. In addition to the Qur'an, Muslims have the example and practices of Muhammad set down in the Sunnah and Hadith to guide them. From early times, Muslim scholars have used these to guide them when drawing up laws for contemporary situations. Today this would include ethical issues such as embryo technology.

Obedience

The name Islam is sometimes translated as 'submission', which stresses the importance to Muslims of giving their lives in obedience to Allah. Every person has certain responsibilities towards their fellow human beings and the rest of creation. Obedience is a way of expressing love for Allah.

Types of behaviour

Actions which are permitted are known as **halal** and those which are forbidden are **haram**. Types of behaviour are classified as follows.

- **Fard** – actions which must be done, such as the five Pillars of Islam. Failure to carry out a fard is thought to be both a crime and a sin.
- **Mandub** – actions which are recommended, such as hospitality to visitors.
- **Mubah** – actions which are decided by one's own conscience.
- **Makruh** – actions which are not forbidden but which are not approved of, such as divorce.

Allah requires Muslims to acknowledge their sins. When they make wrong choices, their weaknesses remind them of their dependence upon a compassionate God who is always ready to forgive. Muslims are taught that being sorry is important and that they should apologize to anyone who has been wronged. Islam teaches that repentance wipes out their sins, but good actions are never wiped out.

Prayers for a surgical half-miracle

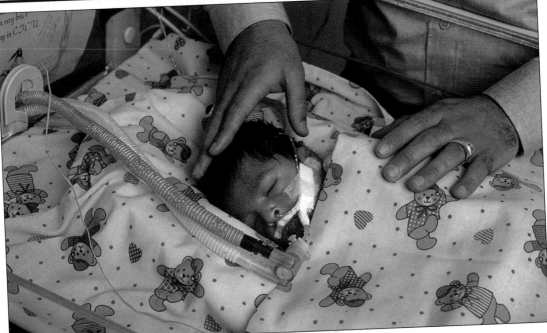

When Hussein and Hassan were born, they were joined at the heart and liver. In a major operation to separate them, one of them was saved. Hassan died, as the doctors had told his parents he would. His death was necessary in order that his brother should live. After his death his father briefly cradled him in his arms: 'I was crying. We knew he would die, but the night before, our family, our friends, we all prayed he would be saved. It is not a good feeling to hold your dead son, but I told myself that out of his death would come good.'

Standing over his living son, the proud but worried father tried to hide his emotion. He quoted the Qur'an ... 'It is difficult for me to explain how I feel. We cannot know what happens now ... it is out of our hands, it is in the hands of Allah.'

Get talking

- What other events are sometimes described as miracles?

- Is there something in your life that you have thought of as a miracle?

- Why do you think the birth of a child is often considered to be a miracle?

Fact file 1

Muslims believe that life is a sacred gift from Allah and should be lived in obedience to him. Each person has a set time span on Earth. *'When their term expires, they would not be able to delay for a single hour, just as they would not be able to anticipate it.' (Surah 16:61)*

It is thought that life on this Earth is a preparation for the next life when the soul, which has been lent by Allah, will live on (see page 152).

Because the soul is created and loved by Allah, Muslims should be grateful for this gift. The wilful taking of one's life is always considered as wrong. *'He who kills himself with a sword or poison or throws himself off a mountain will be tormented on the Day of Resurrection with that very thing.' (Hadith)*

Fact file 2

Euthanasia

As Muslims believe in the sanctity of life, they are opposed to euthanasia or mercy killing (see page 80). Like many people, they are concerned that an individual may not have any choice in the matter and that doctors are put in the position of having to 'play God'. Although it can seem unfair when sick or elderly people are suffering, Islam teaches that life is a test which should be borne with courage. However sick or disabled a body is, the soul of a person is perfect and only Allah can decide when death should come. *'Nor can a soul die except by Allah's leave, the term being fixed as by writing.' (Surah 3:145)*

It is important to show compassion and to do as much as possible to relieve pain and discomfort in others.

Muslim teachings about the sanctity of life influence their beliefs about other life and death issues such as embryo technology, organ transplants and abortion.

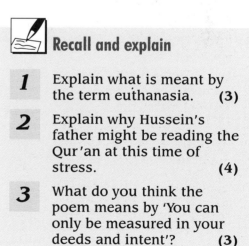

Oh my people

Oh my people, what is your worth?
What is your worth, what is your worth, child of the earth?
Are you like silver, diamonds or gold
increasing in value as you grow old?
Or are you like the dew at the start of the day
like smoke in the wind, slowly fading away?
You cannot be measured in dollars and cents
You can only be measured in your deeds
and intent
And what you achieve and how you relate
And what are your virtues and if you are great
And in your assent you will find that it's true
there is no treasure more precious than you
Oh my people, what is your worth
What is your worth, what is your worth, child of the earth?

Suliaman El Hadi, *The Last Poets*

Recall and explain

1 Explain what is meant by the term euthanasia. **(3)**

2 Explain why Hussein's father might be reading the Qur'an at this time of stress. **(4)**

3 What do you think the poem means by 'You can only be measured in your deeds and intent'? **(3)**

Embryo technology

Appeal for Asian egg donors

A woman who is desperate to start a family has made a plea for women volunteers to donate eggs.

Fact file

An embryo is the first stage of life formed from the fertilization of a female egg by male sperm. Embryo technology is often used to help couples who are unable to have children because one or the other of them is infertile (see page 21). This includes the following.

- **AIH** (artificial insemination by husband) and **IVF** (in-vitro-fertilization)
  In these processes the fertilization of the egg by the sperm takes place in a laboratory. A couple can try this when natural means have failed. These two methods are generally permitted to Muslims as long as absolute security is maintained.
- **AID** (artificial insemination by donor)
  If a husband is sterile, another man's sperm from a donor bank is used to fertilize the wife's egg. This is not . acceptable to Muslims as it involves another man and it is therefore seen as similar to the sin of adultery. Also, Muslims are concerned about the characteristics or diseases that may be inherited from an unknown donor.

Sisters battle for custody of surrogate baby

Two sisters fought each other in a courtroom this week in an attempt to control the life of the baby that one had for the other.

Surrogacy

This is a form of parenting which occurs when a woman is paid to carry and give birth to a child on behalf of a woman unable to become pregnant herself. The husband's sperm will be used to fertilize the egg of the wife or, if necessary, the egg of the other woman. It is then transferred to the surrogate mother who agrees to hand over the child to the parents when it is born. Some Muslims accept this practice, although only if the man were married to both women (see polygamy, page 107). Others are against it because:

- it tampers with the normal processes of nature
- it encourages women to use their bodies for commercial gain
- it creates confusion as to who is the real mother and may lead to wrangling.

Get talking

- Do you think donors should remain unknown?

Get talking

- What difficulties might occur between the 'mother' and 'surrogate mother'?

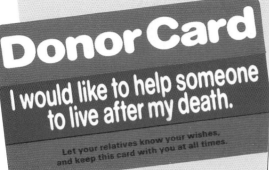

Donor Card

I would like to help someone to live after my death.

Let your relatives know your wishes, and keep this card with you at all times.

Do the stars carry a card?

Most Muslims have refused to carry donor cards as they believe that their body belongs to Allah and therefore they have no say over it. This has caused particular difficulties for the many Asians waiting for a kidney transplant, particularly as kidney failure among Asians can be up to eight times more common than in other groups. In the summer of 1995, the **Muslim Law Council** issued a **fatwa**, a religious ruling, saying Muslims may donate organs, carry donor cards and permit the removal of organs for their closest relatives. This ruling is backed by both Sunni and Shi'ite Muslims (see page 90).

Ahsen Bhatti, actor:
❛I got myself a donor card about seven years ago mainly because the girl that I was going out with carried one. She made me think twice about something that I think a few people actually consider unless they are asked to think about it.

Even though I was brought up as a Muslim, my parents don't object. After all, once you are dead it would be much better to help someone else. I was watching the news the other day and was shocked to see that most of the people featured in a news topic on kidney disease were Asians.

In fact, I think that everyone should automatically qualify to donate unless they specifically state that they don't want to.❜

Get talking

● What are your views on surgery which offers a better life through the transplant of an organ from a dead person?

● What are the advantages of a donor card?

Recall and explain

1 What is a fatwa? **(1)**

2 Why has Ahsen Bhatti decided to carry a donor card? **(4)**

3 Why did Muslims once refuse to have donor cards? **(5)**

Abortion

The last resort

What if the test confirms my worst fears?
What if I'm sick and somebody hears?
What if it shows and they start to suspect?
What if I lose their love and respect?
What if I'm faced with seeing their pain?
What if I'll never feel loved again?
What if, through me, they'll have to lose face?
What if we're spurned by the rest of our race?
What if they make me become his wife?
What if I don't want commitment for life?
What if my thoughts don't dare to find voice?
What if I'm left without any choice?
What if I'm cornered and have to abort?
What if I've no strength for this last resort?

(Aisha)

Cultural

In some cultures there is pressure within the community for women to produce a boy in order to carry on the family name. It is important, though, to realize that this comes from the culture and not from religious teaching.

What are the pressures?

Economic

A young girl, with or without the support of her male partner, might be led into deciding upon an abortion if there are going to be money problems in becoming a parent. This can also apply to married couples who perhaps already have other children who are a strain on the family budget.

Get talking

- After reading the thoughts of Aisha, who suspects she is pregnant, what do you think are her concerns about:

  – her parents

  – her community

  – her boyfriend?

- Can you think of any reasons, other than those mentioned, for people deciding to have an abortion?

Fact file 1

(For general information on abortion, see page 23.)

Although there is no specific teaching on abortion, the Qur'an stresses the sanctity of life (see page 95) and states:

- all life is sacred and cannot be disposed of except for a just cause, such as war
- it is a sin to take the life of a child
- in the next life, when earthly actions are judged, young children who have died will have the right to know why they were killed.

There is clear teaching that relates to the foetus:

- Up to four months
  the mother's rights are greater than those of the foetus.
- After four months
  the child has equal rights with the mother.

The reason for this is that 120 days after conception, Muslims believe that **ensoulment** (the receiving of a soul) takes place. This refers to that part of a human being which some people believe makes a person unique and which continues to exist after the present life on Earth is finished.

Many issues of morality are involved whenever an abortion is considered.

'Of course I didn't want an abortion. It's something I wouldn't wish on anyone – a real ordeal. I just don't see how I had a choice. My baby would have had no quality of life and I couldn't bear that.'

(Fazarna)

'Women, and men for that fact, do not have the right to take the life of an unborn baby …

My first son Qasim had a genetic disease and died. When I fell pregnant for the second time all the doctors took it for granted that I would have an abortion but I really had to fight to have my baby.

I had Hafsa who gave me such joy until she passed away in 1992.

They were my babies and it was destiny to have them even if they weren't perfect according to society's standards.

My life wouldn't have been complete without them.'

(Rashidah)

Recall, explain and evaluate

1 What is meant by the term 'quality of life'? (2)

2 Explain what Rashidah means by 'even if they weren't perfect according to society's standards'. (4)

3 'Every woman has a right to choose if she wants an abortion.' Do you agree? Give reasons for your answer. (4)

A Muslim protest outside an abortion clinic

Fact file 2

Muslims believe that the rights and status of the foetus should be protected although opinions differ as to the exact point at which life begins. The opinions of when life begins are:

● the moment of conception
● when the foetus has recognizable human features
● after 120 days (from ensoulment).

In Islamic countries where the death penalty exists for certain crimes, the execution of pregnant women is postponed until after she has given birth and weaned the child. This preserves the child's right to live.

While it is in the mother's womb, the foetus has rights of inheritance, so, if a relative of a pregnant woman dies, the money is not divided until after the birth. This gives the child the right to inherit.

In the case of a woman having a miscarriage or a stillborn child, the foetus must be given a burial.

Creative assignment

Imagine you are a friend of Aisha (see page 98) in whom she has confided. Write either a conversation or a letter in which you respond to her situation.

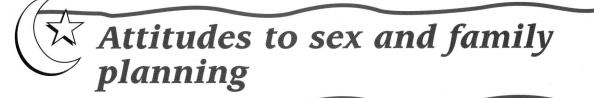

Attitudes to sex and family planning

Let's talk about sex...

Thoughts from the students

❝I'd like to ask questions but if you do, the boys think you're too forward.❞

❝I wish we could have our lessons separate from the girls, it's dead embarrassing.❞

❝Mr parents are withdrawing me from sex education – I think they're afraid I'll start practising what I've been taught!❞

Thoughts from the parents

❝I would want my daughter to be taught earlier than my son. I think girls mature earlier than boys.❞

❝I don't want my child to have lessons which don't take into account our religious rules.❞

❝Learning about contraception is all right, but only in the context of marriage.❞

Get talking

- Is school the best place for sex education? At what age should it take place?
- Do you agree with the rights of parents to withdraw their children from sex education lessons?
- Should it be taught to boys and girls separately?

Fact file 1

Islam teaches that sexual intimacy is only permitted within marriage, and is a gift from Allah. *'When a husband and wife share intimacy it is rewarded, and a blessing from Allah; just as they would be punished if they had engaged in illicit sex.'* (Hadith)

For this reason, men and women are expected to marry and **celibacy** (choosing not to have sexual intercourse and remaining unmarried) is not approved of (see page 26).

Men are taught that they should be kind to their wives so that their sexual relationship becomes a loving gift (sadaqah). Being unfaithful in marriage is considered to be very wrong and those found to have committed adultery are guilty of a serious sin.

Sex outside marriage, often referred to in the past as fornication, is also considered unlawful. Muhammad understood the problems of temptation for those not married and recommended fasting as a way of developing self-restraint.

Fact file 2

Homosexuality (see page 28) is thought to be unnatural and, therefore, unlawful. However, in some instances where it is known to exist, it is ignored rather than punished. A sign of changing attitudes is seen in the setting up of groups such as the Asian organization **Shakti**, which offers counselling services and advice for gay and lesbian Asians.

Masturbation is only considered acceptable if a person is unable to marry or if it will help resist the temptation of committing adultery or having sex before marriage.

A summary of the Muslim attitude to sex:

Faithfulness is all-important.

Adultery is unlawful.

Intimacy is for marriage only.

Treating women with respect is sadaqah.

Homosexuality is considered unnatural.

Fasting helps develop self-control.

Unfaithfulness is a form of stealing.

Loving sexual relationships in marriage are Allah's gift.

In some Muslim countries, such as Saudi Arabia, the teaching of the Qur'an (Shari'ah) is also the law of the land, and the punishment for adultery is severe.

100 lashes bring affair to end

European learns the hard way that Qur'an means what it says

'The woman and the man guilty of adultery or fornication, flog each of them with a hundred stripes.' (Surah 24:2)

Recall and explain

1 What is adultery? (1)

2 Explain the teachings of Islam concerning sexual relationships. (5)

3 What types of advice do you think Shakti might give? (4)

Family planning

Fact file 3

The main teaching about birth control in Islam is that self-control should be exercised. There are differing views about artificial forms (see page 27), with some Muslims accepting modern methods in certain circumstances. The rhythm method which involves having intercourse only during the time of a woman's cycle when she is least fertile and therefore unlikely to conceive is preferred to other ways. In Islam the pill and condom are more widely accepted than methods which cannot be reversed such as vasectomy and female sterilization. These are only permitted in life-threatening situations.

Conference on Islam and Family Planning

At the Conference on Islam and Family Planning (in 1971), the use of all safe and lawful contraception was approved for married couples if (in descending order of importance):

- there was a threat to the wife's health
- it helped lessen the burden of frequent child-bearing
- there was a chance of transmitting genetic disorders (certain conditions which children can inherit from parents)
- there was a serious financial difficulty.

Creative assignment

Write a short talk by a Muslim teacher to Muslim boys or girls on the subject of sexual relationships.

Fact file 4

Infertility

Some couples are unable to have children because one or other of them is sterile. Just as sex is seen as Allah's gift, so too, is the life that comes from it. If couples are not able to produce children it is seen as his will. *'He bestows both males and females, and He leaves barren whom He will …' (Surah 42:50)*

However, in cases of infertility, there are two acceptable steps that can be taken in Islam.

- Polygamy – (see page 107) In certain countries, but not in Britain, if a woman is sterile, her husband may have more than one wife.
- Fostering – couples are encouraged to take over the care of orphaned or abandoned children, although legal adoption, which gives the same status as a natural child born to the couple, is not permitted (see page 109).

Recall, explain and evaluate

1 Name two sources of authority a Muslim might refer to when seeking advice on family planning. **(2)**

2 Explain why Muslims consider some methods of contraception are more acceptable than others. **(4)**

3 'People should live together before they marry or they have no idea what their partners are really like.' Do you agree? In your answer you should consider more than one point of view. **(4)**

Marriage

Nisa and Mandy are college friends and are sitting in the common room chatting. Nisa, a Muslim, is explaining why she has to be at home with her family for the weekend.

Mandy: But you've never even met him. Let's have a look.
(She studies the photo that Nisa shows her.)
OK so he looks quite nice but I can't believe you can even think about marrying someone you don't even know.

Nisa: I'm not yet, but that's the whole idea. His family are old friends of my parents and so we're going to be introduced.

Mandy: How embarrassing – what if you don't fancy him?

Nisa: It's not about fancying him. If he's going to be right for me that will come later. Anyway, no-one's going to force me into anything. If we don't hit it off then that will be that. Don't forget it works both ways – he might not fancy me!

Mandy: I couldn't bear to have my marriage arranged for me. It's like those kids' fairy tales where all the suitors line up for the king to choose a suitable bride, while the princess meekly stands by, hoping for the best.

Nisa: What about your royal family? Can you imagine Prince Harry being allowed to date someone from the local comprehensive?

Mandy: Maybe not, but if I'm going to spend the rest of my life with someone, I want to choose him myself.

Nisa: OK and how many couples in this country who choose a marriage partner stay together for life? Have you looked at the British divorce statistics recently – one in two, isn't it?

Mandy: But where's the romance? It seems so cold and calculated. You can't give in a shopping order for a husband!

Nisa: It doesn't have to be cold. You still go through a period of getting to know each other. You'd be surprised how well it can work. Don't you think that something as important as a commitment for life should be based on a bit more than Bollywood-style* romance? What happens when the novelty wears off? We like to think we grow into love, not out of it.

Mandy: How do you know you're going to get on if you don't live together first?

Nisa: Our religion teaches that we must save ourselves. It's what we believe is right.

*Bollywood is the Asian equivalent of Hollywood.

Get talking

- What other important decisions do young people have to make which affect their future?

- Can you think of any other arguments for either Mandy's or Nisa's point of view that were not mentioned?

Fact file 1

The ideal for marriages in Islam is a life-long union based on trust, morality and devotion. They are arranged by families and are a legal contract. The couple concerned should know each other first and both parties give full consent. The arrangements include a decision about the dowry (**mahr**) paid by the groom to the bride. This will be paid in full, but a separate dowry may be paid later in the unlikely event of a divorce. A mutually agreed, written contract is drawn up (**nikah**). A Muslim man may marry a Christian or Jew but a Muslim woman may only marry a Muslim. The reason for this is that in Islam, children usually take the religion of the father. They may only marry women other than Christian or Jewish if the woman is prepared to convert to Islam, Christianity or Judaism.

Longer meetings will take place, with a chaperone.

Short meetings will be arranged.

Letters may be written.

Photos will be exchanged if the couple don't live near each other.

Information will be given.

Family discussion will begin.

Steps to know each other

In countries such as Britain where Islam is not the main religion, it can sometimes be difficult for Muslims to know about suitable families to approach. Many are now finding the Western-style marriage bureau a useful way of finding suitable partners. In this way, they can be introduced to people of similar interests and backgrounds.

Here is a view from a couple who decided to advertise for a partner for their daughter.

•We were getting worried about our daughter. She has reached the age where she really ought to be settling down and having children, rather than behaving like a child herself.

We want her to get married soon, and to someone who we think would be suitable for her. We worry that she may have had boyfriends in the past, and we didn't want her to come home one night and suddenly announce she was planning to marry someone of a different religion.

She wasn't very happy about it at first. She thought it would be really embarrassing to put herself on the market like that. She is going along with it now because at heart she is a good girl and she respects Islam.

We don't want her to marry someone who she won't be happy with, so we haven't mentioned marriage in the advert. You can't pin someone down to something like that.

We are just going to take things slowly – if she does meet someone she will be able to see them on her own terms for a while before she has to make a commitment to them. It is important for her to be friends with her future husband.

At the end of the day, her happiness is utmost in our hearts. We are willing to wait until she finds someone she really wants. She has had proposals in the past and we allowed her to turn them down because she felt they weren't the right guy for her. Marriage is a two way thing after all.•

Recall and evaluate

1 Describe two of the steps leading to a Muslim marriage. **(3)**

2 What is the meaning of the following words – mahr, convert, nikah? **(3)**

3 'I'm glad my parents helped me find a partner – it took away a lot of pressure.' Would you agree? Give reasons for your answer. **(4)**

Fact file 2

After a marriage has been arranged a date is set for the wedding. The ceremony is simple and brief and, since a recent change in British law, can now take place anywhere. It is often performed in a masjid with the imam leading it. The couple will exchange vows promising to base their marriage on the teaching of Allah and to make it a partnership of love, mercy, peace, faithfulness and co-operation. There will be readings from the Qur'an and prayers will be offered. The couple may exchange rings and sign the contract before two witnesses. This establishes the relationship according to the teachings of Islam. The roles of both partners are of equal importance and in their different ways they are taught to give each other love and support. Their shared responsibilities will extend to the nurturing of children and care of the extended family (see page 108).

Advice to the bride

Advice to the groom

'He has planted affection and mercy between you.' (Surah 30:21)

'The best of treasures is a good wife. She is pleasing to her husband's eyes, obedient to his word and watchful over his possessions in his absence.' (Hadith)

'Do not marry for the sake of beauty; the beauty may become the cause of moral decline.' (Hadith)

'Do not marry for the sake of wealth for this may become the cause of disobedience.' (Hadith)

'… and the best of you are those who treat your wife best.' (Hadith)

'They are your garments and ye are their garments.' (Surah 2:187)

Creative assignment

Imagine Mandy and Nisa (from the dialogue on page 104) meeting five years later. Nisa is married but Mandy is not. Write a new dialogue between them in which they talk about their different roles and lifestyles.

Fact file 3

Polygamy is the practice of a man being married to more than one woman. The teaching of the Qur'an permits a man to have up to four wives, but only with the permission of his first wife. When the marriage contract is drawn up there will often be a promise on behalf of the groom that polygamy will not take place. Where it does happen a man is required to treat all wives equally, both in the time he spends with them and the possessions they receive. *'Marry women of your choice, two, or three, or four; but if ye fear that ye shall not be able to deal justly (with them), then only one.'* (Surah 4:3)

Historically there have often been strong social reasons for polygamy where it has been seen to be a help for the female population. Where there is a larger percentage of women than men, such as after a war, it is a way of offering companionship and financial security to women who might otherwise be driven to desperate lengths such as prostitution. Muhammad married twelve times after the death of his first wife Khadijah. His wives were mostly widows and the marriages were seen as acts of kindness. Today, polygamy is far less common and it has been banned in some countries, such as Tunisia. In Islamic countries where it still exists, men can be taken to court if they are found to be abusing the laws concerning it.

Self-styled preacher is serving 25 months in jail while awaiting trial for violating Islamic law by having more than four wives at a time

Recall and evaluate

1 What is polygamy? (2)

2 What are the only reasons that a Muslim man is allowed to have more than one wife? (4)

3 Do you think a man should be punished for having ten wives if they have all agreed to the marriage? Give reasons for your answer, showing you have considered more than one point of view. (4)

Home and family

•We live in Imran's large family house with his father and two of his sisters and their respective families while their houses are being built across the canal. Imran and I live upstairs in what is basically a self-contained flat, but we spend a lot of time with the family and the various children. I've never seen such appealing adorable children. They're so well brought up. There's something about the extended family system which means that children are stable and loved, yet disciplined. We've also got two dogs and Imran's bought us chickens and a goat so we can have free-range eggs and meat from the garden. Imran's sisters are my protectors.•

Jemima Khan
(née Goldsmith),
the wife of Imran Khan

 **Get talking**

● What do you think is an ideal size for a family?

● What are the advantages and disadvantages of having relatives living with you or living nearby?

What is a family?

In describing family structures, the terms **nuclear** and **extended** are often used. A nuclear family refers to the basic group consisting of mother, father and children. The extended family refers to the larger group which includes grandparents and other relatives, such as aunts, uncles and cousins. Jemima Khan's account of her new life as part of a Muslim family describes an extended family.

Fact file 1

The family is the basis of Islamic society in which the rights and duties of each family member are laid down. It is believed that parents have a strong role in helping to shape and develop children's values, morals and personalities.

A husband and wife's relationship with each other should be one of respect and they should attend to each other's needs.

Children are taught to be considerate to their parents and listen to their advice and instruction. When the time comes, they will support and maintain them in old age.

Parents are expected to show interest in their children and be affectionate towards them. It is part of their role to help them find marriage partners when they are older.

'Your children have the right to receive equal treatment, as you have the right that they should honour you.' (Hadith)

Dear Rashid

Congratulations on your success. Your Aunt and I are so proud of you. As you know, we were not blessed by Allah with children of our own. When your dear parents were tragically killed we knew it was his will that you should come under our care and protection. We could never take their place and we have never pretended that we are more than Uncle and Aunt. But we cannot help being pleased that we have had the opportunity to help you along your way in life.

The blessings of Allah be upon you.

Fostering

Adoption in the legal sense is not allowed in Islam although families are expected to show compassion towards the children of relatives, and fostering is encouraged. Those taken care of are entitled to know about their true parentage. They do not have the same rights or status as the true children of the parents, as it is taught that a child can only have one father. Also, there could be disputes over inheritance.

'… nor has He made your adopted sons your sons … Call them by [the names of] their fathers … But if ye know not their fathers' [names, call them] your brothers in faith.'
(Surah 33:4–5)

Recall and explain

1 How would you define the term 'family'? **(2)**

2 What is the difference between a nuclear and an extended family? **(4)**

3 Explain why the family is considered the basis of Islamic society. **(4)**

Fact file 2

Learning the faith in the home

From the moment a child is born, it is introduced to the faith of Islam. The first words that will be heard are from the Call to Prayer, adhan, which is whispered into the baby's right ear, usually by its father. When the baby is seven days old, its head is shaved and the same weight of the hair in silver is given to the poor. (In the case of bald babies, a donation is still usually given!) This ceremony is known as **aqiqa**. The ceremony of **tahnik** is also practised. This involves touching the lips of the baby with something sweet such as honey as a symbol of the hope that the child grows up to be 'sweet' and obedient. Prayers for the child's well-being are said while this happens. Circumcision (**khitan**), the cutting of the foreskin of the penis, is carried out on Muslim boys and is usually done at the same time as the aqiqa.

From a very early age, children are taught the rituals, beliefs and prayers of their religion. This will involve attending the masjid regularly (see page 129). It is here that they will learn Arabic so that they are able to read and memorize parts of the Qur'an. There is no set coming of age ceremony for them but at the age of puberty they are expected to take responsibility for their actions. This will involve learning about the dietary laws and what is halal (see page 133).

Ramadan (sawm)

'*… it can be a great joy to have a big family … During Ramadan when you're sitting with your family and the time comes to break your fast, that's the moment of true joy.*'
(Emran Md Majid, taxi driver in the sultanate of Brunei.)

When they are old enough to fast during Ramadan (see page 127). Muslim children will learn the importance of self-control and be taught awareness of those less fortunate than themselves. At the end of the month of Ramadan is the festival of Id-ul-Fitr. This is one of the two main Muslim festivals and is a time of joy and celebration. The word Id means 'returning or recurring happiness'. Muslims believe that the occasion ensures that families do not lose touch with each other. They are re-united with extended families and friends who may be living some distance away. The customs of exchanging cards, giving presents and eating special foods all help to make it an enjoyable family occasion.

Recall and explain

1 What is the adhan? (2)

2 Why do most Muslims fast during Ramadan? (4)

3 Explain why Muslims treat the Qur'an with great respect. (4)

Creative assignment

Imagine you are in a similar situation to Jemima Khan (page 108). Write a letter home to a friend describing family life as a Muslim.

Divorce

> Are you looking for an attractive Muslim girl who is sincere, honest caring and loyal? I am 35 years old, a British-born graduate. I am divorced, following a brief, childless marriage. Correspondence invited from genuine and sincere gentleman.

Get talking

- What are the problems for divorced people?
- Do you think advertising for partners in personal columns is a good thing?

Steps to divorce

There is a three month period of waiting (**iddah**) for the couple to reconsider their position. They remain in the same home but without physical contact. If it is the husband seeking the divorce, he must announce it three times over this period. Financial duties to the wife must continue to be met.

The extended family will become involved and a member from each side will try to mediate for the couple.

At the end of the iddah, if the wife has applied for divorce, deferred dowry is often returned and settlements are made. Both partners are free to re-marry. The husband has legal custody of the children. He either pays for their upkeep or looks after them himself.

Fact file

Islam teaches that there is nothing that Allah likes less than for a couple to divorce. *'The most detestable act that God has permitted is divorce.'* (Hadith)

If a marriage has severe difficulties and appears irretrievably broken down, divorce is permitted in Islam. However, it is considered to be the last resort and important steps have to be taken to ensure that a fair settlement is made. According to Islamic teaching, both men and women have equal rights to seek divorce. Apart from a mutual agreement, a wife has grounds if her husband is sterile, refuses to maintain her, abuses her, becomes mentally ill, deserts her or is in prison. *'If a wife fears cruelty or desertion on her husband's part, there is no blame on them if they arrange an amicable settlement between themselves.'* (Surah 4:128)

Explain and evaluate

1. Explain why there is an iddah or three months' waiting period before a Muslim divorce. **(2)**

2. Explain what situations might appear irretrievable. **(3)**

3. 'It's better for children to live with both parents, even if they don't get on.' Do you agree? Give reasons to support your view. **(5)**

Caring for grandmother – 4000 miles from home

Atia Idrees, aged 22 is from Pakistan and is extending her stay in England to care for her sick and elderly grandmother. She has been told that her grandmother, who is half blind and crippled with arthritis, is eligible for a place in a nursing home but Atia has special reasons for not letting her go. Every day she tends for the old woman, feeding and washing her, reading to her from the Qur'an, helping her to dress, taking her to the toilet.

Her grandmother, Alam Bibi, does not speak a word of English and is a devout Muslim. The Manchester Pakistani Welfare Association has attempted to explain to the Home Office the 'shame' Mrs Bibi would feel if she was forced into a home. For a Pakistani female, it would be unacceptable to live with non-Muslims because of her perceptions about the 'pollution' of people who eat pig meat or drink alcohol and who are not ritually clean because of not always washing in running water.

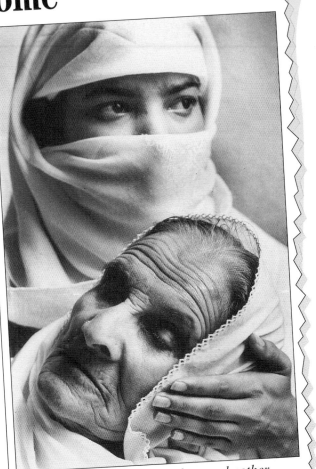

Atia with her sick and elderly grandmother

Get talking

- What are your views about old people's homes?
- To what extent do you think families should be responsible for their elderly relatives?
- What are the reasons given for it being preferable for Atia's grandmother to be cared for at home?

Fact file

Muslims are taught to respect and revere the older members of their families.

'Thy Lord hath decreed that ye ... be kind to parents. Whether one or both of them attain old age in thy life, say not to them a word of contempt, nor repel them, but address them in terms of honour'. (Surah 17:23)

Support for the elderly is important in Islam and the idea of sending ageing members of the family away to an old people's home is something Muslims prefer not to consider. However, for some Muslims the problem of lack of room in which to accommodate the extended family has led to a change in attitudes. In some communities special homes for the elderly are being built.

Dear Sir,

I am writing to ask you if you have a vacancy in your home for my father. He is 78 years old and has severe arthritis and so is no longer mobile. I would much prefer to have continued looking after him myself. Unfortunately, the situation has become impossible for me. I am a widow with three children still living at home. Our space is very limited. My father can no longer climb the stairs which means that our living room has to be used as his bedroom at night. Dua, his personal prayers, are very important to him and he finds it difficult to cope with not having a room where he can be in peace for this. As you may know, our duty of praying five times a day means an early start and my father needs to go to bed very early. As I am sure you will understand, this is very difficult when the rest of the family wishes to stay up later. Equally, it is hard for the children who also need space. I have to go out to work which means he is unattended during the day. He cannot go into a non-Muslim home where he would not have facilities for prayer and halal food would not be provided. I feel that in your home, where he will be with professional carers and Muslims with whom he can relate, his needs will be much better met. I am only concerned for his welfare and happiness.

Yours sincerely

Mira Hussein

Residents in a Muslim home for the elderly

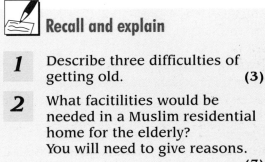

Recall and explain

1 Describe three difficulties of getting old. **(3)**

2 What facilities would be needed in a Muslim residential home for the elderly?
You will need to give reasons.
(7)

Age does not affect a person's religious duties

Older Pilgrims to Get Hajj Priority

First-time pilgrims to Makkah who are aged 55 and above as of 1 January 1996 will be given priority for the annual pilgrimage … Immediate family members who have performed the Hajj before can sign up as joint applicants with the first-timers. This is for elderly pilgrims who may need help on the trip …

Journeying towards Makkah – an elderly man on Hajj

Hajj and the elderly

The pilgrimage to Makkah, one of the five Pillars of Islam (see page 91) is something every Muslim tries to do during his or her lifetime. Although spiritually rewarding, it is very demanding and the elderly and sick are excused from taking part. However, many elderly people have saved all their lives to go on Hajj and those who do are helped by the 1996 ruling. Makkah is in Saudia Arabia. Muslims who live in countries far away, face a long journey even before the Hajj begins. On arrival, there will be many hours of travel, often in intense heat. Because of the tens of thousands of others coming for the Hajj the crowds are dense, which can make it difficult for the elderly and frail. The pilgrimage itself involves long hours of prayer and several days of travel. For instance, one of the requirements is to run between the two hills of **Safa** and **Marwah** in memory of Hajar and her son Ismail's search for water (see page 91). Younger members of the family accompanying the elderly pilgrims will be able to assist and protect them. This might involve the use of wheelchairs in some cases.

Recall, explain and evaluate

1 Hajj is one of the pillars of Islam. Describe another two. **(4)**

2 Why might the elderly want to go on the Hajj pilgrimage? **(2)**

3 'When you get old you're thrown on the scrap-heap. You feel no use to anyone!' In what ways can society value the elderly? **(4)**

Creative assignment

With reference to this chapter, design a collage or poster reflecting the value of the elderly to society.

'Let there be a community among you, advocating what is right and eradicating what is wrong' *(Surah 3:104)*

The questions below give you a chance to re-examine the issues raised in the preceding units. Remember to look at the number of marks for each question and to develop your answer accordingly.

a Name any *two* sources of moral authority a Muslim might refer to before making a decision. **(2)**

b Give a brief description of the preparation before *either* a Muslim marriage *or* a Muslim divorce takes place. **(6)**

c 'It's the children who are our future.'

Explain the role that home and family life plays in a young Muslim's life. **(7)**

d 'Young people should be out having fun – they shouldn't be thinking about religion until they're older.' (Response of a 16 year old in a recent survey.)

Do you agree? Give reasons for your answer showing you have considered other points of views. **(5)**

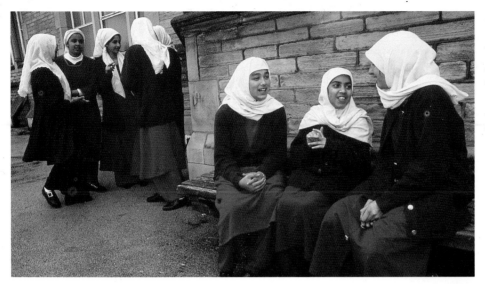

Some schools do not permit Muslim girls to wear headscarves. Many Muslims have campaigned on this issue as they see it as an essential part of their faith to dress modestly

Victory! Muslim sisters win right to wear headscarves in school

Get talking

● Do you have a piece of clothing or jewellery that you feel strongly about being able to wear? Why is it important to you?

● Can you think of other examples of when people take action to show their beliefs (e.g. vegetarianism)?

Fact file 1

Muslim women are required to dress modestly. They must wear clothes that cover all of their bodies, except hands and face, when in the presence of men other than their immediate family. Hair is covered by a head scarf and the body garments must be loose-fitting. Tight trousers would not be acceptable. This is known as wearing **hijab** (see page 128).

'Tell thy wives and daughters, and the believing women, that they should cast their outer garments over their persons (when abroad); that is most convenient, that they should be known (as such) and not molested.' (Surah 33:59)

Wearing hijab is seen as a form of protection. By concealing their bodies, women are not looked upon as sex objects. Hijab is considered a symbol of purity and a way of showing that women are keeping themselves for their husbands. *'Believing women ... should draw their veils over their bosoms and not display their beauty except to their husbands.' (Surah 24:31)*

Some women wear a different form of hijab from others. This has to do with culture rather than religious rules. In some countries, women are required to wear black veils covering most of their face when outside. This is known as **chador** in Iran and women can be arrested if they disobey. Many women, however, do not feel the need to bow to the pressure of others. They choose to wear hijab willingly. They see it as an opportunity to please Allah and as a symbol of their beliefs.

What do women feel about hijab?

Here are three viewpoints – the first from a woman brought up in the Muslim tradition and the other two from English women who have converted to Islam.

Khula's view

In hijab I felt myself different. I felt myself purified and protected. I felt the company of Allah … I found the hijab sheltered me from such impolite stares. I was also very happy and proud in hijab which is not only the sign of my obedience to Allah but also the manifestation of my faith … As a policeman becomes more conscious of his profession in his uniform, I had a stronger feeling of being Muslim with hijab.

Ruqaiyyah's view

I didn't mind not showing a cleavage or covering my ankles, but it's very hard for an English woman to sacrifice her hair. I'd always gone to the hairdresser, but there's no point when you wear a scarf.

Huda's view

Islamic dress is liberating rather than oppressive … In the West, you grow up with the idea that you have to look sexy to look good. If you are not a size 10, forget it. I feel free covered up, not constantly on view as a sex object.

Different forms of hijab

An Iranian woman wearing chador

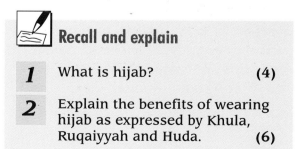

Recall and explain

1 What is hijab? **(4)**

2 Explain the benefits of wearing hijab as expressed by Khula, Ruqaiyyah and Huda. **(6)**

117

Myths and reality

Muslim women are taking an increasingly active role in the world of technology

Many people have a stereotypical view of the life of Muslim women. They think that the women are repressed and are often seen as being inferior to men. It is not always taken into account that, for instance, Pakistanis had Benazir Bhutto as their state leader and that Bosnian and Palestinian women were part of the fighting forces, alongside the men. Although there are certain restrictions put upon women, many of these come from the authority of the state and do not have their origin in religion.

❛*The majority of what is written in the Qur'an is liberating to women but, patriarchy* being what it is, cultural practices grew over the Qur'an which are unjustifiable. Many female theologians are working on reclaiming the Qur'an.*❜

(Saaba – British Muslim from London)

*Patriarchy – a social organization in which the head of the family is always a man.

Fact file 2

The Qur'an teaches that women were created from the same single soul as men (see page 152) and will be judged in the same way as men. Although men and women are of equal importance, each have different roles to play and each should support the other.

'…Reverence your Guardian – Lord, who created you from a single person, created, of like nature, his mate, and from them twain scattered (like seeds) countless men and women.' (Surah 4:1)

The most important function for women is within the home. This, though, is not looked upon as a lesser role but one of great significance. Muslims believe that as long as the responsibilities of the home are not neglected and that there is no clash with their religious rules, women may take up other activities and careers. It is considered that both men and women should be able to use what gifts and skills they have in society. Women can play a valuable role, particularly in some of the caring professions such as nursing, teaching and social work.

Muhammad showed great respect for women and was known to have advised men not to go to war so that they could care for their mothers. He believed that women had the right to work. He himself married Khadijah who was a business woman. At his farewell sermon at Arafat before 124,000 people he spoke about the role of women.

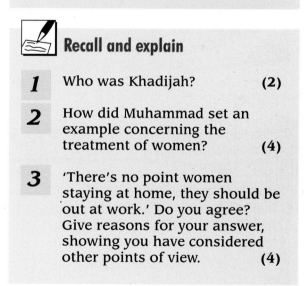

'O People, it is true that you have certain rights with regard to your women, but they also have rights over you. Remember that you have taken them as your wives only under Allah's trust and with His permission. If they abide by your right then to them belongs the right to be fed and clothed in kindness. Do treat your women well and be kind to them for they are your partners and committed helpers. And it is your right that they do not make friends with anyone of whom you do not approve, as well as never to be unchaste.'

(Part of Muhammad's last sermon)

Recall and explain

1 Who was Khadijah? (2)

2 How did Muhammad set an example concerning the treatment of women? (4)

3 'There's no point women staying at home, they should be out at work.' Do you agree? Give reasons for your answer, showing you have considered other points of view. (4)

 Creative assignment

A young Muslim woman is applying for a career post. Decide what the job might be and, using the information about women from this chapter, write her letter of application in which she describes herself. Include questions you think she might want to ask her future employer.

Work

Basketball star Kareem Abdul-Jabbar carries his Muslim beliefs into his working life.

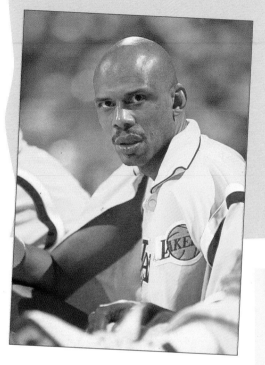

•*The "less moral" way can be very tempting. Like everyone, I am always in a kind of battle between my lower self (the part of me tied to society's pettiest goals: greed, selfishness, narrow-mindedness) and my higher self (the part of me that cares for others and acts for the benefit of the community). The Qur'an guides me. It teaches that some of the reason we're here is to exercise personal responsibility, to evolve the higher self and to influence that development in others.•*

(Kareem Abdul-Jabbar led the Los Angeles Lakers to five NBA championships)

Get talking

- What issues of morality can people's jobs involve them in?
- Which jobs do you consider immoral and why?

Fact file

Muslims believe that it is their duty to work honestly and to the best of their ability. Allah has given them skills which they should strive to develop and put to good use. This means that whatever they are employed in doing should be of benefit to the community and the smooth running of society. It is important for Muslims to gain knowledge as without it they will lack the ability to manage their affairs or play an active part in helping to shape society. No type of work is considered inferior to another if it is done sincerely and it is in keeping with Muslim values. Certain jobs are forbidden.

These include any connected with gambling, magic and fortune-telling, pornography, prostitution, alcohol and harmful drugs.

In Islam men are expected to be the breadwinners and maintain their families. Women have equal rights to work and own or run businesses. They are encouraged to pursue their education and develop their skills which are thought to be particularly suited to working in caring professions such as medicine. Muslim teaching on modesty means that any work in which the body is used provocatively, such as modelling or dancing, is not acceptable.

Sinan abdur-Mennan (1489–1588) designed more buildings than any other architect who has lived. These included forts, mosques and aqueducts. Two of his pupils designed the Taj Mahal in India

Muslims have benefited the world with their highly-developed skills in many fields of work such as science, mathematics and architecture.

Work and prayer

Although Islam teaches that humans have free will, obedience to Allah is an important duty. Muslims are taught that they should not be so involved with work that they become too interested in materialistic values, forgetting their loyalty to Allah. The duty of salah which is performed at intervals throughout the day, helps to remind Muslims where their priority should be. However, work is important and even though Friday is a special day for jumu'ah prayers at the masjid, it is not a rest day and work is expected to be carried out before and after the duty has been performed. A story from the Hadith tells of a man who spent all his time in prayer and meditation at the masjid. When Muhammad asked who fed him he was told that his brother did, to which the Prophet replied that the brother was a better man.

Work and Ramadan

Sawm, fasting at Ramadan (see page 110), can be a test for Muslims as going for long periods without food or drink can sap people's strength. It can be particularly difficult for those in work which demands a great deal of energy or for those working in restaurants and food shops. In Muslim countries, this is easier as everyone is involved and the pace of life is expected to be slower during this month.

Recall and explain

1 Name two jobs forbidden to Muslims. **(2)**

2 What are jumu'ah prayers? **(2)**

3 Many Muslims wish to pray at work during their lunch hour. Explain what facilities would be needed. **(6)**

Creative assignment

Create a collage which is divided into two sections, one headed by a tick and one by a cross, to show examples of kinds of work that would be acceptable and unacceptable for Muslims to do.

Prejudice and discrimination

Malcolm X

'*About twenty of us Muslims who had finished the Hajj were sitting in a huge tent on Mount Arafat. As a Muslim from America, I was at the centre of attraction. They asked me what about the Hajj had impressed me the most. One of the several who spoke English asked; they translated my answers for the others. My answer to that question was not the one they expected, but it drove home my point.*

I said, "The Brotherhood". The people of all races, colours from all over the world coming together as ONE! It has proved to me the power of the One God.'

(An extract from Malcom X's account of his pilgrimage to Makkah)

Fact file 1

One of the most important teachings in Islam is that all people are equal, although not the same. Humankind is seen as being like a large garden in which there are flowers of every kind and colour, each important in its own right. Allah created the whole of humankind from one soul and their differences were his intended design. '*And among His signs is the creation of the heavens and the earth, and the variations in your languages and your colours …*' (Surah 30:22)

Muhammad's example of treating people with equality can be found throughout the Sunnah and Hadith. The person he appointed to be the very first **Mu'adhin** (the caller to prayer) was Bilal ibn Rabah, a black Ethiopian.

This brotherhood of Muslims, ummah, crosses all national and political boundaries. A baby enters it as soon as the adhan is whispered into its ear shortly after its birth and is born with fitrah (without sin). This means that anyone returning to the religion in later life is called a revert, rather than a convert and will not be treated differently from those who have practised Islam since birth.

The ummah

The community of Islam is multi-racial, multi-cultural and multi-lingual. What unites Muslims? – the strength and support of the five pillars. These are the five duties which all Muslims perform.

Hajj

By the wearing of **ihram*** by everyone on the Pilgrimage to Makkah, to show purity and equality, all differences of wealth and status are invisible.

•*I felt myself humbled, as someone from an affluent and privileged family but, before the eyes of Allah, I was at one with all classes of people. Either side of me were poor people, yet they were as rich as I was in the eyes of God.*•

(Zubeida)

* Ihram is two plain white unsewn cloths worn by men. For women it consists of their normal modest clothing.

Shahadah

By stating their creed and truly believing it, they have entered into the community of Islam.

•*When I wished to become a Muslim I realized by saying the shahadah I was equal to those who had kept faith all their lives.*•

(Fatima)

Shahadah | Salah | Zakah | Sawn | Hajj

Salah

By praying five times a day at set times and always facing the Ka'bah in Makkah they are united in their worship.

•*At prayer times I am always reminded of our international brotherhood. My brother in Toronto, my cousin in Lahore, my uncle in Bethlehem and I in Manchester are all praying at the same time, in the same direction with the same purpose. When I stand next to my fellow Muslims in the masjid I mix with people of different ages and races. You don't save the prayer mat next to you for your best friend.*•

(Ali)

Zakah

By giving up 2.5 per cent of their savings held over the year Muslims are sharing with those of their brotherhood who are less fortunate.

•*As I believe it is only by the Grace of Allah that I have money, zakah helps to stop me being selfish.*•

(Imran)

Sawm

By fasting during the month of Ramadan, Muslims are strengthened by the knowledge that all are making the same sacrifice.

•*I look forward to my fast – it has a special atmosphere. It is a time when I feel the strength of the ummah most and it reminds me of those without food and how we shouldn't take it for granted.*•

(Nisa)

 Recall and explain

1 Describe in detail what is meant by Shahadah and salah. (4)

2 Do you think religion can unite people? In your answer you should refer to a range of practices. (6)

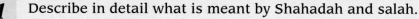

Prejudice and discrimination against Muslims

PIG'S HEAD JIBE

A MUSLIM foundry worker was splattered with blood from a severed pig's head, was urinated against in the shower and taunted with racial abuse, an industrial tribunal heard.

Now 36-year-old Azar Hussain is claiming racial discrimination and unfair dismissal against Westcroft Castings Limited, Bradford, foreman Henry Irvine and company director Alan Scotson.

In one incident a pig's head was brought into the factory. Mr Irvine allegedly urinated against Mr Hussain as he showered, in another. The foreman is also claimed to have called him a 'paki' several times a day.

The tribunal also heard that Mr Hussain's food was called dirty when he brought it into work and he suffered racial taunts during the Gulf War.

The company ignored the abuse, according to Mr Hussain.

The hearing continues.

Get talking

● It has been estimated that approximately 1 in 20 racist attacks are never reported. Why do you think this is?

Attacks on Muslims continue

A petrol bomb was thrown through the living room window of a Muslim family in Kenton, Middlesex. No one was seriously hurt but the furniture was set on fire. Luckily for them, a policeman and a fireman came to their rescue. A month before, two bricks were thrown through the living room window, narrowly missing Babru Miah Begum's head. During the fire bomb attack, he was at his cousin's house. His wife Mina was praying while her daughters, Fatima, Sofina and son Suja were asleep. She heard a crash and ran downstairs to find the furniture on fire. Fatima and Sofina suffered from smoke inhalation.

In Rotherham, a gang of around 14 men and women attacked Khurseed Ahmed, 36, while his terrified wife and young children looked on helpless.

… Mr Qureshi said his two children, Rosina, 11, and Iran, 8, were on a ride at the Falmingo Land fun park near Malton when a gang began punching and pulling the hair of the children. 'They came out with a lot of racial abuse and then someone pushed or hit me from behind and I fell on the ground.' They continued to kick and punch him. His daughter was punched a couple of times.

Fact file 2

Racism is a result of prejudice (see page 58). There is evidence that Asian Muslims are 50 times more likely to be at the receiving end of racially-motivated attacks than whites. The **Anti-Racist Alliance**, detailing racist murders, has reported that over 65 per cent of the victims since 1991 were Muslims. In response to this situation, a group called Muslims Against Racism has been set up to campaign against anti-Muslim discrimination. Its aims are to:
● give comfort and support to victims
● focus on an action plan to combat the problems.

The group feels that more needs to be done to help Muslims. With high unemployment there is pressure on parents to work very long hours (see page 36).

Muslims Against Racism has made contact with Muslim communities in other European countries in order to share their experiences and show solidarity. They see themselves as a means of uniting Muslims and, through a series of programmes, they aim to educate them to lead the way in overcoming the evils of racism.

When East meets West

Barriers caused by ignorance

Building bridges between people of different beliefs and cultures requires knowledge. Ignorance can lead to misunderstanding and may cause offence.

Lack of knowledge can lead to prejudice when the media give a false or stereotypical picture. Many people judge Islam from press coverage of the activities and views of a few extremist groups which most Muslims would not want to be a part of.

The French fashion house Chanel apologized to Muslims for showing a low-cut dress on which they had unknowingly embroidered verses of the Qur'an

Post Office refuses to withdraw offensive leaflets

The leaflet called 'A Celebration of Cats' contained a picture claiming to be of Muhammad placed alongside photos of political leaders Lenin and Mussolini. A spokesperson apologized and said that no offence was intended and that they only wanted to show a display of historical cat lovers.

The importance Muslims attach to Muhammad means it would be considered wrong for him to be represented in any way other than through his words and example.

Recall and explain

1 Why is Muhammad such an important prophet for Muslims? **(2)**

2 On a visit to Egypt, Prince Charles said:
'The West has formed a mistaken view of the Islamic world. What binds our two worlds together is much more powerful than what divides us.'
What do you think he meant? **(2)**

3 Explain why the Chanel dress and the Post Office leaflet would cause offence to Muslims? **(6)**

Muslims in Britain

British Muslims

> *"it's difficult to pray at my school. I need a room and washing facilities."*

> *"I want to wear hijab but I'm the only girl in school who does."*

> *"I don't think a separate school would prepare me for the multi-faith society I'll later work in."*

> *"I think there'll be more ignorance about Islam unless all religions mix from an early age."*

Fact file 3

Islam is a fast-growing religion both in Britain and throughout the world. People who are not born into the faith but who convert to it are usually referred to as reverts. This is because in Islam it is believed that as everyone is created by Allah, all people are born as Muslims and those who join are reclaiming their inheritance. A well-known example of this is Jemima Khan (see page 108).

In the United Kingdom 60 per cent of British Muslims are under the age of 25 and have English as their first language. Living in a country where the rest of the population does not share their beliefs is a challenge for many Muslims and it is not without its difficulties. Although there are now many more facilities for them, such as an increase in shops selling halal meat and many schools allowing girls to wear hijab, education is still a problem. The requirements of their religion can often bring young British Muslims into conflict with the rules and practices of the school they are in. There is currently much discussion about separate Muslim schools and several state funded Muslim schools have recently been established.

> *"It's difficult during Ramadan when so few children in my class fast."*

> *"My mum wants my two sisters to be taught by female teachers but the school they go to can't provide this."*

Get talking

● What are your views on the advantages and disadvantages of religious schools.

A family gets together for a festive dinner at Id

Fact file 4

In the month of Ramadan, Muslims commemorate the time when Muhammad received the first revelation from Allah. During the hours of daylight they are not allowed to let any food or liquid pass their lips. Very young children, the sick, elderly and pregnant are exempt, as too are those whose work requires precision, such as surgeons. It is easier to fast during Ramadan in Muslim countries where everyone is involved and geared to it. Restaurants close and eating, drinking and smoking in public places are prohibited. It is accepted that the pace of life will necessarily be slower. Going for long periods without food or water can sap people's strength. In Britain it can be a problem for Muslims having to work alongside others who are eating and drinking and where employers and teachers do not always allow for a reduction in energy.

Here in the UK, where there is no declared holiday for the festival of Id at the end of Ramadan, families are often forced to postpone the actual celebration to the weekend, for the sake of convenience. Speaking about Asian Muslims here, Mrs Shama Contractor, President of Muslim Women's Welfare Association, feels that 'those in full-time jobs have to make a real effort' to find time for prayer times between appointments, and finding a place for prayer within an office.

Recall and explain

1 Why do Muslims fast during Ramadan? **(5)**

2 What difficulties might they experience keeping the fast in Britain? **(5)**

'There was in Islam a tradition which painted the devil as being in the West. That won't do for us, we are the West.'

(Jamil Ali)

Fact file 5

Some second and third generation Muslims growing up in the West feel that many of the practices of the older generation have more to do with Eastern culture than actual teaching from the Qur'an. As a result, they are interpreting religion for themselves in a way that takes on parts of Western traditions but which is still firmly rooted in Islamic teaching. They will eat pizza but it must be halal. Girls will still choose to wear hijab (see page 116) but it will often be designed to suit the European climate.

 Get talking

- How important do you think it is to keep traditions?

- Are there traditions you have been brought up with that you feel strongly about?

Pizza...Pizza...Pizza...

Try our delicious PIZZA

whatever toppings you like – just ask!

WE USE ONLY HALAL MEAT

101 High St.

Seeboard advice at the Mosque

A CUSTOMER service desk in the Croydon Mosque is one of the new services being considered by electricity company Seeboard.

The move comes after a series of recent meetings with members of the Asian community and the Race Equality Council in Croydon aimed at improving the service Seeboard offers them.

Ethnic leaders said customers who had trouble with English found it hard to raise queries about bills. A weekly surgery at the London Road mosque with an interpreter on hand was deemed to be the best solution.

The mosque was chosen as the favourite location for a weekly surgery after Iffat Rizvi, who was present at the meetings with Seeboard, pointed out it was a major meeting place for those in need of help.

Fact file

The masjid has an important role in any Muslim community but particularly in places where Islam is not the majority religion. It is a place which can provide the facilities and fulfil the needs of Muslims which can be difficult to find elsewhere. In Britain the masjid is a communal place for prayer, relaxation, social functions and education. Many masjids have a school (**madrasah**) where Muslims can learn Arabic to help the study of their Qur'an. Equality is emphasized and old, young, rich, poor, black and white stand together in prayer. Classes are held for refugees and there are sometimes health units with female doctors for the women. Funerals and circumcisions are arranged and conducted.

Many masjids promote inter-faith activities by holding open days when non-Muslims can visit, and they join with other religions to campaign on world issues. They often give support to local communities in time of difficulty.

Mourners shed tears for Afghan refugee Ruhullah Aramesh at his funeral on Monday. A service was held at the mosque ... Crowds of people of different cultures and religions turned up outside the mosque to peacefully pay their respects. ... Ruhullah died after being attacked by a gang near his home.

Recall and explain

1 What happens at a madrasah? **(4)**

2 How do you think a masjid could give support to local communities? **(6)**

The natural world

I the world, who used to be free
Am imprisoned by your disloyalty to me.
For your own benefit
You have used me
Regardless of my infinite beauty.
Was this the way I was meant to be?

(Hend Hawas, 16, Egypt)

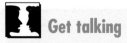 **Get talking**

● In what ways do you think the writer of the poem thinks people have been 'disloyal' to the Earth?

● What are your concerns about the environment?

Fact file 1

Muslims believe that Allah made the world and everything in it. Human beings are his most important creation and have been given the role of **khalifah**. This means that they have inherited the responsibility of being guardians to look after and care for all of nature. *'It is He who hath made you (His agents) inheritors of the Earth.' (Surah 6:165)*

There is a pattern and balance in the universe, known as the fitrah, which cannot be changed. It is for humans to maintain that balance by being aware of the needs of the rest of creation.

'So set thou thy face steadily and truly to the Faith. (Establish) Allah's handiwork according to the pattern on which He has made mankind: no change (let there be) in the work (wrought) by Allah …' (Surah 30:30)

From this Muslims learn that they should use their skills to look after the environment and not allow it to be spoiled through wrong use. Muslims believe that on Judgement Day (see page 152) they will be questioned about their role as caretakers of the Earth and its resources.

The preciousness of water

Three-quarters of the Earth's surface is covered by water. Ninety-eight per cent of this is sea water. Humans depend on the small percentage that is left. About 1.2 billion people have to use water that is unsafe.

Islam originated in an area of the world where water is scarce. Because of this, Muslims have always regarded it as one of the most precious of all the Earth's resources, not to be taken for granted.

An artistic impression of a Muslim preparing for salat

Muhammad and water

A man came to Muhammad and asked, 'What is prayer?' The Prophet answered, *'Prayer is a refreshing stream into which one dips five times a day.'*

When the Prophet and his companion were once on a long, hard journey, they stopped by a clear stream. It was a hot day and Muhammad's companions immediately went into the water and let it freely splash over them. When they looked up, the Prophet had taken a small bowl from his carrier and had scooped a small amount to wash in. Amazed, they asked him why. 'Who gave us these good gifts but Allah and he gave enough for all but we should only take what we need and not waste any part.'

Wudu

An important feature of a masjid might be a fountain. Ritual cleansing with water before prayer is a part of Islamic practice. This is known as wudu and involves the washing of hands, face, arms and feet. The mouth, nose and ears are wiped clean. In this way, the cleansing power of water is shown as a symbol of the purification of the worshipper from sin by hand or mouth.

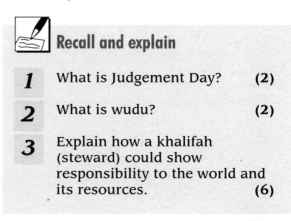

Recall and explain

1 What is Judgement Day? (2)

2 What is wudu? (2)

3 Explain how a khalifah (steward) could show responsibility to the world and its resources. (6)

Animals

Muhammad and his travelling companions once stopped on a journey and set up camp to rest. One of them lit a fire to keep warm. The Prophet was walking around to check that all was well when he noticed an ant hill. Some of the ants were scurrying in the direction of the fire. He quickly called to the man who had lit it to put it out. Muhammad was teaching him that Allah forbids that any creature, however small, should ever be harmed.

Get talking

- To what extent should people be concerned about the welfare of animals?

Fact file 2

In the Qur'an there are many references to the relationship between Allah and the world of birds and animals. *'Seest thou not that it is Allah whose praises all beings in the heavens and on earth do celebrate, and the birds (of the air) with wings outspread?'* (Surah 24:41) The Qur'an teaches that animals have feelings and that their lives have a purpose which, like humans', is part of Allah's plan. *'There is not an animal that lives on the Earth, nor a being that flies on its wings, but [forms part of] communities like you … and they all [shall] be gathered to their Lord in the end.'* (Surah 6:38) Muhammad told many stories in which he stressed the importance of caring for animals. This became an important part of Islam and as early as the 13th century, a Muslim legal scholar formed a bill of Animal Rights.

All domestic animals such as farm animals should be well cared for and not be over-burdened. Owners of cows are instructed to cut their nails before milking, and not to buy or sell an animal when it is still in need of its mother.

Hunting is only allowed for food and never for pleasure. The use of animals for scientific experiment is not approved of if there is known to be cruelty involved and if it is done for non-essential reasons such as the making of cosmetics.

Assisi Declarations

At the 25th anniversary of the Worldwide Fund For Nature in Assisi (see page 57), Islam was represented with the other five major world faiths to meditate on the theme of nature and to declare its message to the world.

'His trustees are responsible for maintaining the unity of his creation, the integrity of the Earth, its flora and fauna, its wildlife and natural environment.'

(The Muslim Declaration on Nature)

Food

Lynn has been given a topic to research for homework on 'Food in Islam'. She has arranged for her Muslim friend to help her.

Lynn: Thanks for sparing the time – I'll do the same for you some time. (*tucking into a snack she has been given*) If all I had to do was write about your Mum's gorgeous samosas I'd have no problem.

Yasmin: So, what *is* your problem?

Lynn: Well all I really know is that you get your meat from the halal butcher and that you don't eat pork. I'm afraid that's about it.

Yasmin: OK. Get your note book and we'll see what we can do. You're right that we don't eat pork but we can eat other meat if it's halal. That means it has to have been slaughtered in a special way. It will always be a Muslim butcher and he has a special sharp knife so that it's done with one clean cut and the animal doesn't suffer unnecessarily. An animal that has already died cannot be used.

Lynn: I've suddenly lost my appetite!

Yasmin: Have you ever stopped to think about the slaughter of the animals *you* eat?

Lynn: Come to think of it, no. Anyway, carry on. This is similar to kosher laws with Jews, isn't it?

Yasmin: Sure. Anyway, the animal is kept away from the other animals so it doesn't see any suffering. It faces Makkah, our holy city in Saudi Arabia. A special prayer called the **Bismillah** which uses Allah's name is spoken as it is done.

Lynn: So are there other rules?

Yasmin: The other things that are haram – that means forbidden – are carnivorous or flesh-eating animals and blood.

Lynn: So provided you always buy from a halal butcher it's not too much of a problem, is it?

Yasmin: No, not really, and they usually have a certificate on display to show it's an approved halal butcher.

Lynn: I suppose you can't just go anywhere for a meal, then?

Yasmin: That's right and it can be difficult to buy food without gelatine, which we can't have because it contains animal extract which is not allowed.

Lynn: Seriously, I'm not being rude, do you think these are good rules?

Yasmin: Apart from being Allah's will, there's a discipline about not being able to eat just anything. It teaches us to respect food. This is true, too, at Ramadan when we fast during daylight hours for a whole month. It certainly makes us appreciate food after that. That's why our festival of Id-ul-Fitr which comes straight after it is so great. By the way, the food rules are in Surah 5:3–4.

Lynn: (*scribbling it down and closing her note book*) Well, this is going to give Mrs Raven a bit of a shock. She'll wonder if I'm all right when she sees I've actually quoted a reference!

Recall and explain

1 What does the term 'halal' mean? **(1)**

2 Explain how Islam believes animals should be treated. **(4)**

3 'There is no point in following a dietary course for your religion. It's just sheer fancy.' Do you agree? In your answer you need to show you have considered other points of view. **(5)**

Creative assignment

Either create a poem or piece of artwork called 'The Preciousness of Water'

Or use *Surah 24:41* as the centre-piece or title for a poster or collage on compassion for animals in today's society.

Wealth and poverty

'Gambling, without exception, is forbidden by Islam'

Get talking

- Why do you think the National Lottery is so popular?

- What can you learn from the news extract about Muslim views on gambling?

Muslim man in a £17.8m religious dilemma

The Muslim who won the National Lottery jackpot of £17.8 million will face a testing religious dilemma when he returns home to Blackburn: having broken Islamic law, how can he make his peace with God?

Islamic Relief, a charity for the poor and needy throughout the world, was equally baffled. Yesterday's Daily Mail reported that an offer of £1 million had been rejected because the money was 'tainted'.

Whether the winner will ever be able to enjoy his fortune is a matter of dispute. Gambling, without exception, is forbidden by Islam.

Abdul Hamid Qureshi, the director of the Lancashire council of mosques explained yesterday:

'Gambling is one of the absolute harams. It is against the rule of God.'

According to Islamic law the winner will not be able to use any of the money for his own benefit or his children's, but will be free to give it to charity.

Fact file 1

It is forbidden by the Qur'an to take part in gambling and lotteries or to do any work connected with them. *'Shaytan's plan is (but) to excite enmity and hatred between you, with intoxicants and gambling.' (Surah 5:91)*

Receiving interest, **riba**, on money loaned is not seen as a good idea as it makes the rich richer. Many Islamic banks have been set up which work out honourable ways of investing the deposited money.

Charity is an important part of Muslim life. Muslims are taught that all giving should be done through love and not just duty. *'But it is righteousness to believe in Allah … to spend of your substance out of love for Him, for your kin, for orphans, for the needy, for the wayfarer.' (Surah 2:177)*

In addition to money given to the poor, contributions also go towards the education of young Muslims at the madrasah, the school attached to the masjid (see page 129).

Zakah

What is it?

Payment

It is the *payment* each year of about 2.5 per cent of all wealth on cash savings, cattle, land and crops.

Pillar

It is the fourth *pillar* of Islam (see page 123), making it a religious duty, next in importance to prayer. *'And be steadfast in prayer and regular in charity; and whatever good ye send forth for your souls before you, ye shall find it again with Allah; for Allah sees well all that ye do.'* (Surah 2:110)

Purification

It is what is done by Muslims to *purify* their wealth, in the form of helping others. It is a form of worship, benefiting both the giver and receiver.

What is it for?

Problem-solving

It has been used for centuries as a way of tackling the difficulties of poverty, greed and envy.

Passing the test

Muslims believe that wealth is Allah's wealth. Life is a test in which one has to use freedom of choice and responsibility. The test for the poor is to have patience and to earn a living by lawful means. This will be rewarded by Allah.

The test for the rich is greater. It involves realizing that wealth is a gift which must be used for doing good and sharing with the poor. The temptation to use it for wrong purposes must be resisted.

Muslim children may be helped to learn about zakah through simple poems. Here is an example.

We have to share with those in need
And not give in to thoughts of greed,
Zakah then helps us in this way,
Lest we should err and go astray.
The receiver and the giver of aid,
All feel good when zakah is paid,
And society as a whole will be,
Enriched by acts of charity.

(Mymona Hendricks)

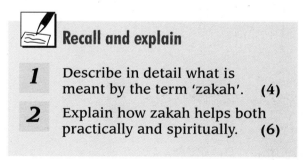

Recall and explain

1 Describe in detail what is meant by the term 'zakah'. **(4)**

2 Explain how zakah helps both practically and spiritually. **(6)**

What is zakah used for?

- Zakah cannot be given to non-Muslims, nor is it usually given to support international disasters. For this, **sadaqah** would be used (see page 137).

- A Muslim must look after his family's needs first. Zakah is collected on surplus money and goods that remain after this is done.

- Zakah cannot be given for building or repairing a masjid (mosque). As a place of worship it belongs to everyone.

A summary of the use of zakah:

Ransoms may be paid for releasing hostages or prisoners of war.

Education for promoting Islam, including payment for teachers at the madrasah, can be funded.

Stranded travellers, such as those on pilgrimage (Hajj) are given aid.

Converts to Islam can receive financial assistance.

Underprivileged and poor members of the community are given support.

Employees collecting zakah are paid wages.

Debts are met on behalf of those owing money.

A young Afghan is fascinated by his first ever book – bought for him with money paid as zakah

Fact file 2

Sadaqah

This is any act which is done out of love, generosity or compassion. In addition to the compulsory zakah, Muslims are encouraged to show concern and care for others in voluntary action and giving. Muhammad is reported to have said, *'He is not a believer who eats his fill while his neighbour remains hungry by his side.'* (Hadith)

At festivals such as **Id-ul-Adha**, when the willingness of Ibrahim to sacrifice his son Ismail is commemorated, Muslims sacrifice an animal and the meat is then cut up and distributed to the poor.

Qurbani is the meat of animals given in sacrifice. When Muhammad was asked 'What is qurbani?' he answered, *'It is the Sunnah of your father Ibrahim. For every hair of the Qurbani you will receive a reward from Allah and from every hair in the wool you will receive a reward.'* (Hadith)

Red Crescent is one of many organizations that carry out sadaqah (see also page 138)

Red Crescent

Red Crescent is the Islamic section of the international relief agency known as the Red Cross. The two work as one and are active in bringing humanitarian relief to 150 countries around the world. This includes both medical care for those living through war, and emergency aid for those affected by famine.

 Recall and evaluate

1 What is the difference between zakah and sadaqah? (5)

2 Do you think it's a good idea for everyone to give a percentage of their wage to charity? Give reasons for your answer, showing you have considered other points of view. (5)

Islamic Relief

Fact file 3

Islamic Relief is an independent charity that aims to help those in need, by upholding the principles of Islam. It began in 1984 as the first Muslim relief agency in Europe. Islamic Relief works throughout the world and is not allied to any government or country. It has both short- and long-term projects with 81.8 per cent of its money coming from voluntary donations.

During the 1980s much of its work was concentrated upon alleviating suffering caused by flooding, earthquakes and other natural disasters. In the 1990s it focused more on areas of need caused by humans such as in Bosnia and Somalia.

Projects included:
● Emergency relief
● Education
● Sponsorship of orphans
● Ramadan programme
● Social and economic development
● Health care
● Zakat
● Building wells
● Qurbani programme.

A boy receiving his share of the Islamic Relief bread distribution in Sarajevo, Bosnia

Aqiqah is the offering of sheep etc. made when a new-born baby is named. Donations from this are used by Islamic Relief to help other children.

Every new born has the right to an Aqiqah

 **Creative assignment**

Imagine you are a Muslim working for Islamic Relief and that you have been asked to talk to young Muslims about your work and how it fits in with Islamic teaching. Write what you are going to say to them.

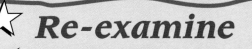

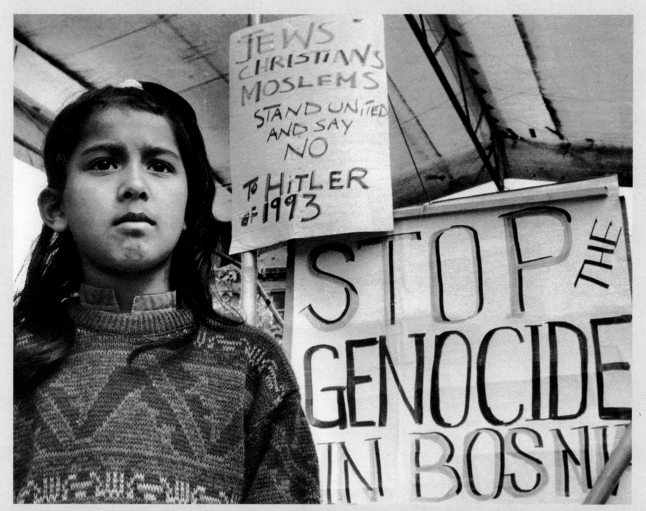

Showing solidarity – members of three religions in Bradford came together to stage a week of protest over the war in Bosnia

The following questions give you a chance to re-examine the issues raised in the preceding units. Remember to look at the number of marks for each question and to develop your answer accordingly.

a What is the difference between prejudice and discrimination? **(4)**

b Describe the example of Muhammad concerning responsibility towards *either* humankind *or* the environment. **(6)**

c Explain how Muslims might practise good akhlaq (conduct) concerning the care of the environment. **(7)**

d 'What's the point in teenagers protesting about world issues – they can't even vote until they're 18!'

Do you agree? You need to refer to a range of references in support of your argument. **(5)**

GAOL DRINK DRIVERS

Alcohol is the root of all evil

Drug pushers must be punished

Get talking

- In what ways do alcohol and drug abuse affect both users and the people they come into contact with?

Islam teaches that all people are equal in the eyes of the law and that on Judgement Day everyone will stand before Allah who is all-knowing (see page 152). The Hadith tells how an important woman was arrested for theft, but because of her high position it was suggested that she should not be punished. Muhammad replied that it was this unfairness which Allah had been angry with and that if the theft had been committed by his own daughter, Fatima, he would expect her to receive the same punishment as anyone else. 'O ye who believe! stand out firmly for justice, as witnesses to Allah … and if ye distort justice, verily Allah is acquainted with all that ye do.' (Surah 4:135)

In Islam, in addition to murder, there are three crimes that are particularly condemned. These are theft, adultery and the making or taking of alcohol and drugs. These are seen as the cause of many social evils. Theft is an abuse of others' property and possessions, and unfaithfulness in marriage leads to the break-up of families.

Alcohol and drug abuse are often responsible for crimes of violence. They affect both the mind and body, preventing Muslims from true communication with Allah. 'Approach not prayers with a mind befogged, until ye understand all that ye say.' (Surah 4:43)

Alcohol and drugs are intoxicants and are known as **khamr** or poison. Temptation to use them is thought by Muslims to come from Shaytan (see page 90). 'Intoxicants … are an abomination of Shaytan's handiwork.' (Surah 5:90)

The Shari'ah

The Shari'ah (straight path) is the code of law for the Islamic way of life giving both rules and punishment. It is based on the Qur'an and Sunnah and is believed to be relevant for all time and for Muslims in all nations. Many Muslim countries have adopted the Shari'ah as their law as they believe it was revealed by Allah and will make good triumph over evil.

Punishment

Muslims believe that punishment helps to prevent people from repeating their crimes and others from copying. Some critics think that the punishments are too severe, particularly the cutting off of the right hand for theft. Those who support the law point out that as well as being a deterrent, it is only carried out for persistent offenders and when the crime has been testified by two witnesses.

Capital punishment

In Islam there are two crimes which are thought to be serious enough for execution. These are:
● murder
● openly attacking Islam.

'Nor take life – which Allah has made sacred – except for just cause.' (Surah 17:33)

In some countries, political events can clash with religious laws. The headline below refers to a political activist whom many Muslims believe was unlawfully executed for opposing the regime of his country. This was condemned not only by the human rights organization **Amnesty International** but by many Muslims.

Islamic activist beheaded
It is unIslamic

This includes **The Committee for the Defence of Legitimate Rights**, of which the executed man was leader, and **Liberty for the Muslim World**. The killing has been described as an act against the Shari'ah law.

Forgiveness

Although it is important for justice to be done, forgiveness also plays an important part in Islam and it is believed that Allah will always forgive a person who is truly sorry and repents their sins. Those who are forgiving towards others too will be rewarded. '… but if a person forgives and makes reconciliation, his reward is due from Allah …' (Surah 42:40)

Muslim countries often grant a pardon to some prisoners at festival times.

Prisoners released for Id

100 prisoners were released in a special amnesty granted for Id-ul-Adha, the feast of sacrifice, in Bangladesh this week.

Recall, explain and evaluate

1 Give two reasons why people are punished. (2)

2 Explain how alcohol and drug abuse can be the cause of crime. (4)

3 'If we want less crime then we must start to use harsher punishment.' Do you agree? Give two reasons to support your answer, to show you've considered other points of view. (4)

Jihad

Mujahedin pray five times a day. Most put aside their guns to do so

Get talking

- What are the reasons for the existence of wars?

- Can wars ever be right? If so, in what circumstances?

Fact file 1

Although the word **jihad** is used in connection with war, it has a much wider meaning. It is considered by many Muslims to be a sixth pillar of Islam and it refers to the personal striving against evil in the way of Allah. This also involves the defence of the ummah (see page 123) against attack or unjust government. Muhammad once compared the ummah to a strong wall made up of separate bricks, each supporting the rest.

To keep the 'wall' intact may involve fighting an enemy which threatens to destroy it. There are two kinds of jihad – greater and lesser.

Greater jihad is the personal struggle against temptations to behave wrongly, which would be against the wishes of Allah. Muslims are taught that they must resist selfishness by putting effort into their duties and by showing a caring attitude to others.

Defending the faith

In the passage headed 'To die for faith and country' are the words of a **mujahedin**, a Muslim soldier fighting for what is thought to be a just cause. He believes that it is the duty of Muslims to defend themselves against any force or power that poses a threat to Islam and which prevents Muslims from practising their religion.

To die for faith and country

The war that we Afghans are waging against the Soviet Union is jihad, a holy war, because it is a war to defend the faith and to defend against the infidel*, an atheistic power that believes in no religion.

It is the duty of every Afghan to fight back, to defend the faith and to defend his country. So that is why it is a great deed to fight jihad. God gives to the mujahedin who fights jihad a special place in Paradise.

* Infidel means an unbeliever.

Fact file 2

Lesser jihad is military jihad. The Qur'an states that war should not be fought for reasons of greed or ambition to capture and possess other people's lands. Neither should it be for the purpose of forcing others to become Muslims. The only time it is permitted is in defence of Islam.

'To those against whom war is made, permission is given (to fight), because they are wronged and verily, Allah is most powerful for their aid.' (Surah 22:39)

There are clear conditions set out for military jihad:

- fighting should only be used in defence
- it should be the last resort
- it should be led by a spiritual leader who has knowledge and understanding of the situation and will be fair in his judgement
- trees, crops and animals should be protected

- fighting should not continue when the enemy has laid down arms, and prisoners should be released
- civilians should not be harmed
- its aim should be to restore peace and freedom.

'If two parties among the believers fall into a quarrel, make ye peace between them: but if one of them transgresses beyond bounds against the other, then fight … until it complies with the command of Allah; but if it complies, then make peace between them with justice and be fair: for Allah loves those who are fair.' (Surah 49:9)

(It should be remembered that there are some extremist groups who adopt the label jihad but who do not keep these conditions.)

The Qur'an states that for those killed in jihad, there is entry into Paradise on the Day of Judgement.

Recall and explain

1 What is the greater jihad? (2)

2 What is the lesser jihad? (2)

3 Explain what temptations a Muslim might have to strive against in their daily life. (6)

Creative assignment

Imagine that a non-Muslim has read from newspapers about an extremist group of Muslims in another country and is overheard criticizing their attitude to war. Create a dialogue between him and a Muslim who explains what the true Islamic teaching about jihad is.

Peace

The ummah – the community which strives for peace and harmony

 Get talking

- What does 'being at peace' mean to you in *your* life?
- How important is it to you?
- Which people or organizations can you think of that are associated with peace?

Fact file

Muslims are expected to fight in the name of Islam but it is considered important actively to promote peace. This is reflected in the words which conclude the daily prayers of every Muslim when they turn to either side of them, saying, 'peace be on you'.

The Qur'an teaches that the ideal is not to seek revenge for wrongs but to pursue ways which will help reconciliation. This involves trying to turn hatred into friendship by forgiveness and love. It is up to Allah to punish and it is not good to return evil for evil. '*Nor can goodness and evil be equal. Repel [evil] with what is better. Then will he between whom and thee was hatred become as it were thy friend and intimate.*' (Surah 41:34).

Human rights

The protection of human rights is important to Muslims. They believe that Allah created all humankind and that everyone has the right to be treated fairly. '*Stand out firmly for Allah, as witnesses to fair dealing, and let not the hatred of others to you make you swerve to wrong and depart from justice.*' (Surah 5:8)

The example of Muhammad

In the Hadith, Muhammad showed by his own treatment of prisoners the importance of treating the enemy humanely. He taught that the plight of their children should be considered.

Once Muhammed was told that in a battle some children of the enemy had been killed. His companions were surprised to see that he was greatly distressed by the news. He made it clear to them that he believed strongly that children were innocent victims, whatever side they were on. He reminded them that wars are brought about by adults and that children should be protected and kept free from danger. He strictly forbade the killing of children, no matter who they were.

A Muslim subhah with 99 beads – one for each of the names of Allah

The example of Allah

The basic Muslim belief that Allah is Tawhid means not only is he the Creator, existing outside and beyond time, but also that he is concerned with what he has created. Throughout the Qur'an there are 99 names or attributes given to Allah, e.g. 'the one who gives safety and peace' and 'the gentle and tolerant'. There are no names describing Allah as a warrior or a soldier.

Muslims remember these attributes when they use the subhah. This is a string of 99 beads (one for each attribute) which are used as an aid to praising Allah.

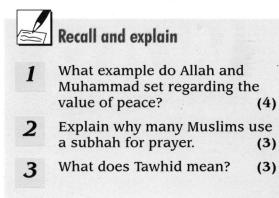

Recall and explain

1   What example do Allah and Muhammad set regarding the value of peace?   **(4)**

2   Explain why many Muslims use a subhah for prayer.   **(3)**

3   What does Tawhid mean?   **(3)**

Creative assignment

Write and illustrate a poem which reflects your views about peace.

'The giver of safety and peace'

WAR CHILD

Get talking

● What are your views on pop stars and other famous people becoming involved in charity?

● How much good do you think charity does in the short and long term to reduce suffering?

The album called 'Help' was made in response to the suffering caused by the war in the former Yugoslavia, and was produced by the Bosnian children's charity, **War Child** under the direction of Brian Eno. One of its contributors was Ian Brown of the Stone Roses who, when asked his reasons for becoming involved, said:

❛I have kids of my own, but you feel it anyway if you're conscious. Do I hear about kids dying on the news, and then feel lucky that my kids are safe? Every day, yeah. Which is another good reason for getting involved in this.❜

Fact file 1

Compassion

One of the names of Allah is The Compassionate. Muslims believe that although there is suffering in this life there will be joy in the life to come. It is believed that life is a series of tests and it is up to people to find their own answers and face up to what happens to them. Allah knows everything and nothing that is said or done will go unaccounted for.

'Be sure we shall test you with something of fear and hunger, some loss in goods or lives or the fruits (of your toil), but give glad tidings to those who patiently persevere – who say, when afflicted with calamity: To Allah we belong, and to him is our return.' (Surah 2:155–6)

Islam teaches that compassion should be shown to others who suffer and relief given to them whenever possible (see page 138).

Fact file 2

Evil

Muslims are taught that evil comes from Shaytan (see page 93) who tries to turn them away from Allah by putting wrong thoughts and temptations into their minds. Muslims must resist this through constant prayer and reading of the Qur'an. Evil is hateful to Allah and must be punished. Even if the wicked escape punishment in this life they will not escape it in the next. Those who sin must make their peace with Allah in penitence and prayer. He will always forgive those who are truly sorry. Just as Allah is compassionate, those who have been sinned against must also forgive but they have the right to seek justice first. *'Nor can goodness and evil be equal. Repel evil with what is better.'* (Surah 41:34)

Every Muslim has been given free will to be tempted by or reject evil.

Throughout history there have been many times when Muslims have suffered for their faith. Agencies such as Amnesty International actively support people who have been victims of human rights abuses.

I sat next to a 13-year-old boy whose body looked blue. I asked him, "What have you confessed to?" He said: "My crime was to shout 'Allahu Akbar'* at every oppressor, and I was tortured with electricity for four days. The skin on my back was peeling and I can only sleep when sitting." There was another young man who was unable to stand or hold anything because the skin on his hands and feet had peeled from being tortured with flames.

(From interview conducted by Amnesty International)

*Allahu Akbar means 'Allah is great' and is the first line of the adhan (the call to prayer).

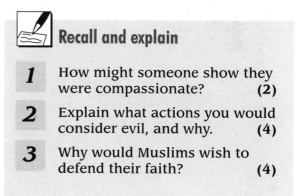

Recall and explain

1 How might someone show they were compassionate? **(2)**

2 Explain what actions you would consider evil, and why. **(4)**

3 Why would Muslims wish to defend their faith? **(4)**

The importance of prayer

Two women from Bhopal in India find that prayer has helped them to cope with suffering – the first in her personal life and the second after a chemical explosion which caused great loss of life.

'I would have collapsed after my broken marriage. It was prayer that saved me. I now teach a group of women how to pray and find peace.'

(Tayeba Begum)

'Even while I was breathing the gas I was praying. The neighbourhood was torn by cries of women and children. I sat here with my beads chanting the 99 names of Allah. I was in control. I had the strength to walk out of my door, collect the children in the street and take them to safety.'

(Sajida Biya)

Imran Khan, former Pakistan cricket captain is pictured here at prayer. It was the witnessing of suffering that brought great change to his life

 **Get talking**

- In what way do you think prayer can help people who suffer?

- In what other ways do people seek help?

The relief of suffering

Imran Khan was deeply affected by watching his mother die of cancer. After her death he felt the need to do something about it. He had been particularly appalled to see many cancer patients lying in corridors because they were not able to afford to pay medical bills. His dream was to relieve suffering by building a hospital which would offer free treatment to the poor. To raise the money he organized door-to-door collections, charity launches and a Ramadan appeal.

IMRAN'S RAMADAN APPEAL

The Shaukat Khanum Memorial Cancer Hospital

Cricket legend-turned-fund-raiser, Imran Khan, dropped into his cancer appeal headquarters in London yesterday to announce the launch of his latest fund-raising efforts.

On the first day of Ramadan on 26 January mosques nation-wide will be asked to donate cash towards his cancer hospital in Pakistan.

So far, 22,000 patients have visited the hospital, of whom 92 per cent have been treated free of charge.

Imran realizes his dream. The Shaukat Khanum Memorial Cancer Hospital and Research Centre is named in memory of his mother

On a personal level it has been one of the most fulfilling and satisfying periods of my life. It has been a humbling experience, one which can only be compared with creation itself. No one can even begin to imagine the effect on a mother when she gives birth to a child, except those themselves that have given birth … But it has been a struggle for me and the people who have been supporting me. My faith has kept my spirits up in this battle to raise the target of 21 million dollars.

Imran Khan

SHAUKAT KHANUM MEMORIAL TRUST
CANCER HOSPITAL & RESEARCH CENTRE
ZAKAH FUND

The need:
- There are 200,00 – 700,000 new cases of cancer every year in Pakistan.
- 80% of the population is not capable of paying their own expenses.
- 50% of these patients will require complete funding.
- 30% of these patients will receive subsidized treatment.

The concept and elligibility for zakah:
It is confirmed by religious authorities that in Islam zakah money can be used for the treatment of poor patients and it is already being used for the treatment of patients in Pakistan.

How you can contribute to the fund:
Contribution can be made by:
- sponsoring a bed or unit.
- you can also give a general donation to the zakah fund.

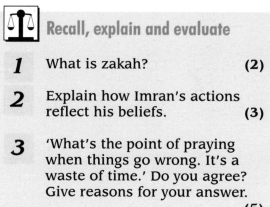

Recall, explain and evaluate

1 What is zakah? **(2)**

2 Explain how Imran's actions reflect his beliefs. **(3)**

3 'What's the point of praying when things go wrong. It's a waste of time.' Do you agree? Give reasons for your answer. **(5)**

Creative assignment

Either as a game of snakes and ladders or an illustrated diagram show different ways in which evil can lead to suffering

Or write a story or draw a cartoon with the title 'Suffering is never in vain'.

Death and beyond

Interviewer: When you began your training, were you aware of the needs of each religion?

Nurse: Not really. I believe in God, I think, but I don't go to a place of worship. We never really learned other religions at school – so I had some quick catching up to do!

Interviewer: Is it important to know about the practices in each religion?

Nurse: Oh yes, definitely. Many people think more about their religion when they're in hospital. So it can be a great comfort to help them keep their practice.

Interviewer: Don't you find it all a bit confusing, with all the different traditions?

Nurse: I think you mean fascinating! Even *within* each religion, different families may have different requirements, but there tends to be a structure to follow. Take Islam for instance. We know how important it is for patients to be able to have halal food and for women to be treated by female doctors. For those who are very ill, we know that they must be allowed to face Makkah. We all had a lesson in how to find the direction – it's called the **qiblah** – and we now have a compass to help us. The family play such an important part and should be at the bedside if their relative is dying. This is to whisper the adhan, the 'call to prayer' so it

will be the last words that are heard on Earth.

Actually, if I go down to the maternity unit, I'll hear the same words whispered into the baby's ear. The first and last words – makes sense, doesn't it?

Interviewer: Then, after the death, the family leave?

Nurse: People from the community come and wash the body and cover it with a shroud. Sometimes the men who are **Hajji**, those who have been on the pilgrimage to Makkah, will have the robe that they wore draped over them. It's called the ihram (see page 123).

Interviewer: That's a fair amount to remember.

Nurse: It's taken a lot of study. I wish I'd learned it at school.

Get talking

- What other jobs or out-of-school activities would be helped by a good knowledge of religious beliefs and practices?

- Have you had experience of not knowing how to help someone who is grieving?

Exclusive ground for Muslim graves

South London is to get a new graveyard dedicated to members of the Muslim faith.

The initiative will create space for around 80 graves and has been welcomed by the Muslim community.

Councillor Shafi Khan said: 'I am delighted that the local Muslim community could soon have its own dedicated space in a local cemetery.

'It will mean a great deal to people of Muslim faith to have their own allotted area.'

Muslims have to be buried in areas exclusive to their faith. Other stipulations are that the graves must point towards Makkah, burials should take place within 24 hours and graves should be raised to stop people sitting or walking on them.

The plot will have enough space to last four years of burials and the planned extension of the Greenlawn cemetery should mean the exclusive area will be added to.

A Muslim grave

Fact file 1

The burial

Muslims believe the soul leaves the body at death and so the body becomes an empty shell. The body will be treated with great respect, with only Muslims washing it. It will be placed in several garments called a **shroud**. Muslims who die in battle are not washed but buried in their blood-stained clothes. As in Judaism, the burial will take place as soon as possible after death, preferably within 24 hours, by which time prayers will have been performed at the mosque.

The funeral

A Muslim funeral is expected to be simple with no great show, as all are believed to be equal before Allah at death. The grave should be plain and facing towards Makkah. A little earth is sprinkled over the grave as words from the Qur'an are recited: *'From the (earth) did We create you, and into it We return you, and from it shall We bring you out once again.'* (Surah 20:55)

Often the grave is marked with a headstone with writing on it for identification purposes. Expensive memorials should not be set up.

The mourning period for a wife will last for four months, and for ten days and three days for other relatives and for friends.

Recall and explain

1 Why is it important for Muslims to hear the adhan before they die? **(2)**

2 Explain why it's considered important for Muslims to have their own burial area. **(4)**

3 Why do many people think about their religion when they're in hospital? **(4)**

'That to thy Lord is the final goal, that it is he who has granted laughter and tears; that it is he who granted death and life ... that he hath promised a Second Creation (raising the dead).' (Surah 53:42–7)

Fact file 2

Life after death

Muslims believe in an after-life which they call **Akhirah**. The soul is taken by the Angel of Death to a state of waiting until the Day of Judgement. When this comes the universe will be destroyed and the dead will be brought to stand before Allah.

Life on Earth is seen as a preparation for the life to come. Everyone will be judged according to their actions on Earth towards both people and animals. Those who have performed ibadah, and so obeyed Allah's will with their actions, will be rewarded in Paradise (Heaven). Those who have not will suffer in Hell. *'The decision of the Hour (of Judgement) will be swift as the twinkling of an eye – for Allah has power over all things.'* (Surah 16:77)

Heaven and Hell

The descriptions of Heaven and Hell are very graphic, with Heaven like a beautiful garden with rivers flowing with milk and honey, and Hell a terrifying place of heat and torment. For centuries, people have taken these descriptions literally, and some still do. Others interpret them as symbolic picture-language. For them it is enough to know and believe that Paradise means the bliss of being at one with Allah and that Hell is the unhappiness felt by being confronted with all one's wrong-doings. The Qur'an teaches that no matter what sins have been committed in this life, if a person is repentant, forgiveness will be given. Repentance wipes out sin, while good actions are never wiped out.

 Creative assignment

Divide a circle into three sections and give them the headings 'My hopes', 'My fears', 'My beliefs'. In the appropriate section, put words and symbols which express *your* views about death and beyond.

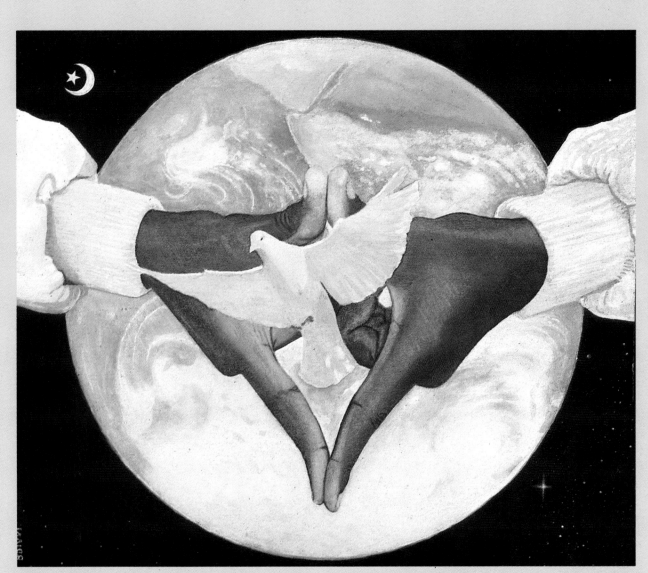

'You are the best community ever raised, you enforce what is right; fight what is wrong and believe in Allah.'
(*Surah 3:110*)

The following questions give you a chance to re-examine the issues raised in the preceding units. Remember to look at the number of marks for each question and to develop your answer accordingly.

a What do Muslims mean when they refer to the Tawhid? **(4)**

b Describe what is meant by Ibadah and Shahadah in Islam. **(4)**

c Explain the importance of following the five Pillars to a Muslim's daily life. **(7)**

d 'Following religious rules or laws does not make you a better person.'

Do you agree? Give reasons showing you have considered other points of view. **(5)**

Introduction

Jews

Judaism is the religion of the world-wide community of Jews and it traces its history back to the 20th century BCE. The largest group of Jews live in America and the second largest in Israel. Jews who come from Central and Eastern Europe are called **Ashkenazim** and those from Mediterranean countries as **Sephardim**.

Judaism is a way of life that influences Jews in everything they do. This whole code of conduct is known as the **Halakhah** (The Way).

Groups or movements

Practising Jews fall into two broad categories. The majority group is the **Orthodox** Jews who believe they must observe the **Torah** and its development in **Talmud**. They believe the laws are the will of God and so are timeless. The **Hasidim** are an ultra-Orthodox movement which refuses to wear western clothes.

The **Progressive** movement believes that Jews should keep to the basic beliefs and principles but have adopted many practices to suit the modern world. **Liberal** and **Reform** Jews make up the Progressive movement but there are a variety of names depending on the country in which they live.

History

The story of the Jews began with a man called **Abraham**, the founder of a tribe who became known as **Hebrews**. They were later called Israelites after one of Abraham's descendants, Israel.

Later still they came to be known as Jews, which comes from the word Judah, the name of one of Israel's sons. Abraham, who came from ancient city of Ur near the Persian Gulf, heard God telling him to leave his country and go to a new land. In return, he was promised that he would be the father of God's chosen race of people. This **Covenant** or agreement, was to mark the beginning of the bond which gave the Jews the special relationship which they have with God today. Abraham travelled and settled in Canaan, the land which was to become Israel.

In later years, Abraham's descendants were forced into slavery in Egypt, where they remained for 400 years until rescued by **Moses** who led the **Exodus** to their 'promised land'. They lived there until they were captured and exiled in Babylonia some hundreds of years later. Although some did eventually return, many were dispersed around what was soon to become the Roman empire. This scattering was known as the **diaspora** and is one of the reasons for the widespread nature of the Jewish community today.

Throughout history Jewish people have suffered much persecution, known as **anti-Semitism**. The worst persecution of Jews was in Europe during the time of Nazism in Germany. The **Shoah** (Holocaust) is the name given to Hitler's systematic extermination of over six million Jews in the 1930s and 1940s.

Although, understandably, many questioned why God could let the Holocaust happen, most Jews kept their faith and Judaism remained alive. Many of the survivors found themselves homeless and some went to Israel and settled in the land of their ancestors. In 1948 the State of Israel was set up, fulfilling the dream of a Jew from Austria named Theodor Hertzl who fifty years earlier had founded a movement called **Zionism** to make a land for the Jews. After years of conflict between the Jews and neighbouring countries peace treaties have now been signed.

Holy books

Jewish beliefs and practices come mainly from the teachings of the Torah. These are written in Hebrew and form the first five books of the **Tenakh** (the same as the Old Testament in the Christian Bible). They were given to Moses on Mount Sinai when the covenant between God and his people was renewed. In return for keeping his **mitzvot** (commandments) they would be his people.

The Torah, which contains 613 mitzvot, is sacred to the Jews and the scrolls on which they are written are brought out ceremoniously to be read aloud as an important part of worship in the synagogue. Teachings and explanations about the laws were collected over the centuries and were written down into the **Mishnah** and later the **Gemara**. These two together form the Talmud. There are other collections of commentaries which are known as the **Midrash**. Among these is the work of **Maimonides**, a leading 12th century philosopher whose *Thirteen Principles of Faith* form part of the **Siddur**, the Jewish daily prayer book.

The synagogue

The synagogue is the place for public worship and its focal point is the **Aron Hakodesh**, the Holy Ark, which contains the sefer Torah. For worship to take place among Orthodox Jews there has to be a minimum of ten men, known as a **minyan**. In Progressive communities this may include women but in these communities a minyan is not always needed. Prayers and readings are usually led by the **rabbi**, an ordained Jewish teacher. In the Orthodox tradition this will always be a man but is not necessarily so in other movements.

Prayer

Jews may pray whenever they wish but men should pray in the morning, afternoon and evening. The Jewish prayer book, the siddur, contains different types of prayer but it is the **Shema** which is repeated both morning and evening. The Shema can be found in the Torah and affirms the belief in One God. Copies of it are often fixed inside a decorative case (**mezuzah**) and placed on the doorposts of Jewish homes (see page 169). It is also rolled into **tefillin** boxes which are strapped onto the forehead and arms for morning prayers on weekdays.

Festivals

There are many important festivals in Judaism. The main one is the annual festival of **Pesach** (Passover) when families gather to remember the Exodus from Egypt.

Rosh Hashanah is the Jewish New Year and is a time when Jews remember their wrongs in the year that has passed. A sign of its importance is the sounding of the shofar (a ram's horn) in the synagogue each day for a month beforehand. It ends with **Yom Kippur**, the Day of Atonement, the holiest day of the year, when Jews fast and ask for forgiveness for their sins.

The home

For Jews the home is an important place of worship and is where the weekly **Shabbat** (Sabbath) is observed. Shabbat is a holy day of rest and renewal beginning at sunset on Friday and finishing at nightfall on Saturday. No work is done during this time.

Bringing up children to follow the Jewish faith is an important part of Jewish life and it is in the home that children will learn the beliefs, values and traditions of their religion.

The nature of God

The important aspects of Jewish belief in God are summed up in the *Thirteen Principles of Faith* laid down by Maimonides. These form part of the Jewish prayer book and are sung in the synagogue. They are:

1 God exists as Creator

Jews believe in a living creator God. This important belief is stated in the very first sentence of the Torah (*Genesis 1:1*). Nothing in nature can exist without God's continuing activity within it.

2 The unity of God

He is the only God and there is no other. This 'oneness' is reflected in the words:

'Hear, O Israel: the Lord our God is one Lord: And thou shalt love the Lord thy God with all thine heart, and with all thy soul and with all thy might.' (Deuteronomy 6:4)

These words begin the Shema (see page 155).

3 God is Spirit

He is not in human form and is everywhere. His divine presence is called Shekhina.

4 God is eternal

He is infinite and, unlike humans, he is not bound by the limits of time.

5 Only God must be worshipped

Loyalty to God is stated as the first Commandment.

6 God has communicated through the prophets

Throughout history, spiritual leaders became spokesmen of God and through their revelations Jews came to know God. It was to Abraham, the father of the Jewish people, that God and his purpose were first revealed. The Covenant or agreement made between them led to the circumcising of all the men in Abraham's family. This sign of being God's chosen ones has been used in Jewish families ever since (see page 170).

7 Moses was the greatest of the prophets

It was through Moses that the most important revelations came. Moses experienced the presence of God at the 'burning bush'. Such was the awe he felt that he removed his shoes, believing himself to be on holy ground when God revealed that his purpose, through Moses, was for the Israelites to be taken to the land of Canaan where they would settle and become God's nation as had been promised to Abraham.

8 The Torah given to Moses is from God

When Moses was on Mount Sinai, God renewed the Covenant with him and gave him the laws which set out the Jewish code for living.

9 The Torah is sacred

They are the words of God and cannot be changed. When a copy of the sefer Torah is read, a **yad** (pointer) is used so that the words are not soiled or damaged by touch. When a copy of the Torah has to be replaced it is buried and not destroyed.

10 God is omniscient

He knows all that humans think and do.

11 God punishes evil and rewards good

Jews believe that the two main principles of God's relationship with them are justice and mercy (which includes loving kindness).

12 God will send a Messiah

A specially chosen spiritual leader will bring in a new age for Jews and all humankind.

13 God will resurrect the dead

Humans will be with God after death.

Morality

In becoming God's chosen people the Jews believed they were called upon to become 'holy unto God' and to separate themselves from anything that went against his will.

The **Noachide laws** are considered the very basic framework of morality. They were given to Noah after the flood and tell Jews: to worship only God, not to blaspheme, not to murder or steal, not to commit adultery, not to be cruel to animals and to promote justice.

The Torah

God gave the Jews 613 mitzvot (commandments), including the **Decalogue** (the Ten Commandments) which provided them with moral framework to live by. These are contained in the Torah, which makes up the first five books of the Tenakh. Although the **Neviim** (the second section of the Tenakh, containing the words of prophets such as Isaiah) and the **Ketuvim** (the third section with books such as *1* and *2 Kings*) are considered to be written under divine guidance, the Torah is believed to have been revealed by God to Moses on Mount Sinai. The specialness of the Torah can be seen by its use at home, in synagogues and through such festivals as **Simchat Torah** which celebrates the completion and recommencement of the cycle of weekly Torah readings.

In addition to the written Torah, God revealed an oral Torah which was passed down through generations of Jews until it was eventually recorded in 200 CE as the Mishnah. This document, along with its commentary, the Gemara, forms the Talmud. The relationship between the Torah and Talmud is that the Torah states the Law and the Talmud gives the details of how it should be carried out. For instance, in *Exodus 20:8* we read, 'Observe the Sabbath and keep it holy', and the Talmud specifies the 39 types of work that are prohibited on that day.

Interpretations and commentaries

There are various interpretations among Jews as to how literally the Torah and Talmud should be followed. The Orthodox movement believes that both oral and written Torah are revelations from God and can never change. The Progressive movement believes that they do contain some human development and so do not need to be taken so literally. It is this difference in interpretations that has led to Jews following a wide range of practices in **kashrut** (rules governing lifestyle and home) and Shabbat.

Studying sacred texts has always been an important part of Judaism and there are many colleges called **Yeshivot** for this purpose. Jews today have their own Jewish courts called **Bet Din** (House of Judgement) based upon *Deuteronomy 16:18*. The judges in this rabbinic court spend much time hearing divorce cases and have been involved in a recent debate about the issue of gets. In addition, many people go to their rabbi for moral guidance.

Jews believe that humans were given free will and that true morality can never be just a matter of outward adherence to a set of rules. Instead it must come from within and be a development of their own moral conscience, based on *Leviticus 19:18*: *'Love your neighbour as yourself'*.

CONGRATULATIONS YOU HAVE WON A LIFETIME SUPPLY OF LIFE!

 **Get talking**

As with all religions, Judaism considers life to be most precious, but what you put into it can often mirror what you get out of it.

● In what ways do you think people get out of life what they put into it?

Ben & Jerry's Recipe for Life

Ingredients:

1 US military budget (liquefied)
1 pound dreams
⅓ cup chutzpah*
3 cups love
2 cups political action
1 pound fun

Directions:

1 Mix together chutzpah, love, dreams, political action and fun.
2 Transfer into saucepan and add military budget. Reduce by half over high heat, stirring constantly.
3 Yields health, education and playgrounds for all the world's kids.

*Chutzpah means nerve.

Ben & Jerry
(Ben Cohen and Jerry Greenfield) are the founders of Vermont's all-natural ice cream empire.

Get talking

● What would be your own recipe for life?

Fact file

Judaism teaches that God is the Creator and Sustainer. He alone can give and take life. It is God's greatest gift and the saving or preservation of life should take priority over all else. It is an important **mitzvah** (commandment) in Judaism to practise **pikuakh nefesh**, the term used to describe the setting aside of certain laws in order to save a life. There are many references to this mitzvah in the Jewish sources of authority.

In the Mishnah (part of the Talmud) it says:
'Whoever destroys a single life is considered as if he had destroyed the whole world, and whoever saves a single life as if he had saved the whole world.'

These beliefs on the sanctity of life govern Jewish actions and influence their views on such things as embryo technology, abortion and all other issues of life and death.

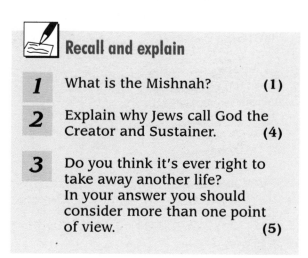

Recall and explain

1 What is the Mishnah? **(1)**

2 Explain why Jews call God the Creator and Sustainer. **(4)**

3 Do you think it's ever right to take away another life? In your answer you should consider more than one point of view. **(5)**

"How can I help you, Mr and Mrs Frankenstein?"

Infertility can cause suffering in all families and it is up to individuals to consider the lengths they might go to for a child.

'I want no more treatment'

Louise, 36, and her husband, Michael, have been trying to conceive for five years.

'As a Jewish person, I find it much worse not having children. Everything in Judaism is centred on the family. If you can't have children, you are not really a woman. And with Pesach coming up, it is even more painful.

'I don't want to undergo any further medical intervention ... There comes a point when you must come to terms with infertility.'

Fact file

Judaism lays great emphasis on the importance of having a family. According to Jewish teaching, God created man and woman to populate the Earth and make it holy. *'Be fertile and increase'* (*Genesis 1:22*) is the first mitzvah in the Torah. There is a sympathetic approach to infertility among Jews and childless couples often seek spiritual help from a rabbi. There are a variety of aids to infertility (see page 21). Many Jews would consider the following:

- Egg donation from one woman to another is an accepted practice, although some would want it to be from another Jewess in order to ensure the child's Jewish status (see page 180). Others say that this can be maintained through upbringing.
- Surrogacy is not approved of and is seen as damaging to the ideals of motherhood and beliefs about the sanctity of life.
- AIH is permitted by many authorities but not AID as this would be seen as a form of adultery.
- IVF is also accepted as long as both the sperm and egg come from husband and wife.

Get talking

- Why might it be especially painful to be without a family at festival times?

- Do you think there should be any rules about having children with the aid of embryo technology, e.g. an age limit?

Abortion

Can I bear that this life has potential within?
Will God who knows all forgive me this sin?
Does he know that I simply haven't reserves
To give it the chance it surely deserves?
I've searched in my soul through each painful day
But questions that torture me won't go away.
I'd give this child life if only I could
But sometimes a wrong seems the greater good.

Fact file

In the *Thirteen Principles of Faith,* written by Maimonides (see page 155), it states that God is Creator of life. Judaism teaches that only God can decide when life is given and taken away.

'Naked came I out of my mother's womb, and naked shall I return there; the Lord has given, and the Lord has taken away.' (Job 1:21)

However, as a mother's life is considered to be more important than that of an unborn child, abortion is permitted in certain circumstances, such as if her life is in danger during pregnancy or childbirth. *'If a woman in labour has a life-threatening difficulty, one dismembers the embryo within her, removing it limb by limb, for her life takes precedence over its life. But once its greater part has emerged it may not be harmed, for we do not set aside one life for another.' (Talmud)*

Some authorities also allow an abortion in situations of rape, incest and when the mother's general health is poor. However, poverty would not be considered a valid reason as many believe that God will provide.

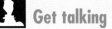 Get talking

● What are the pressures upon women to have abortions?

● What is the link between the last line of the poem and relative and absolute morality (see page 11)?

 Recall and explain

1 Describe the reasons why a Jewish woman might be allowed an abortion. **(3)**

2 What are the sources of authority a Jew might consult when making moral decisions? **(3)**

3 How do you think a rabbi could help people who are considering embryo technology or abortion? **(4)**

Rachel Green,
Jewish Women's Advice Bureau,
P.O. Box 31,
Ilford

Dear Rachel

My fiance and I plan to marry next year.
Although we wish to have children, we would
like to plan our family and not rush into
parenthood. I should be grateful if you
would advise me about what is permitted
according to Jewish teaching about
contraception.

Yours sincerely

Betty Leigh

Dear Rachel
Many of my friends are living with
their partners before marriage. I
sometimes feel they think I'm old-
fashioned and my boyfriend and I
have had many soul-searching
discussions about it. We are both
Jews but he does not feel as
strongly as I do that we should wait
until marriage. I'm very mixed up in
my mind about the rights and wrongs
of it.
I'd like your advice
Sarah James

Get talking

- To what extent should couples getting married share their views with each other about planning for a family?

- What thoughts need to be taken into consideration when deciding upon different means of contraception?

Fact file 1

Casual sexual relationships and cohabitation (living together) are not approved of in Judaism and Jews are taught that sexual intimacy should be part of a stable relationship within the framework of marriage. Fidelity (faithfulness) is considered to be important and in the seventh Commandment it says, *'You shall not commit adultery'. (Exodus 20:13)*

In the Torah it states that God created man and woman to populate the Earth and make it holy. *'Be fertile and increase' (Genesis 1:22)*. Within marriage sex is seen as the husband's duty and the wife's right. In addition to creating a family, sexual relationships help the companionship of a marriage. No virtue is seen in practising celibacy (abstinence from sex) within marriage and the only time the Torah prohibits sex between a married couple is when the wife is menstruating and during the following week (see Mikveh, page 182).

Fact file 2

Many Jews consider a large family as a blessing from God and for this reason, contraception is often seen as interference with the Divine plan. Among Jews, however, there are differing viewpoints on the subject. It is generally considered acceptable to use contraceptives if the physical or mental health of a woman is at risk. The same is true if the welfare of the rest of the family is likely to be affected by the addition of more children.

Oral contraceptives such as the pill, are a preferred method of birth control as they do not interfere with intercourse and the male seed is not directly destroyed. The use of an IUD (see page 27) can present problems for Orthodox Jews as it can lead to spotting of blood between periods. (See Mikveh, page 182.) Sterilization and vasectomy are not approved of as they are regarded as a mutilation of the body.

Condoms are considered unacceptable by many people as they prevent the true bonding of bodies, which is referred to in *Genesis 2:24*: '*a man leaves his father and mother and clings to his wife, so that they become one flesh'*. This causes difficulties when agencies such as the Jewish AIDS Trust are trying to promote safe sex.

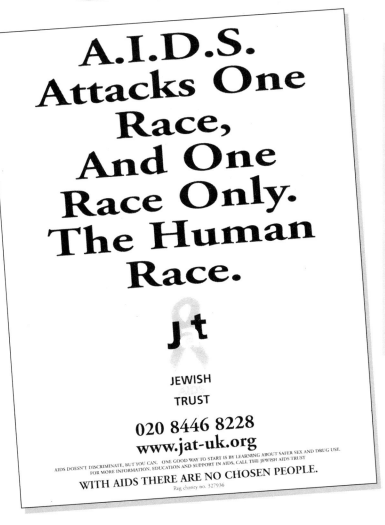

A.I.D.S.
Attacks One
Race,
And One
Race Only.
The Human
Race.

Jt

JEWISH
TRUST

020 8446 8228
www.jat-uk.org

AIDS DOESN'T DISCRIMINATE, BUT YOU CAN. ONE GOOD WAY TO START IS BY LEARNING ABOUT SAFER SEX AND DRUG USE.
FOR MORE INFORMATION, EDUCATION AND SUPPORT IN AIDS, CALL THE JEWISH AIDS TRUST

WITH AIDS THERE ARE NO CHOSEN PEOPLE.
Reg. charity no. 327936

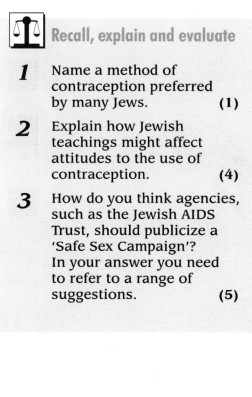

Recall, explain and evaluate

1 Name a method of contraception preferred by many Jews. **(1)**

2 Explain how Jewish teachings might affect attitudes to the use of contraception. **(4)**

3 How do you think agencies, such as the Jewish AIDS Trust, should publicize a 'Safe Sex Campaign'? In your answer you need to refer to a range of suggestions. **(5)**

Get talking

- What symbols can you see in this poster and why are they being used?
- What kind of help do you think is needed and offered?

Rabbi Lionel Blue, well-known writer and broadcaster is famous for humour and down-to-earth compassion. In his autobiography, *A Backdoor to Heaven*, he tells of his decision, after a life-time of secrecy, to 'come out' and state openly that he was a homosexual.

I am gay or homosexual, and was so used to living life in two parts … it was time to come clean. Being gay meant a more difficult fit socially, psychologically and physically, but it led to the same goals as straight relationships, commitment, loyalty and fulfilment. You just had to pay more for them, that's all. Now I had always been angry with God – an emotion most pious people find difficult to admit. Being Jewish, poor and plump was difficult enough. Why did he have to gild the lily by making me gay too? It was an older, wiser colleague, more conforming, and heterosexual too, who told me to ponder the opportunities God had given me by being gay. And doing so in a silent chapel I was overwhelmed by the riches I had received and never regarded. Because I had been an underdog myself, I felt for the "outsiders" who waited nervously outside my little tribunal. I too knew what it was like to have no place in the "happy family" pictures which illustrated Sunday school textbooks. My gayness had saved me from self-righteousness. And this was useful because the number of outsiders was growing, and there was more spirituality among them than they realized, just as there was more doubt among "insiders" than they cared to admit.

Fact file

The Torah condemns male homosexuality, describing it as an abomination (*Leviticus 18:22*). No mention is made of lesbianism, although the condemning of women who '*copy the practices of the land of Egypt*' (*Leviticus 18:3*) is sometimes interpreted as meaning that it is also forbidden. While Orthodox Jews continue to follow this teaching, others have different views.

Many Jews make a distinction by accepting the homosexual person but condemning the homosexual act. Some believe that although a heterosexual relationship is the ideal model for the raising of children and the nurturing of faith, their religious laws make it clear that they should treat others as they would wish to be treated themselves. They interpret this to mean that they must develop tolerance and empathy. They are aware that homosexuals can become scapegoats for people's fears and prejudices, particularly in relation to AIDS, which can lead to homophobia (the fear and dislike of homosexuality). This they strongly condemn, remembering all too well that homosexuals died alongside Jews in Hitler's concentration camps during the Holocaust.

Recall and explain

1 What is meant by the term scapegoat? **(2)**

2 Explain why there are different veiws on homosexuality amongst Jews. **(4)**

3 With reference to the extract, explain how Rabbi Blue's homosexuality has affected his life. **(4)**

Marriage

 **Get talking**

- What can be learned about Jewish wedding traditions from this card?

Marriage ceremony

At the wedding, a **Ketubah** or marriage contract is read out. This will include the husband's vow: 'I will cherish and honour and maintain thee in truth and faithfulness as it becometh a Jewish husband to do' and the bride's that she will cherish and honour her husband 'as beseemeth a daughter of Israel'. Many Jews are now suggesting that arrangements concerning the unlikely happening of divorce should also be included through a Pre-nuptial Agreement. (See Divorce, page 174.)

The wedding takes place under a **huppah** or canopy which symbolizes harmony, enclosing the couple who stand beneath it but open at the sides to signify that they belong to the rest of the community. The bridegroom offers a ring to the bride and says, 'Behold you are sanctified to me with this ring, according to the law of Moses and Israel'.

The bride accepts the ring as a sign of her commitment to the marriage.

Are you looking for a partner? Let **PARTNERS**, the Jewish Marriage Bureau help you. Our professional and strictly confidential consultants are here to help you. Write for details.

MATCHING BRIEF

The young adults task group of the organization Jewish Continuity has come up with an idea. They want there to be a register of matchmakers known as rent-a-Yenta to help people find the right partner. This is in response to the continuing fall in Jewish marriages.

Fact file

Marriage is seen as extremely important as both physical and spiritual fulfilment. This can be seen by the Hebrew word for marriage, **Kiddushin** which means holiness. Marriage is considered to be important for a number of reasons:

Kids! The first Commandment to people in Genesis is to be fertile and increase. A child is seen as a gift from God.

It's not good to be alone. God showed the necessity for companionship by creating Adam and Eve. *(Genesis 2:18–22)*

Delays of marriage should only happen if extensive study of the Torah is taking place. Eighteen used to be considered the ideal age to begin a loving life of growing together. Celibacy is not considered a virtue.

Develops the individual's personality within a special relationship.

Underpins society and promotes the continuity of Judaism.

Sins are forgiven when one marries, according to Jewish teaching.

Happiness! In the Talmud, it says that an unmarried man lives without joy, without blessing and without good.

Increases stability and security in a changing and troubled world.

Natural state for all, including rabbis. The only people who should delay being married are those who study in the **Yeshiva**, a college for the study of the Torah.

Finding a partner

For Jews the ideal marriage would be where the couple are both Jewish, with Jewish children. This used to be easier when each community had a **Shadchan** – a matchmaker who would weigh up the suitability of couples before introductions went ahead. This custom is illustrated in drama and song in the musical *Fiddler on the Roof*. Now, other ways have to be considered such as events for single people organized by synagogues and marriage bureaux.

Recall, explain and evaluate

1   What do the words kiddushin and huppah mean?   **(2)**

2   Why is marrriage considered important in Judaism?   **(4)**

3   'Before I get married I want to have worked out what happens if we divorce.' Do you agree? Give reasons for your answer, showing you've considered other points of view.   **(4)**

Creative assignment

Design a wedding greeting card, both inside and out, which has words and symbols that reflect some of the important aspects of marriage in Judaism.

Trends in UK synagogue marriages

Graph: Number of marriages per year (vertical axis: 750, 950, 1150, 1350, 1550, 1750, 1950) against Year (horizontal axis: '67 to '93). Values decline from around 1950 in 1950 to 1100 by 1993.

Marriage in decline

Nationally, as many couples choose to cohabit (live together), the number of weddings has decreased in all religions, but there are several situations causing a decline in Jewish marriage:

● smaller families have resulted in fewer Jews being born
● Jewish people are facing difficulties in meeting other young people.

Intermarriage between Jews and non-Jews has increased. In Britain and America, one in two young Jews are marrying 'out' of their religion and not bringing up their children as Jewish. The **Jewish Continuity** project helped to combat this problem (see page 173).

It is now being recognized that intermarriage between religions can succeed but it is recommended that the couple should sit and talk about ways they might overcome difficulties.

‘It didn't seem to matter at first. Love conquered all I believed. Looking back, our marriage was doomed from the start. Parental disappointment that I was marrying out, no big announcement, no synagogue wedding. A friendly vicar allowed us to marry in his church as my husband had been in the choir, but it wasn't the same, it couldn't be.

Trying to select hymns and prayers that would offend neither set of relations was an art in itself. I'd read in the Jewish Chronicle about "marrying out" and the decline of the Jewish race. I felt nothing but pure guilt. All my husband's workmates presumed I was Christian, too, and I felt I'd lost my identity as I'd write the countless Christmas cards and suffer their anti-Semitic jokes. Pesach and Rosh Hashanah were the worst times. The isolation was unbearable. Then we discussed our future children. If we had a boy, would he be circumcized? What about schools and would we celebrate Christmas, Hanukkah – both or nothing? It took a long time for me to realize I was Jewish in outlook, culture and beliefs. My religion was not like an overcoat I could slip on and off at will. When I denied my religion, I denied myself. Love couldn't conquer all.’

Get talking

● How could the couple in the story above have better prepared themselves for marriage?

If You're Looking for G-d, Go Home

- What do you think the words 'If you're looking for G-d, go home' mean?

- Compare with each other some of the things you have been taught at home.

- In what ways will these things be an advantage to you in the near or distant future?

Note: Some Orthodox Jews consider the divine name so holy they do not write it in full.

The photo shows a **mezuzah**, a section from the Torah on a small scroll inside a case. It is placed on the doorposts of Jewish homes and is often touched on entering and leaving the house to remind the family of God's presence in their home.

The family is incredibly important to me, and if there is one thing I insist on, it is that everyone gets together on Friday nights for the Sabbath. There's usually about 22 of us around the table, and it's a warm and happy time.

(Naf Naf co-founder Gerard Pariente, *Sunday Times*.)

Jonathan Sachs, Chief Rabbi, in *Faith in The Future* cited the family as the most powerful influence.

Its effects stay with us for a lifetime. It is where one generation passes on its values to the next and ensures the continuity of a civilization.

Fact file 1

The importance of the family home is greatly valued by many Jews who consider it as a sanctuary. It is where the practices of Judaism and virtues of charity and hospitality are learned and reinforced.

Each week mothers usher the Sabbath into Jewish homes by lighting the candles. From sunset on Friday until the stars appear on Saturday, there should be no work. For the Orthodox, even the preparation of food will have been done beforehand so that the mother will not have to cook. In this way, the family has time for each other and is freed from the stresses of the week. The home is where the **Kashrut**, the laws relating to kosher food, will be learned and practised (see page 201).

Fact file 2

The home plays an important role in the celebration of festivals. At **Pesach**, all bread made with yeast (leaven) must be removed from the house before the eight days of festival begin. During the ceremonial meal or **seder**, families remember and recount the Exodus of their ancestors from Egypt.

In the autumn festival of thanksgiving called **Sukkot** a temporary building called a **sukkah** is built as an extension of the family home. This reminds Jews of the shelters built and used by the Israelites in the desert after the Exodus from Egypt. Many families eat their meals and sleep out in it, looking through the roof of leaves at the stars. (See also page 200.)

The nurturing of children is an important mitzvah (commandment) in Judaism, second only to the preserving of life. It is often in the home that a boy's **brit milah** (circumcision) takes place as a sign of the covenant or bond between the Jews and God. It is carried out when the child is eight days old and is performed by a **mohel**, who is specially trained and who represents the father.

Parents have an important role in educating their children in Jewish practices and values until they reach a time of maturity. This is at twelve for girls and thirteen for boys. To mark the passage to manhood, boys have a ceremony and family celebration called **Bar Mitzvah**. Fathers will have overseen their learning the laws and the reading of the Torah in preparation for it. For girls, some families choose to have a similar event called a **Bat Mitzvah**, or they might decide to have a **Bat Chayil**. These occasions are considered to be the time of entering a special covenant relationship with God and taking responsibilities for one's actions.

A Bat Mitzvah card

A Bar Mitzvah card

Recall and explain

1 Name two Jewish festivals. (2)

2 Why is the home considered so important in Judaism? (4)

3 Look at the illustrations on this page. Explain the use of any two symbols. (4)

Creative assignment

Imagine you are a Jew who has received a letter from a student asking for information about Jewish home life. Write an interesting and helpful reply. Illustrate it if you can.

Family life for Jews in Britain

It is important to Jews to be able to keep the beliefs, values and traditions of their religion, but this can be difficult when mixing with communities which have a different or no religion. Many of these situations need the support of the family and synagogue (see page 183).

School

Many Jewish children go to non-Jewish schools where kosher food is not provided at lunch time. Daily school collective worship will probably have a broadly Christian bias. Jewish boys might want to wear the head covering (**kippah**) as a mark of respect for God.

Synagogue

Many people live in an area where there is not a synagogue and have to travel a long distance for communal worship. Orthodox Jews are expected to walk. Apart from the inconvenience of this, it makes it harder for them to get to know and share activities with other Jewish families. A **minyan**, a minimum of ten men, is needed for a service to take place in many synagogues.

Shabbat

The Sabbath begins at sunset on Friday. In order to be ready for it, some people have to leave school or work early. It carries through to Saturday which means that no work should be done. (See also page 184.)

Kosher

There are relatively few kosher foodshops (see page 201) and they tend to be only in areas where there is a substantial Jewish population.

Festivals

Most festivals are at different times from Christian ones and require time off from work or school. **Rosh Hashanah**, the Jewish New Year, usually falls in September near the start of the term and begins the Ten Days of Returning, which end in the fast of **Yom Kippur** (the Day of Atonement). Many Jews spend much of this day in the synagogue (see page 204).

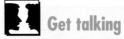 **Get talking**

● **Can you think of other situations which pose problems for people of other religions because of different beliefs, values or traditions?**

When asked why she was not made head girl at school, author and radio presenter, Edwina Currie replied:

❝Because I was Jewish … When I was taking time off for Rosh Hashanah, the acting head said to me, "You do have the most inconvenient religion, you know."❞

Janis Goodman

As Hanukkah, the Festival of Light, often falls in mid-December, near Christmas, the two festivals can often appear integrated. Hanukkah is an eight-day celebration. It marks the Jews' victory, nearly 22 centuries ago, over Antiochus IV who tried to abolish Judaism.

The celebrations at Hanukkah include lighting lamps or candles for eight days and giving gifts.

Gary Jacobs, boxer
'I give gifts all year round, not just at Hanukkah. This year, I'll probably buy my two children toys. They're just babies. As a child, we celebrated Christmas and Hanukkah, so we wouldn't feel left out when our non-Jewish friends got presents.'

* 'gelt' means spending money
+ menorah – see page 183

Vanessa Felz, TV presenter and columnist
'I'll be buying presents only for my two daughters this year. I've succumbed to the material world – we'll be giving them eight presents, one for each day. When I was little we used to get a 10 shilling note (50p) from my Grandpa Willy – Hanukkah gelt*. I'm not expecting anything myself, but last year a wonderful box from Janet Reger arrived – a fantastic bathrobe, my best-ever present.'

Chief Rabbi Dr Jonathan Sachs
'What do I give for Hanukkah? Books. What do I like to receive? Books. But the best present I ever had was the menorah+ made by our son, Joshua, when he was five. It was made out of cardboard and bottle tops, but to receive such a gift from our first child, and to see in our own family the miracle of Jewish continuity, was the most beautiful present.'

Jewish Continuity

Fact file 3

Jewish Continuity

The family has always been the most effective and important means by which Judaism has stayed alive and been passed on to each new generation. In recent years, there has been concern at the decline in the number of Jews choosing to continue in the Jewish faith and way of life. Many factors have led to this situation, including assimilation into non-Jewish life (see page 168). In order to overcome this problem, the Jewish Continuity project was created.

It was set up in 1993 to encourage and fund a variety of programmes to bring people closer to the beliefs, values and traditions of Jewish life. The main focus is on the 13–35 age group, whom it believes are the ones who will be making key life choices which will affect their future as Jews. It has 90 projects around the country including crash courses in reading Hebrew, trips to Israel, a communal database and Schools J-link in non-Jewish schools.

Dear Grandma and Grandpa,

Hi, how are you? I am having a brill time on Israel Tour. Last night we climbed Massada (a very HIGH mountain) at 3am, we watched the sun rise and ate breakfast looking over the Dead Sea — it was amazing. We then went to swim in it. I could even read my Mizz magazine while floating in the water, it's sooo salty. Apart from that the tour has been quite ordinary. We went camel riding, slept in a Bedouin tent, went to the beach, met an Israeli MP, saw a show at King David's Tower (not uncle David, Gran, King David!), visited a kibbutz, went to a water park, windsurfed in Eilat, saw the Western Wall* and met some really cool Israelis.

Israel is just the most happening place in the world. My group has people from all over the country and they are really OK, apart from one group of girls from London

*(see page 196)

— can you believe it, they are Robbie Williams fans! I'm going out with a boy called Chas from Birmingham who is also in to Heavy Metal.

I know I was going to work for that touring rock band this year but I'm thinking of staying in London and doing my A Levels and then going to Israel for my gap year. I hope Mum and Dad won't be too disappointed.

We are going to watch the sun set on the beach front so I must run. Lehitraot (that means see you soon in Hebrew).

Love

Katie

Recall and explain

1 Describe the work of the Jewish Continuity project. (4)

2 Explain how Katie's religious indentity has been developed by her visit to Israel. (6)

Divorce

Get talking

- Should couples be allowed to divorce as and when they want to?

- Do you think divorce is harder on women than men?

- Who or what might help a couple seeking a divorce?

Fact file

Although it is Jewish belief that marriage should be permanent, divorce is permitted if a couple have found it impossible to stay together. The Talmud says, *'Whoever divorces his first wife even the altar sheds tears on her behalf'*. In all countries, apart from Israel, a civil divorce must be given first where the marriage will be annulled in a court of law. There are differences of practice between Orthodox and Liberal Jews. The Orthodox base their beliefs on *Deuteronomy 24:* which states: *'and he writes her a bill of divorcement, hands it to her and sends her away from his house'*. Before the partners are free to re-marry, the husband must give his wife a religious bill of divorce (**get**). This is a document which dissolves the partnership. This can present difficulties if the husband refuses, disappears or is incapable of doing so through illness. Women caught in this trap are called **agunot**, 'chained women'. The Israel Women's network claims that there are about 10,000 agunot living in Israel and 15,000 in America. A woman may not re-marry for 90 days in case she was pregnant before the divorce. If the Orthodox woman re-marries after only having had a civil divorce, children born within that marriage are considered to be **mamzerim** (offspring of a forbidden man). According to the Mishnah, such children can only themselves marry people of that same status.

Women from the Liberal community do not require a get to re-marry.

'Chained women' protesting outside a Bet Din

The get

The get will generally be written on a piece of parchment with special non-erasable ink. It is given from husband to wife who removes any rings so that nothing comes between the document and her hands accepting it. The document should have a special mark so that if its validity is later challenged, it can be checked by the person who wrote it. The document has to be cut so that it cannot be re-used.

Things are changing

In December 1995, the United Kingdom's main Orthodox courts introduced a new document which will help the 'chained women'. It will include the following.

1 A pre-nuptial agreement (PNA) which will commit couples signing it to attend a religious court in the event of a divorce.
2 A set of sanctions against husbands who refuse to agree to a get, such as a denial of certain privileges in the synagogue.

London-born Sandra, 56, comes from an Orthodox background. Her marriage broke down eight years ago but, to this day, she has still not obtained a get, although she is divorced according to civil law.

'My ex-husband has never actually said he won't give me a get. And indeed, when the Bet Din★ has contacted him, he has always been very pleasant.

'In the meantime, I have not been given a get.

'It is so very unjust that an ex-husband in this situation can go ahead and re-marry if he wants to and have children, and there will be no slur on those children.

'Being an agunah,[+] I cannot be introduced to any men. I feel it would be dishonest of me.

'I have a daughter and two granddaughters. I think of their future too. Is it wrong of me to expect equality before the law for half of the Jewish population?'

★The **Bet Din** is a Rabbinic court of law which deals with matters relating to issues among Jews.
[+] Agunah (singular), agunot (plural).

Recall, explain and evaluate

1 What is a get? **(1)**

2 Explain why it was difficult for Sandra being an agunah. **(4)**

3 Do you think men should be forced to grant their wives a get? In your answer you should refer to a number of possible alternatives. **(5)**

Yahrzeit poem

In her later years she took to speaking
Russian once again – strange syllables that we
Had never heard – words long forgotten which found
Their way into her speech by some cerebral
Short-circuit unexplained by science and yet,
After all, only a common miracle.
'It happens all the time,' the doctor told us,
And we accepted it and tried to make do only
Half understanding her, hearing sentences
With all the crucial words in an alien tongue.

She never seemed quite at home in the world,
Technology amazed her, and she would spend her
Days staring out the window of her apartment,
Trying, it seemed, to comprehend it all. 'What
Does she do all day?' I asked my mother. 'She
Counts the cars,' my mother replied, as if this
Were a proper activity for an elderly woman,
A simple strategy to order things not understood.

A pious woman, she was unknowingly an animist,
A technological mystic who believed in the souls
Of things. As when our car was stopped at a traffic
Light one day and we fumed, late for some appointment,
She suggested that it was good,
For after all cars too needed to take a rest.

She passed away on a hot July day, and I,
Away on vacation, almost missed hearing
About it: a mix-up with the telephones –
It seemed appropriate. She always called
The operator when she wanted a number, a human
Voice helped explain the mystery of bodiless speech.

Today I saw an old woman try to enter a supermarket
The wrong way. She hadn't mastered the electric doors.
What a world for her, I thought, where doors
Never get touched by hands and only open one way.

Barry Holtz

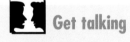

Get talking

- What are the difficulties of getting old?

- Is it easier or harder for the elderly living in today's society compared with when their grandparents were old?

Note: In Judaism, **yahrzeit** refers to the anniversary of someone's death (see page 219).

Fact file

Care of the elderly is an important duty in Judaism. The fifth Commandment says, *'Honour your father and your mother'.* *(Exodus 20:12)*

Although living a long life is seen as a blessing and is given as a reward *(Isaiah 65:20)*, the needs and difficulties of the elderly are also highlighted. *Psalm 71:9* says: *'Do not cast me off in old age, when my* *strength fails, do not forsake me'.* Respect for parents is an important part of Jewish family life.

Society cares for the elderly in many ways, but there are increasing difficulties with a higher percentage of people living beyond eighty and many carers of seventy-plus looking after relatives of ninety-plus.

Community centres can make a difference

A growing number of community centres nationwide have been shown to answer many of the needs of elderly and lonely people.

‘They're so kind at the Centre and I get taken and brought home afterwards.’

‘I used to be a barber so I cut the people's hair here.’

‘This place is fantastic. I never did any art before – I didn't have the time.’

‘I enjoy reminiscing with my friends.’

‘I sometimes go for whole days without seeing a soul.’

‘My grandson and I have a special relationship.’

‘I'm afraid to go out after all you hear on the news.’

Recall, explain and evaluate

1 What do the Jewish Scriptures say about the care of the elderly? **(4)**

2 Why are the Ten Commandments so important to Jews? **(2)**

3 In what ways can respect for parents be shown? Does it change as the children get older? In your answer refer to a range of suggestions. **(4)**

Jewish Care

The organization **Jewish Care** has six centres, the largest one of which is Sinclair House, in Ilford, Essex. Among its many features is a range of care for 3500 users and it has 450 elderly and disabled people from the Jewish community relying upon it. It has 82 volunteers and organizes the delivery of meals on wheels to the house-bound.

As well as this, it is a centre where the elderly may go. It enables them to mix with other Jewish people which they might find difficult if they have lost a partner or cannot travel with ease. It aims to combat social isolation and develop physical and creative skills in a Jewish environment. All the Jewish festivals are celebrated at Sinclair House.

For a small charge members are provided with transport, a kosher meal and entertainment. Other facilities include:

Dance classes

Chiropodist

Flower arranging

Aid for the visually impaired, stroke and arthritis sufferers

Religious festivals are observed

Hairdresser

Reminiscence and discussion groups

Arts and crafts

Drama

Manicurist

Many members have found a new lease of life; others a new skill in the art class or at discussion groups. For some, just a simple perm at the hairdresser's has made all the difference.

Creative assignment

Using the fifth Commandment as the centre-piece, create a collage of images and words about respect for the elderly.

'What the child speaks out of doors he has learned indoors.' (*Talmud*)

The following questions give you a chance to re-examine the issues raised in the preceding units. Remember to look at the number of marks for each question and to develop your answer accordingly.

a Name any *two* sources of moral authority a Jew might refer to before making a decision. **(2)**

b Describe the Jewish attitude concerning *either* family planning *or* sex outside marriage. **(6)**

c Explain how and why the family and home are so important in Judaism. **(7)**

d 'It's the duty of parents to care for children and, in time, for children to care for parents. No one else should be involved.'

Do you agree? Give reasons for your answer showing you have considered other points of view. **(5)**

The role of women

The story of Ina Shalom

Non-Jew: 'Your God is a thief because in your Bible it says he stole a rib from Adam.'

Ina: 'Last night a stranger broke into my house and stole my silver coins, leaving gold ones in their place.'

Non-Jew: *(laughing)* 'That was hardly a thief!'

Ina: 'Well, so it was with God who took a rib from man and gave him a wife instead!'

(A story from Rabbinic literature)

Get talking

● What do you think the writer of the story is teaching about women?

● Why are some men against sexual equality?

● How hard can it be for men to accept it?

Fact file 1

Equality between men and women is found in many places in the Torah and throughout Jewish history women have always played a significant part. Stories in the Bible tell of women such as Miriam, Deborah, Hannah and Ruth who had great influence on events. The annual festival of **Purim** focuses upon the courage of Queen Esther. In Jewish teaching, the roles of men and women are different but equally important. They are seen to complement each other. Although men traditionally have a greater prominence in the synagogue, much religious practice takes place in the home, where the woman takes the leading role. Here a woman has distinct responsibilities such as bringing in Shabbat, saying prayers and lighting the candles.

At festival times, the home is often the focal point for the religious celebrations. Candles are lit daily during Hanukkah, the house is specially prepared for Pesach and important rules are observed concerning food. These are all the responsibility of the woman in both the Orthodox and Reform movements (see page 181). The Jewish identity of a person is established through the female line.

In recent years, groups of women have sometimes used the time of **Rosh Chodesh**, which marks the beginning of each Jewish month, to strengthen their Jewish faith. They have adapted ancient customs and given them a distinctive women's identity. Their activities often focus on charity work.

Women in Orthodox and Progressive Judaism

Judaism regards men and women as equals with shared responsibilities. The differences between the branches of Judaism are most marked where the role of women is concerned. These affect rules concerning marriage, divorce, and public worship. In 1993 the Jewish Women's Network was established to help communication between women from different branches of Judaism.

Orthodox Judaism

In Orthodox synagogues women sit separately from the men in an area called the women's gallery. This is to ensure that they do not distract each other. Women do not read from the Sefer Torah, but in 1992 a group of Orthodox women organized a Women's Only Service so that they would be able to. This caused the Chief Rabbi to intervene. It was pointed out that for communal worship to take place a minyan of ten men was needed. However, this is because of religious teaching which states that women are not obliged to pray in a synagogue. A compromise was reached and women's services can take place where the parts needing a minyan are omitted.

Some Orthodox women will cover their hair at all times except when they are alone with their husbands and will use the mikveh (see page 182).

Progressive Judaism

Within the Progressive movement women may sit with men in the synagogue, lead services and even become rabbis. The first female rabbi was ordained in 1972, although some felt this was against Jewish law.

Women are also allowed to wear the **tallit** or prayer shawl and kippah, the head covering worn during prayers. They are permitted to say the **kaddish**, the prayer publicly recited by mourners (see page 218).

An Orthodox synagogue, where men sit separately from women

A Progressive synagogue, where men and women sit together

 Creative assignment

Make up a collage about a woman (or women) you admire for the contribution she has (or they have) made to society.

Mikveh

Fact file 2

Among Orthodox Jewish women there is a tradition which involves the use of a **mikveh**. This is the name given to a special pool of rain water (usually heated) which is used for ritual bathing. Attached to the bathing area is a room where everything must be removed so that complete physical and spiritual cleansing can take place. A woman's first experience of the mikveh will be just before marriage. After that, she will go every month. Orthodox and many Reform Jewish women practise the Niddah (separation) in accordance with the teaching in *Leviticus 15:19–24* which states that while a woman is having her period and for seven days afterwards, she is impure and so sexual relations are not permitted. At the end of this time, she will go to the mikveh where she will say a blessing and immerse herself in the water three times.

An advert from a Jewish newspaper

Women's views on the use of a mikveh:

•*Why should women be considered impure because of periods?*•

•*The mikveh is a real cleansing each month. I feel renewed spiritually and physically.*•

•*The time of not being allowed to have sex gives breathing space for non-physical love to grow.*•

•*It encourages adultery when you have to go so long without sex.*•

A rabbi responds to a woman traumatized by rape, who asked for a mikveh ceremony:

•*When Laura was raped, I wanted to find a way to support her as a friend. As a rabbi I needed to find a way for Judaism to respond to her … The mikveh seemed the most appropriate ritual … its waters symbolically flow from Eden, a place of wholeness … water itself is cleansing, supportive, and life-sustaining.*•

Recall, explain and evaluate

1 Give two differences between the Orthodox and Progressive movements concerning the role of women. **(2)**

2 Explain the role of women in Judaism. **(4)**

3 'The mikveh has no role in the twentieth century.' Do you agree? In your answer refer to other points of view. **(4)**

The role of the synagogue

A synagogue or **Bet ha Knesset** has developed as a community centre where Jewish people gather for sacred, cultural and social activities.

1 Festivals

Although the home is the central place for celebrating many festivals, the synagogue plays an important role at Rosh Hashanah, Shabbat, Purim and Simchat Torah. At Sukkot a large sukkah is often built in which communities can share meals. On Yom Kippur some may spend the whole day in the synagogue.

7 Social activities

At the synagogue there are many opportunities for Jews to get together, providing activities such as boys' and girls' brigades; summer camps; quiz nights; cultural exchanges; inter-faith activities and exhibitions.

6 Fund-raising

Through the synagogue, money is raised for charities both in England and Israel.

2 Advice

A number of people are available to give advice and education to the community. The rabbi is experienced in matters relating to the **Halakhah** (see page 154) and can advise on it.

5 Education

Sunday schools are often held where Jewish children can have lessons in Hebrew and learn about festivals and Jewish customs.

3 Prayer

In addition to daily prayers at home, many Jewish people choose to say them in the synagogue with the minyan (see page 171). Certain parts of prayer and readings from the Sefer Torah are specifically for use in community prayer.

4 Initiation

The ceremonies of Bar Mitzvah, Bat Mitzvah, Bat Chayil and many marriages take place in the synagogue. Many are also used as centres for the celebration afterwards.

Note: the seven-branched candlestick, known as the **menorah**, is an important symbol in Judaism.

Work

Shabbat

Sunset on Friday is the start of Shabbat.

Holy day set apart from the week.

All the family together.

Bringing in the Shabbat is done by mother.

Blessings are given and the candle is lit.

All work stops.

Time for rest and reflection.

 **Get talking**

● What kinds of work within the home have to be done, regardless of what day of the week it is?

Shabbat begins in **London** tonight at **4.01pm**; Leeds, **3.55pm**; Manchester, **3.59pm**; Tyneside, **3.49pm**; Glasgow **3.55pm**

Shabbat times for one week in winter, printed in a Jewish newspaper

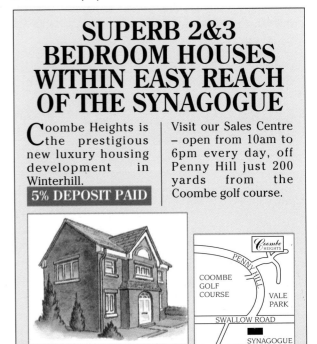
Fact file

The Jewish Sabbath or Shabbat is one of the most important festivals that takes place in Jewish homes. It celebrates God's creation of the Earth and the command recorded in *Exodus 20:8–10* not to work.

'Remember the Sabbath day and keep it holy. Six days you shall labour and do all your work, but the seventh day is a Sabbath of the Lord your God: you shall not do any work …'

The Mishnah and Talmud have interpreted this by drawing up 39 different types of work or **melakhah** which are prohibited.

For many Jews the observance of Shabbat allows them to switch off from the bustle and pressures of the working week. Orthodox Jews may not do any cooking during Shabbat but prepare food beforehand using time-switches on their cookers. They also do not use transport and try to live within easy reach of their synagogue so that they can walk to it for the Saturday service. As with all Jewish laws, a matter of life and death would mean that pikuakh nefesh would take priority (see page 159).

3 Newbury Road
Giant Hill
Essex

Dear Rabbi,

I wonder if you could help me in my quandary. I am a qualified doctor, new to the area and seeking a post as a general practitioner. The only one I have been offered is a position in a group practice nearby which would suit me very well. However, I have come up against a problem. On studying the job description I see that I shall be required to work every other Saturday. With family commitments and mortgage payments to consider I feel it would be foolish to reject such an offer. However, as you know, I am Orthodox. I wonder if you would advise me.

Yours sincerely

Alex Levitt

Fact file 2

As Jews believe they are answerable to God for every action they are aware of, they need to be just in their business dealings. According to Rabbinic teaching, the first question Jews will be asked at the Judgement is if they have conducted themselves fairly in matters of work. Within the Torah and Talmud there are references in which dishonesty in trade and business are condemned. The prophet Amos criticized people for '*tilting a dishonest scale and selling grain refuse as grain*'. (Amos 8:5–6)

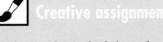
Some things never change!

Recall and evaluate

1 Describe some of the ways that Orthodox Jews keep to the fourth Commandment. **(5)**

2 Do you think it's a good idea to have one day a week when no work should be done? Give reasons showing you have considered other points of view. **(5)**

Creative assignment

Write a thoughtful reply from the rabbi to Alex Levitt.

Wealth and poverty

If I were a rich man
I'd have the time that I lack
To sit in the synagogue and pray
And maybe have a seat by the Eastern Wall
And I'd discuss the holy books
With the learned men
Seven hours every day.
This would be the sweetest thing of all.

from *Fiddler on the Roof*

"He secures justice for those who are wronged and gives food to the hungry." (Psalm 146:7)

"I tend to buy cars for the fun of it. I drive them around for three weeks and then I get bored, dump them in the garage and let the batteries go completely flat."
(Eddie Murphy)

"Now I'm a millionaire I'm going to invest my money in wine, women and fun, fun, fun!" (Lottery winner)

 **Get talking**

● **Can money make you happy?**

● **What are the dangers of being rich?**

● **If you were rich, what would you do with your wealth? What would your priorities be?**

Modern society is often criticized for being too interested in materialism, the desire for money and possessions. We are living in an age of consumerism and people's success is often judged by the amount of wealth they have.

Fact file

Judaism realizes that some material possessions are necessary but that they should not lead people away from God. The Mishnah points out: *'When a man leaves the world, neither silver nor gold nor precious stones nor pearls accompany him, but only the Torah he has learnt and the good works he has carried out.'*

There are two broad types of charity:

Tzedaka = financial support to the poor. As it is believed that all possessions belong to God, there are many occasions when Jews are expected to give money to charities. This includes certain occasions, for example before the weekly lighting of the Sabbath candles and at the annual festival of Purim.

Thought should be given to the person receiving by:

- giving anonymously – this allows the recipient to retain pride and self-esteem
- supporting long-term aid – this involves giving to projects which help people to become self-supporting.

This would follow the teaching of Isaiah: *'to share your bread with the hungry, and to take the wretched poor into your home; when you see the naked, to clothe him, and not to ignore your own kin'. (Isaiah 58:7)*

Gemilut hasadim = kind actions. It is considered important to show compassion towards those who are in difficulties and who need moral support. This can be done by giving up one's time. Maimonides wrote: *'the best way of giving is to help a person help themselves so that they may become self-supporting'.*

The annual 25-hour fast of Yom Kippur promotes compassion through learning what it is like to be hungry.

Tzedaka. Some Jewish homes have collecting boxes called **pushkes** in which money is put towards charity. Children are encouraged from an early age to begin thinking about others by adding small contributions from their pocket money

Gemilut hasadim. There are many examples of charitable work. This soup kitchen began in 1902 to help the poor in Whitechapel. It has now moved to another location.

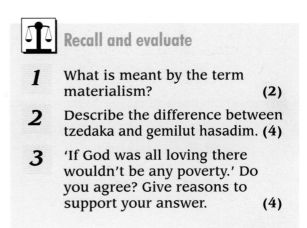

Recall and evaluate

1 What is meant by the term materialism? **(2)**

2 Describe the difference between tzedaka and gemilut hasadim. **(4)**

3 'If God was all loving there wouldn't be any poverty.' Do you agree? Give reasons to support your answer. **(4)**

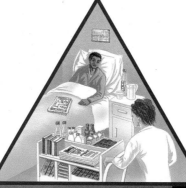

WAYS OF GIVING

10% SALARY

NEWS
Jewish Students join Charity Aid Project

CHARITY SHOP

THIS IS A PESACH APPEAL

JEWISH CARE

Note: This star is the **Magen David**, meaning Shield of David, popularly known as the Star of David.

 **Get talking**

● Look at the illustrations above. Which show examples of
  a) tzedaka,   **b)** gemilut hasadim?

Tzedek

Tzedek is a charity formed in 1990 by a group of young Jews who were concerned to encourage the Jewish community to become more involved in global issues. Tzedek is based on the important Jewish principles of compassion, justice, partnership and respect. Its aim is to provide opportunities for Jews to be aware of poverty and to *respond*.

Relief from poverty is offered to people regardless of race and religion in all parts of the world.

Education programmes are arranged which include seminars on 'Aid', 'Trade and Debt', 'Environment and Development' and 'Refugees'. Activities and programmes are organized for schools and youth clubs.

Support is given to small-scale projects which enable poor communities to be independent.

Practical action and participation are encouraged through fund-raising and events such as collecting tools for self-reliance. Annual events to raise awareness take place including a Spielathon, linking the annual festival of Purim with Comic Relief and a Frugal Family Week where families make a commitment to halve their food bill for a week and donate the other half.

Overseas support is given to the poor in Africa and the Indian sub-continent, working alongside other experienced agencies. People without homes are given assistance to buy land.

New Year festival for trees – a **Tu b'Shvat** seder (meal) is linked with environmental and global concerns.

Development in the long term provides partnership with communities in projects on housing, education and craft skills.

TZEDEK

JEWISH ACTION FOR A JUST WORLD

'… the best way of giving is to help a person help themselves so that they may become self-supporting.' (Maimonides, Gifts to the Poor 10:7)

 Recall and explain

1 What does Judaism teach about how people should behave towards the poor? **(4)**

2 Explain how the work of Tzedek helps to relieve poverty. You need to explore long and short term relief. **(6)**

Creative assignment

Make up two strip cartoons showing
a) good use of wealth
b) the wrong use of wealth.

Find suitable references from this chapter as titles or captions.

Prejudice and discrimination

COPYRIGHT BY HEB. PUB.

Americans welcoming
East European Jews to
the USA

Get talking

- What are some of the reasons for people leaving their countries and settling down in new ones?

- What difficulties can they face?

Fact file

Discrimination against the Jews, **anti-Semitism**, has had a long history stretching back to events in the Bible. Jews have often been made scapegoats for a nation's problems. They were frequently blamed for the death of Jesus and so were refused freedom to worship. In the countries where they had made their homes, they were often forced to leave or suffer forced conversions or organized massacres called **pogroms**. These were especially frequent in the 19th and early 20th centuries in Eastern Europe.

With the rise of Nazism, under the leadership of Hitler in the 1930s, came the beginning of a detailed plan to exterminate all Jews from the world. It began with a gradual undermining of freedom and resulted in the systematic murder of over six million Jews in concentration or death camps. This great crime against humanity is known as the **Shoah** (Holocaust). Others, too, including gypsies, homosexuals, Muslims, Jehovah's Witnesses and any who spoke out against what was happening, suffered the same fate.

Auschwitz: Crematorium 1.
In Auschwitz-Birkenau five crematoriums with gas chambers were in operation. Six to seven kilograms of Cyclone B gas was enough to kill about 1500 people in just over twelve minutes

Shoah (Holocaust)

There are many accounts of the horrors in each death camp – the de-humanizing often incomprehensible. The Jews who were old, sick and unable to work were sent to the gas chambers. The rest were forced to work until they were no longer useful when they, too, met the same fate. Others died from beatings, shootings, illness or starvation.

Recall and evaluate

1 What is anti-Semitism? (2)

2 What do you think makes people treat others in such an inhumane way? You may make reference to past or present situations. (8)

'Stripped down to their underclothes, the Jews had to move forward along the narrow path in a steady flow towards the pits, which they entered by a ramp, in single file and in groups of ten. Occasionally, the flow would come to a standstill when someone tarried at one of the undressing points; or else, if the undressing went faster than expected, or if the columns advanced too quickly from the city, too many Jews would arrive at the pits at once. In such cases, the supervisors stepped in to ensure a steady and moderate flow, since it was feared that the Jews would grow edgy if they had to linger in the immediate vicinity of the pits … .

In the pits the Jews had to lie flat, side by side, face down. They were killed with a single bullet in the neck, the marksmen standing at close range – their semi-automatic pistols set for a single fire. To make the best of available space, and particularly of the gaps between bodies, the victims next in line had to lie down on top of those who had been shot immediately before them. The handicapped, the aged, and the young were helped into the pits by the sturdier Jews, laid by them on top of the bodies, and then shot by marksmen who in the large pit actually stood on the dead. In this way the pits gradually filled.'

Testimony of a survivor: *Approaches to Auschwitz*

Resistance

Within the Jewish community there were many resistance fighters and people who, despite the conditions, displayed concern and charity for others.

⁶*We who lived in concentration camps can remember the men who walked through the huts comforting others, giving away their last piece of bread. They may have been few in number, but they offer sufficient proof that anything can be taken from a man but one thing: the last of human freedoms – to choose one's attitude in any given set of circumstances, to choose one's own way.*⁹

 Get talking

- What do you think is meant by 'to choose one's own way'?
- To which questions about the Shoah (Holocaust) would you like to find answers?
- From whom would you like to find your answers?

One of the many examples of courageous resistance was that of Janusz Korczak, a physician and writer who devoted his life to children. After qualifying as a doctor, he turned his attention to the poor, and in particular, children. He headed two orphanages in Poland, one Jewish and one non-Jewish. When his country was taken over by the Nazis, he refused to let non-Jewish friends smuggle him to safety as he was not prepared to leave his orphans to face their fate alone. On 5 August, 1942, the Germans rounded up Dr Korczak, his staff and his 200 children to march them the three miles (5 km) to the deportation train. He led them, holding a child's hand in each of his. On arrival at Treblinka they were all gassed to death.

Where was God?

Throughout their history, the Jews' belief in God has played a great part in their survival. For those who lived through the Holocaust, many questions were raised, such as: How could humankind behave in this way? Where was God? Was the suffering sent for a purpose? In spite of everything, there is evidence that the faith of many remained intact.

I BELIEVE IN THE SUN WHEN IT'S NOT SHINING.

I BELIEVE IN LOVE EVEN WHEN FEELING IT NOT.

I BELIEVE IN GOD EVEN WHEN HE IS SILENT.

An inscription on the walls of a cellar where Jews hid

A sculpture showing Janusz Korczak, which can be seen at Yad Vashem

Responses to the Holocaust

Among the survivors themselves, there have been a variety of responses to the Holocaust. Some were so severely traumatized that even 50 years later they are not able to talk about it. A number of memorials and museums have been set up, the most famous being Yad Vashem in Jerusalem.

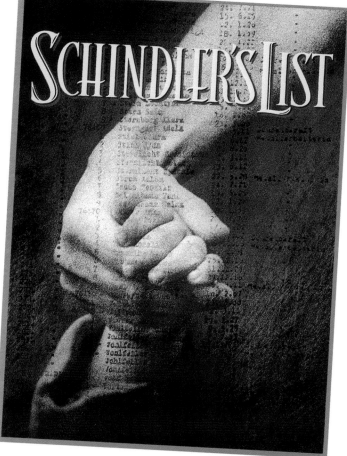

Logo of Yad Vashem

Yad Vashem

The memorial contains extensive pictures, artefacts and documents which remind and educate people about the Holocaust. A Hall of Names records the names of the victims and an eternal flame burns in the Memorial Hall. Here too is the Avenue of the Righteous where trees are planted in memory of non-Jews who helped Jews (e.g. Oscar Schindler). Many Jews visit Yad Vashem as a personal pilgrimage.

Yom Hashoah (Holocaust Remembrance Day)

Each year, (27th Nisan*), prayers are offered for the victims of the Holocaust at Yad Vashem and at synagogues around the world there is a short period of silence. The day was established in 1951 by the **Knesset** – the Israeli Parliament. This day was chosen as it marks the anniversary of the Warsaw ghetto uprising when a brave stand was made by Jews refusing to be taken to death camps. Most were killed in the reprisals that followed.

Some Jews prefer to remember the Holocaust during the fast of **Tishah b'Av** which is a day of penitance and mourning for the destruction of the two Temples in Jerusalem. In the synagogue, the curtain covering the ark is taken down to symbolize this destruction and people sit on low stools as when mourning.

*Nisan is a Jewish month usually March-April.

You should care about this film if you care about humanity, and if you care about the Holocaust never happening again … You go to some movies to be entertained, but you go to this movie to be informed and to be changed, I hope.

(Steven Spielberg, in his Oscar acceptance speech for *Schindler's List*. The film depicts the German Oscar Schindler who saved the lives of many Jews.)

Stones placed as a mark of respect at the foot of Oscar Schindler's tree at Yad Vashem

There are many survivor groups who go to schools to explain what happened in the death camps. They hope that by explaining all the horrors of the Holocaust it will never happen again. But for those who lived through it, it can never be forgotten.

Never shall I forget that night,
the first night in the camp
which has turned my life into one long night,
seven times cursed and seven times sealed.

Never shall I forget that smoke.
Never shall I forget the little faces of the children
whose bodies I saw turned into wreaths of smoke
beneath a silent blue sky.

Never shall I forget those flames
which consumed my faith forever.
Never shall I forget that nocturnal silence
which deprived me for all eternity of the desire to live.

Never shall I forget those moments
which murdered my God and my soul
and turned my dreams to dust.

Never shall I forget these things,
even if I am condemned to live
as long as God himself.
Never.

Elie Wiesel

Note: Born in 1928, Elie Wiesel was interned in both Auschwitz and Buchenwald. He was awarded the Nobel Peace Prize in 1986.

And *still* it goes on…

Outrage at 'death camps' pyjama fashion

Magazine folds following article denying Holocaust

Attack on Jews at new time high

Stalked by the shadows of history – Britain, once a safe haven for European Jews, now has the worst record for anti-Semitic attacks.

Jewish refugee killed herself after seeing Auschwitz film

Recall, explain and evaluate

1 What is Yad Vashem? (2)

2 If God is all-knowing how could an event such as the Holocaust take place? (4)

3 'There is no point making memorials and films about an event that happened over fifty years ago.' Do you agree? In your answer you should refer to other points of view. (4)

Israel

In recent years aliyah has been made by many Jews suffering persecution in their homelands of Russia, Bosnia and Iraq. In one month alone 7000 Ethiopian Jews were air-lifted to Israel in the so-called Operation Moses.

Many people go to Israel and one of the important places visited is the Western Wall, the only remaining part of the Temple not destroyed by the Romans. Men and women pray there separately. Written messages and prayers are often placed in the cracks of the wall. Special occasions such as Bar Mitzvahs and weddings often include a visit.

There are many different expectations from the State of Israel and this can be seen by the numerous conflicts ranging from the decision to open shops on Shabbat to the disputes over land boundaries. With eighteen per cent of Israel's population being non-Jewish, the need for inter-faith dialogue such as in the **Neve Shalom** initiative (see page 209) is seen as vital in achieving the peace that so many Jews long for.

The belief that Israel is the homeland of Jewish people has played a prominent part since God's promise to Abraham (see page 154). Whenever Jews have been exiled or persecuted they have thought of their homeland with longing.

'How can we sing a song of the Lord on alien soil?' (Psalm 137:4)

Although the greatest number of Jews live in America, what happens in Israel affects Jews worldwide.

Jews have marked the role of Israel in daily prayers, festivals and fund-raising. It was during the 19th-century pogroms that the political movement of **Zionism** began. It was established to secure the land of Israel for the Jews. After the Holocaust many surviving Jews went to live in Israel (then called Palestine), which in May 1948 was declared an Independent Jewish State. The Prime Minister of the time, David Ben Gurion, declared that this State of Israel would grant freedom of religion, conscience, language, education and culture to all living there. The State adopted a 'Law of Return' which allowed Jews **aliyah**, migration to Israel.

A newly-married couple after their separate prayers at the Western Wall in Jerusalem

Inter-faith dialogue

Jews do not believe that there is single religion for all people but that believers can be led to God as long as they follow the **Noachide laws** (see page 157). At local and national levels many Jews take part in dialogue where they discuss their own and others' religion.

The Council of Christians and Jews

The Council of Christians and Jews came into being in 1942. It brings together the Christian and Jewish Communities in a common effort to combat prejudice, intolerance, discrimination and anti-Semitism. It encourages Christians and Jews to appreciate and respect each others' distinctive beliefs while recognizing their common ground through:

Recommending inter-faith dialogue at local, national and international level.

Explanations concerning festivals and worship held in synagogues and churches.

Seminars and lectures arranged about Israel and Christian/Jewish relations.

Press and the media being monitored to help prevent inflammatory coverage of race issues.

Events arranged such as Holocaust Memorial Day. The first Holocaust Memorial Day took place on 27 January 2001, which marked the anniversary of the liberation of Auschwitz.

Common Ground Journal, produced and distributed to about 5000 people.

Tours to Israel arranged as an introduction to Israeli society and to meet Jews, Muslims and Christians across the political spectrum.

1998 NUMBER 2

Common Ground

JUBILEE 2000

The Journal of the Council of Christians & Jews

Recall and evaluate

1 What is meant by the term Zionism? **(2)**

2 'All the dialogue in the world won't help people treat others any better.' Do you agree? Give reasons for your answer. **(8)**

Creative assignment

Write a speech suitable to be given to a group of young children who know nothing about the Holocaust. Explain why you think it is important for them to know about it. Think carefully about what they should be told and how the information is expressed.

The natural world

Creation in reverse

And the smog and the radio-active material fell on the sea,
and the dry land and contaminated every herb yielding
seed and every fruit tree yielding fruit.
And man said:
'It is not very good but we cannot put the clock back.'
This was the fifth day before the end.
And by his work, man created great deserts and changed
climatic conditions so that winds swept dust of the Earth
skywards to mingle with the smog which blotted out the Sun by
day and Moon by night so that night and day became the same.
And man saw the work of his hands and said,
'Our conquest of Nature is nearly complete.'
And this was the fourth day before the end.
The third day before the end man said,
'Let us dump our industrial effluents, raw sewage and garbage
into the streams and waterways and seas.'
And it was so.
The waters upon the Earth became foul so that all life in the
waters died.

The words on the left are a stark reminder of what humans have done to God's creation described in *Genesis*.

 **Get talking**

- Do you think people are sufficiently concerned about what is happening to the environment?

- What reasons might non-religious people have for believing in the importance of looking after creation?

Fact file

The Creation story in *Genesis* chapters 1 and 2 states that God created the world and that humankind was given the responsibility of acting as steward for its owner. In *Psalm 24:1* the Jews are reminded that the owner is God.

'The earth is the Lord's and all that it holds, the world and its inhabitants.' (Psalm 24:1)

Jews believe that the Creation caused divine sparks to be scattered throughout the whole universe and that humankind needs to reunite the world into harmony and to care for the environment. This is called **Tikkun Olam** (see page 213).

At the 1986 gathering in Assisi for the 25th anniversary of the WWF – The Global Environment Network, Rabbi Hertzberg reinforced the positive role Jews should take concerning the environment:

'The rebirth of nature, day after day, is God's gift; but humans are responsible for making sure that this rebirth can occur. As we consume any one of the products of God's world we must say first the appropriate grace. At the very least, we must leave the palace of our Host no worse than we found it.'

'The earth brought forth vegetation … and trees of every kind bearing fruit with the seed in it. And God saw that this was good.'
(Genesis 1:12)

THIS TREE WAS PLANTED AS A SYMBOL OF HOPE IN THE FUTURE

Bark Ode

I think that I shall never see
A burger lovely as a tree
Perhaps if we can beat the ranchers
The forest yet may keep its branches.

If people protect trees …

In the Torah it is seen that trees are important and should be protected. Instructions were given about how they should be treated during war. *'When in your war against a city you have to besiege it a long time in order to capture it, you must not destroy its trees, wielding the axe against them. You may eat them, but you must not cut them down.'*
(Deuteronomy 20:19)

In memory: a tree being planted in memory of assassinated Israeli Prime Minister Yitzhak Rabin

… trees protect people

Trees have played a vital role in the rebuilding of the State of Israel since 1948 as so much of the soil had been blown into the desert. Through programmes such as those organized by **Jewish National Fund**, millions of trees have been planted which have helped regenerate the soil.

Trees are planted in Israel to celebrate Tu b'Shvat, the New Year for Trees. Jews throughout the world send money to support tree-planting projects.

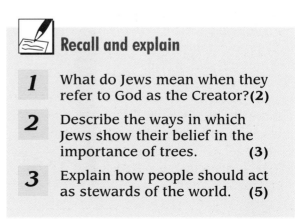

Recall and explain

1 What do Jews mean when they refer to God as the Creator? **(2)**

2 Describe the ways in which Jews show their belief in the importance of trees. **(3)**

3 Explain how people should act as stewards of the world. **(5)**

In touch with the environment in Israel

Neot Kedumim is dedicated to exploring and demonstrating the ties between the Biblical tradition and Israel's nature and agriculture, as expressed in prayers, holidays and symbols

Neot Kedumim is the world's only Biblical landscape reserve. Stone by stone and tree by tree, workers have transformed the once barren hills and valleys of Neot Kedumim into a network of landscapes. It includes 280 nature reserves and the work there is recognized as pioneering restoration landscape.

Many people from all over the world go to Israel to work on the land in communities called **Kibbutzim** where half of the nation's agricultural exports are produced.

Jews throughout the world are reminded how humanity is dependent on God's protection when celebrating Sukkot. This is an eight-day festival when Jews live in leaf-covered temporary buildings to mark the forty-year journey of their ancestors through the wilderness (see page 154). It is also a time of thanksgiving for harvest.

Many homes in Israel have their own sukkah, or Jews go on pilgrimage to the giant tabernacle on Mount Zion and pray at the Western Wall (see page 196).

In Britain too, many homes and synagogues have a sukkah.

A sukkah

A change from the burger bar

Sarah is Jewish and she has invited her non-Jewish friend Mandy to a meal out at Bloom's restaurant to celebrate the end of exams.

Sarah: Well don't look so worried – you're not going to be poisoned! Here's the menu.

Mandy: Sorry, it's only because I know you have strict rules about food and I'm not quite sure what to expect.

Sarah: Don't worry. I'm sure you'll love it. We'll start with braised caterpillars and then I think we'll go for the roast hyena or maybe you'd prefer skunk soup to start with – it's got a lovely aroma.

Mandy: OK, OK, stop mucking about. Just put me in the picture. What about fish. It's not allowed, is it?

Sarah: Yes it is, we don't eat shellfish but we are allowed fish with scales so there's plenty of choice there.

Mandy: Oh, good, I might go for fish. I know you're not allowed pork but what about other meat. Doesn't it have to be specially kosher or whatever you call it?

Sarah: Well it's hardly likely *not* to be here is it, stupid!

Mandy: Yes I realize that but how about other places?

Sarah: You just look for the sign or notice. You can even get kosher pizzas delivered from some of the big restaurants. Anyway, we can eat other meat as long as it's been prepared according to the laws of kashrut.

Mandy: (*looking at menu*) Mmm … there's nice things here – I don't think this is going to be a problem, which is just as well – I'm starving. It's chicken for me, I think. What are we doing about drink?

Sarah: As long as it doesn't have milk in it, anything you want.

Mandy: What's wrong with milk? Anyway, I've seen you drink it.

Sarah: You can, but not at the same meal as meat. You can't mix meat and milk.

Mandy: Where do all these rules come from and why do you have to keep them?

Bloom's kosher restaurant

Sarah: They're in the Torah – *Leviticus* chapter 17 to be precise. If you read it, though I can't imagine you ever will, knowing you, you'll see it's because it shows the 'holiness' – of the people God made a covenant with. It's hard to explain but it's part of our roots.

Mandy: Well I've never thought of you as holy but seeing as you're treating me I'll at least agree that you're special. Shall we order now? I hope you've got the cash.

Sarah: Cash for Kashrut, you could say, 'cos that's what our dietary code is called!

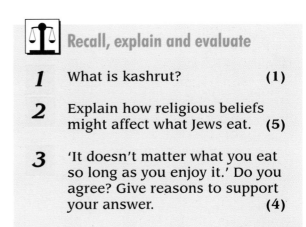

Recall, explain and evaluate

1 What is kashrut? **(1)**

2 Explain how religious beliefs might affect what Jews eat. **(5)**

3 'It doesn't matter what you eat so long as you enjoy it.' Do you agree? Give reasons to support your answer. **(4)**

Animals

1 'A righteous man knows the needs of his beast, but the compassion of the wicked is cruelty.' (Proverbs 12:10)

2 *'I now establish my covenant with you and your offspring to come, and with every living thing that is with you – birds, cattle, and every wild beast as well.' (Genesis 9:9–10)*

3 *'The seventh day is a sabbath of the Lord your God: you shall not do any work – you ... or your cattle.' (Exodus 20:10)*

4 *'If you see your fellow's ass or ox fallen on the road, do not ignore it; you must help him raise it.' (Deuteronomy 22:4)*

5 *'You shall not muzzle an ox while it is threshing.' (Deuteronomy 25:4)*

 Creative assignment

Either draw up a charter suitable for going in the school entrance entitled 'A Young Person's Guide to the Care of the Earth'

Or using one of the references in the chapter, design a poster highlighting any aspect of wrong behaviour towards animals in today's world.

Fact file

Although Judaism teaches that humans have authority over animals, *'They shall rule the fish of the sea, the birds of the sky, the cattle, the whole earth, and all the creeping things that creep on earth'* (Genesis 1:26), it is considered important to show great compassion for them. One of the rules given to Noah and his family in the Noachide laws was to be kind to animals. Meat-eating may not have happened until this time: *'Every creature that lives shall be yours to eat; as with the green grasses, I give you all these. You must not, however, eat flesh with its life-blood in it.' (Genesis 9: 3-4)*

There is no general ruling for Jews about vegetarianism and it is considered to be a matter of personal choice. It is important, though, that the slaughter of animals for food must be done according to **shechitah**. This is the term used to describe the special method of slaughtering. It is one of the oldest Jewish rituals and it is believed that the laws governing it were given to Moses on Mount Sinai. It is devised to reduce animal suffering to a second by cutting the oesophagus and trachea with a knife specially tested for its sharpness. The slaughter is carried out by a learned and religious Jew known as a **shochet** who will recite a blessing over the animal. The work is very specialized and it takes years of training to acquire the skill. After it is killed, the animal is inspected to check that it is not diseased before being passed over to a kosher butcher. Because Jews are exempt from the accepted method of stunning the animal to render it unconscious, the RSPCA has concerns. Although it recognizes that the religious practices of people must be respected, it is campaigning for changes.

The sculpture by Nador Glid at Yad Vashem, Jerusalem, in memory of the victims of the concentration camps

The following questions give you a chance to re-examine the issues raised in the preceding units. Remember to look at the number of marks for each question and to develop your answer accordingly.

a What is the difference between racism and anti-Semitism? **(2)**

b Select *one* of the following issues and describe the relevant teachings from the Tenakh: prejudice and discrimination *or* wealth and materialism. **(6)**

c Why is Israel so important to many Jews today? **(7)**

d 'There are too many problems in the world for us to do anything about them.'
Do you agree? Give reasons for your answer showing you have considered other points of view. **(5)**

A SUSPECTED WAR CRIMINAL

Accused of the slaughter of 4000 Jews and other civilians said this week he had saved lives rather than taken them.

Simeon Serafimowicz, 84, is said to have ordered the deaths when in command of a 500-strong paramilitary police unit for four years in Mir, Belorussia during World War II.

It has been claimed that of the 4000 Jews living in Mir only 30 survived the war.

Mr Serafimowicz, who lives with his son Kazimierz, said he always wanted to come to England because at the age of 12 he read in a book that immortal phrase, "The sun never sets on the British Empire".

He said: "But now I live here and all these people come to me after so many years and and say you are murderer.

"Why they come after so many years, I'm innocent man, I have never done this.

"All people to me are the same, black, white, yellow, Jews, they all the same, I have never hurt anyone."

War crimes suspect Simeon Serafimowicz was found guilty

 **Get talking**

- What are the problems of assessing a person's guilt or innocence so many years after the crime was committed?

- Do you think there are crimes for which the death penalty should be used? What reasons do you have for your views?

Fact file

Jews believe that everyone has been given free will and must take responsibility for their actions. The Torah and Talmud contain many laws giving instruction and guidance about behaviour as well as how crime should be punished. The basic rules for morality can be found in the Noachide laws (see page 157).

Justice has always been important and in *Deuteronomy 16:18–20* it states that judges must be appointed who should be fair and not accept bribes.

Sins against God have always been considered the worst of crimes but there is always the choice to repent and turn back to God. This is called **teshuva** (repentance) and includes the stages of recognizing and regretting the wrongs done, trying to make amends, repenting to God and never committing the sin again. Although teshuva can happen at any time, it is at the Ten Days of Returning before Yom Kippur that special significance is given to this.

Although Jews are taught that they should be forgiving towards others, only the victim can do this and not others on her or his behalf.

Capital punishment

Although certain crimes in the past were punishable by death the Torah states that evidence for the offence must be beyond reasonable doubt. The Jews were instructed to make sure that there was more than one witness to the crime.

'A person shall be put to death only on the testimony of two or more witnesses; he must not be put to death on the testimony of a single witness.' (Deuteronomy 17:6)

As with many groups of people, Jews today are divided in their views about the use of capital punishment. Some who are in favour often refer to *Leviticus 24:17–18* in support of their argument: *'Anyone who commits murder shall be put to death … The principle is a life for a life.'* Those who are opposed to it take the view that as life is given by God, only he can take it away.

In Israel the death sentence can only be used for genocide or treason. This only happened once in the twentieth century when Nazi war criminal Adolf Eichmann was executed in Israel in 1962.

Raising awareness

Drug-related crimes in today's society are a serious issue. Jews are finding ways of raising awareness of the problem through publicity campaigns and education.

Rabbi Isaac Sufrin sounds a shofar (ram's horn) to start Drugsline Chabad's taxi campaign, taking the anti-drugs message onto London's streets

'BE MORE AWARE'
says Ecstasy victim's father

Leah Betts

The father of Ecstasy victim Leah Betts urged parents to be more aware of their children's whereabouts and activities during a drugs awareness evening run by Drugsline at Ilford's Chabad House.

Recalling the harrowing story of how his 18-year-old daughter, Leah, died, Paul Betts stunned the 250 people attending the fund-raising event by declaring: 'We think we know where our children are now, but right now we are here in this hall and they are somewhere else.'

Recall and explain

1 What is the difference between capital and corporal punishment? **(2)**

2 How do you think the taxi and Mr Betts' talk will help deter drug taking? **(4)**

3 Why is Yom Kippur such an important time for Jews? **(4)**

War and peace

Salute to a 'soldier for peace'. Two Israeli soldiers stand guard over the coffin

 **Get talking**

- The caption for this news photo refers to the assassinated Prime Minister of Israel, Yitzhak Rabin, as a 'soldier for peace'. Can you have such a thing as a 'soldier for peace'? Is it a contradiction in terms or a fitting description?

Fact file 1

Jews regard peace as the ideal state. However, they believe there are certain situations when fighting is considered to be the right action.

Obligatory war (milchemet mitzvah)
Traditionally, this has applied to occasions when Jews have believed that it was God's will for them to go to war in order to capture land that he had promised their ancestors. An example of this was when Joshua led the Israelites into battle against Jericho.

They are also obliged to defend themselves, their families or land against attack.

Optional or discretionary war (milchemet reshut)
Jews consider it acceptable to strike first if an attack from another country is suspected. Similarly, it is thought to be right to defend another country under attack, in order to stop the war from spreading.

A soldier in Jerusalem praying by the Western Wall. It is a place of prayer and pilgrimage for Jews

Fact file 2

The emphasis on defence is reflected in the name of Israel's army which is called the Israel Defence Force. This was formed to help survivors of World War II who were returning to Israel to build new lives for themselves in the land of their ancestors.

Judaism teaches that war is a last resort and that, where possible, other means such as discussion and negotiation should be first used to resolve conflict.

When Elisha, a prophet of God, was asked if the enemy should be killed, he answered, *'Did you take them captive with your sword and bow that you would strike them down? Rather, set food and drink before them, and let them eat and drink and return to their master.'* (2 Kings 6:22)

Below are some thoughts of a soldier involved in optional or discretionary war. He is a sergeant in the intelligence unit of the Israeli army.

As an Israeli soldier (three years' compulsory service and subsequent years doing reserve duty), my meaning of life is not a struggle for personal survival but more to help achieve peace so that my children will not need to go to war.

In battle I also give a lot of thought to the enemy facing me. He too has a wife and children and he too cares for them and wants to save his family from the tragic consequences of war. I pray that our next generation will have a new meaning of life unbeknown in the Middle East region for nearly half a century, a life of sincere comradeship enjoying neighbourly peace and happiness.

Recall and explain

1. What is the army in Israel called? **(1)**

2. What is the Jewish teaching about war? **(3)**

3. With reference to the soldier's thoughts above, explain why Jews have sometimes felt it necessary to fight. **(6)**

Peace

Protecting the right to be in a safe place

Ending intrusion of each other's space

Absence of war that turns race against race

Candles reflecting the hope on each face

Envy forgotten in friendship's embrace

is … SHALOM

The dove of peace embroidered on the cover of the sefer Torah, the scrolls containing the Jewish laws. The dove design is made up of the word 'Shalom' (peace) in Hebrew script

 **Get talking**

● **What does the word peace mean to you?**

Fact file 3

Jews look forward to a time of peace as this is a condition for the **Messianic Age** (see page 220). The Jewish word for peace, **shalom**, is a common greeting. Each week Jews use it when they wish each other **Shabbat Shalom**. The word does not just mean the absence of war but a condition of well-being necessary for growth. As it says in the Talmud:

'Great is peace, because peace is to the Earth what yeast is to the dough.'

Although Jews have taken part in many wars, it has not stopped them from seeking peace and taking an active part in working towards reconciliation. The most significant development was the historic signing of the peace agreement by Israel's Prime Minister Yitzhak Rabin and Chairman Yasser Arafat in Washington. The assassination of the Prime Minister on 4 November 1995 later put an end to his own work towards the peace process.

Education for peace

Many people realize that it is not enough to sign peace treaties. The Israelis and Palestinians who have grown up in areas of conflict have never known a different situation. They cannot change overnight. The next generation in particular have to be educated about peace.

The little girl, eleven years old, has freckles on her nose and wears a red ribbon at the top of a long braid …
She has never spoken to a Jew and says she never wants to.
'Do you like Jews?' she is asked.
'No.'
'Why not?'
'They attack our homes, breaking everything, building settlements.'
'Why wouldn't you want to talk to any Jew?'
'Because they are our enemies.'
'What if you met a Jewish girl your age? What would you talk about?'
'Nothing!'
'Wouldn't you be interested in learning about the Jewish girl's life?'
'No.'
'Why not?'
'Because I don't know her, and she doesn't know me.'

Does this cute little Amal with the freckles on her nose have a dream in her life I wonder.
'To get back our land,' she says.
'How?'
'Demonstrate.'
Then after a moment's thought she adds, 'We must use guns.' The young men who brought her to talk with me explode in a roar of approving laughter.

(David Shipler from *Arab and Jew*)

Neve Shalom/Wahat al-Salam

This is the name given to a peace village in Israel. The community was begun in 1970 with the idea of giving Christians, Jews and Muslims the opportunity of living and working together. It has developed and expanded and now includes a primary school and a School for Peace. It also runs workshops and activities for visitors from other countries and for all faiths.

Sesame Street to help Peace Process

A new joint Israeli-American-Palestinian version of *Sesame Street* has been praised. The programme's aims are to encourage understanding between children of different nationalities.

Recall and explain

1. What does reconciliation mean? **(1)**

2. What does the Hebrew word 'shalom' mean? **(3)**

3. Describe the ways that Jews are working towards reconciliation. **(6)**

Creative assignment

Take the letters of a key word, e.g. war, peace, conflict or shalom and create a poem or collage around them.

Suffering and evil

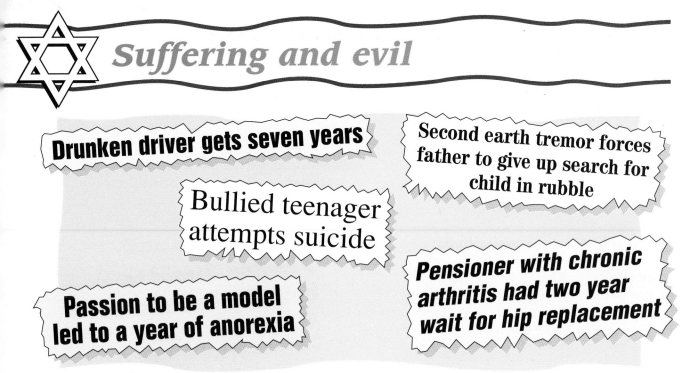

Drunken driver gets seven years

Second earth tremor forces father to give up search for child in rubble

Bullied teenager attempts suicide

Pensioner with chronic arthritis had two year wait for hip replacement

Passion to be a model led to a year of anorexia

Get talking

Suffering is an important part of life for which there often seems to be no reason.

- What kinds of suffering do you most fear?
- Could you put types of suffering into categories according to whether they are caused by people or by nature?

Fact file

Within the Tenakh there are many stories of individuals who experienced physical, mental, emotional and spiritual suffering. For example there is the story of Ruth, who not only suffered poverty but became a young widow. The book of *Job* tells of a man of God who experienced illness, the loss of his family, friends and livestock. These were cases of apparently undeserved suffering, which call into question whether a righteous and just God could allow such things to happen. Job's faith seemed finally to be strengthened by the sure knowledge of God's presence. No explanation was given but it seemed enough for him to know that, despite all the sorrow that he had experienced, he was in God's care. '*… but I would behold God while still in my flesh.*' (Job 19:26)

In Jewish teaching several reasons can be found for certain kinds of suffering. In *Genesis*, suffering is seen as a test of faith when Abraham is asked to sacrifice his son Isaac. There are other examples in the Old Testament which show the belief that God punishes disobedience. This can result in suffering, which encourages people to repent and return to God.

Within Judaism suffering is often thought to have some positive value:

When my baby was born, I suffered – how I suffered! But every second of the pain of labour was worth it – all 28 hours. (New mother)

The last four months of my son's life brought us together as a family. Now it has helped me in my work as a counsellor. (Bereavement counsellor)

In the Midrash it says: *Not to have known suffering is not to be truly human.*

Many Jews suffered during the Holocaust. For some it destroyed their faith. For others, suffering could be seen to have some positive value.

Jews believe that suffering can be helped by developing and drawing on one's inner strength.

Shalom
Shalom
Shalom

Guard your inner spirit more than any treasure, for it is the source of life

- An Ancient Sage (Proverbs 4:23)

1944 — 11 DECEMBER

… How can I believe in God, this callous God who has allowed the slaughter of children, the gas chambers, my people's martyrdom? … I belong to the Jews. Not because I was born one or because I share their faith — I never have done. I belong to the Jews because I have suffered as one of them. It's suffering that has made me Jewish. I belong to people who have been murdered or who are still struggling to escape death. If some of them do survive the war, and if I survive myself, I'll join them. Our shared experience of this ordeal will bring us together. We'll build a home of our own, a place for all homeless Jews where we can live in peace and dignity, respected by other nations and respecting their rights in turn.

Janina Bauman

Recall and evaluate

1 What is the Tenakh? (1)

2 Describe how either Ruth or Job suffered. (4)

3 Explain how suffering can have some kind of purpose. (5)

'It could always be worse' – a Jewish tale

🖌 **Creative assignment**

Make up a modern strip cartoon for a friend who needs cheering up, using the same title as above: 'It could always be worse'.

The actor and storyteller David Kossoff has given pleasure to many people and he now uses his talents to communicate to audiences around the country the evil of drugs. This work is born out of his own experience of suffering as a result of his son's addiction and death from drugs.

How handsome you looked, how elegant my Paul, in your well-cut, brown, elegant suit. How well I remember when you bought it one Wednesday in Windsor High Street – off-the-peg. To you my Paul, just another suit. To your mother and me, so much more! A symbol of hope, a new sign of new life. Celebration clothes for a given back son. For given back you were my Paul. Fought for by young doctors and tireless nurses with swift competent hands. You died my Paul. You were dead and then alive again. Gone away and brought back by doctors and nurses and … God. Monitor screens and tubes and wires and drugs and … God. A tolerant smile you had for Dad with his talk of thanks to God. But we will call things by their right name and the giver of life is God … By your bed we sat, my Paul, and looked at our reborn son … our family miracle.

Soon well enough to celebrate your 25th birthday in your hospital room with loving friends and cards and champagne and a cake with both your birth dates. Our miracle son, soon ready to go home, and buy a light-brown, pin-striped suit. Soon to re-enter your world and life-style where lurks such danger. Soon to re-start habits – now doubly perilous, soon to give up the warnings of loving friends …

To God who gave you back once, we prayed again for your safe return. Did the good Lord, I wonder, hear and give careful thought to what was best. Did he allow you a glimpse, I wonder, that first time, offering you rest. For bring you home safe to us he certainly did. Safe and secure and in perfect peace. Lying down in an open box, elegant in your light-brown pin-striped suit.

Fact file 2

Judaism teaches that humankind has free will to perform good or bad deeds. In the **Kabbalah**, which contains Jewish spiritual writings, the teaching of Tikkun Olam can be found. This is the belief that at the moment of Creation, sparks of God's holiness were scattered through the world into all living beings. When a person performs a mitzvah, then that spark is reclaimed by God – but bad deeds prevent God's love from flowing through the universe. It is only when God has reclaimed all the holy sparks through good actions that the world can be redeemed.

Although it is believed that God created both good and evil, *'I form light and create darkness, I make weal and create woe' (Isaiah 45:7)*, Jews do not believe in a devil or evil force who is opposed to God and tempts people to do wrong.

Note: 'weal' mean well-being.

Recall and evaluate

1 What is meant by Tikkun Olam? **(3)**

2 Do you think a religious belief can help suffering? **(2)**

3 'If God was all powerful then he'd get rid of evil and suffering.' Do you agree? Give reasons showing you have considered other points of view. **(5)**

Death and beyond

Euthanasia

I have to make the journey alone
I'd like to make it now.
I'd like to gently slip away
if only I knew how.
I cannot bear the helpless stare,
I'm ready to let go of the hand.
If I asked for my heart to stop its beat,
would they ever understand?
'All in God's time,' is what they'd say,
'you may go into remission.
We hate it, too – what you're going through
but we cannot give permission.'
Can they not see the indignity,
the dependence that fills me with shame?
Would it be such a sin to release my soul
from its helpless tortured frame?

Fact file 1

Euthanasia is considered to be wrong in Judaism. To lessen pain is seen as a virtue but deliberately to give a person a lethal dose of a drug is against Jewish tradition. Life is believed to be the gift of God and to shorten that life is looked upon as murder. *'The Lord has given, and the Lord has taken away.' (Job 1:21)*

The **Shulchan Aruch** (Jewish legal code) reinforces the view that no matter how ill the patient is, he or she has the gift of life and it is forbidden to take that gift away. Only God, who is the Creator of life, can do so.

If a person is being kept alive on a life-support machine, this should not be switched off unless all the person's functions have stopped (see page 80). Although medicines should not be administered to cause death, if the suffering is so great, it is permissible to pray for a release from that suffering. The answer to the prayer will then be left to God to decide. So although it would be forbidden to give a lethal injection, witholding treatment might be allowed in some cases.

Get talking

- Are there any circumstances in which you would approve of euthanasia (mercy killing)? What reasons do you have for your veiws?

Recall and explain

1 What does euthanasia mean? **(2)**

2 Explain the beliefs of Judaism about euthanasia. **(3)**

3 Explain how prayer might help people who are suffering. **(5)**

Organ transplants and autopsies

Donor Card

I would like to help someone to live after my death.

Let your relatives know your wishes, and keep this card with you at all times.

Life in the balance

Pikuakh nefesh
- Saving of life should come above all else

- Often delays burial
- Requires desecration of the body
- Derives benefit from the dead

 Get talking

- What are your views on whether people should be encouraged to donate their organs for transplant after their death?

Organ transplant refers to the process of removing part of a dead person's body and implanting it in a living person. This will only be done with permission of the next of kin or prior agreement from the deceased.

Many issues have to be taken into consideration, although Jewish teaching on the importance of pikuakh nefesh (see page 159) tips the balance in favour of organ transplants. Some Orthodox Jews are against heart transplants as the organ will be removed before it has stopped beating. However, the Rabbinate in Jerusalem has given permission for it to take place once the brain stem is pronounced dead.

Autopsies

An autopsy means the dissection of bodies after death for medical, scientific or legal purposes such as for a post-mortem. Judaism is opposed to autopsies, as the body should not be cut after death, but returned to God in as natural a condition as possible. If, as a result, the autopsy could help save lives in the future then the importance of pikuakh nefesh might allow it to go ahead.

Recall and explain

1 What is the difference between organ transplants and autopsies? **(4)**

2 What role does a belief in God play when looking at issues connected with the sanctity of life? **(6)**

Death

This prayer was read by actor David Kossoff (see page 213) in his radio appeal for The Compassionate Friends. It is believed to be the burial prayer of the Makah tribe of North American Indians.

Do not stand at my grave and weep

Do not stand at my grave and weep,
I am not there, I do not sleep.

I am a thousand winds that blow,
I am the diamond glints on snow.
I am the sunlight on ripened grain,
I am the gentle autumn rain.

When you awaken in the morning's hush,
I am the uplifting rush
of quiet birds in circled flight.
I am the soft stars that shine at night.

Do not stand at my grave and cry,
I am not there, I did not die.

William Holman Hunt. Lived here.

June 17 Monday 18 Tuesday

Get talking

- In what ways shown in the words and images above, are people remembered after their death?

- Can you think of any other ways?

Reform Jews tend to be more concerned with the present life than with the afterlife, and in their prayer books are the words, 'What can we know of death, we who cannot understand life?' They believe that the soul continues after death irrespective of the body.

The following words are from the Reform Judaism prayer book.

> *In the rising of the sun*
> *and its going down*
> *We remember them.*
>
> *In the blowing of the wind*
> *and in the chill of winter,*
> *We remember them.*
>
> *In the opening of buds*
> *and in the warmth of summer,*
> *We remember them.*
>
> *In the beginning of the year*
> *and when it ends,*
> *We remember them.*

Fact file 2

Judaism teaches that a person's soul continues after death. This is made possible through good works on Earth and in the memories of others.

In the past it was thought that after death there was an existence in a place beneath the Earth, called **sheol**. This is largely rejected and most Jews prefer to accept that it is beyond human understanding to know what it will be like. It is believed that God will judge everyone and that the evil will be punished. '*Many of those that sleep in the dust of the earth will awake, some to eternal life, others to reproaches, to everlasting abhorrence.*' *(Daniel 12:2)*

Orthodox Jews follow the teaching of Maimonides who declared a belief in the resurrection to be one of the thirteen Principles of Judaism. They re-affirm this in their daily prayers and in the fact that the cemetery is called **Bet ha-Hayyim** (House of Life). They believe that the body itself will be resurrected at the time of the Messianic Age (see page 220). For this reason, they do not allow cremation.

Liberal Jews do not believe in physical resurrection but think that the body is just a vessel. Some now have cremation, believing it to be more ecologically sound.

Recall and explain

1 What is sheol? **(2)**

2 Explain what is meant by: 'what can we know of death, we who cannot understand life?' **(2)**

3 Explain the Jewish belief about the afterlife, referring to the differences between Orthodox and Liberal and Reform beliefs. **(6)**

The journey of death

There is an important pattern of rituals that takes place when someone dies in the Jewish community. The degree to which they are followed varies according to which movement of Judaism people belong.

At Death

- Many Jews will traditionally rent (tear) their clothes on hearing of a close relative's death, as a sign of grief (*Genesis 27:35*).
- The body is cleansed, washed and dried by members of the Burial Society and put in plain white garments.
- A lit candle is placed near the head of the deceased and someone remains with the body at all times.
- As all should be equal in death, the body is usually placed in a plain wooden coffin.
- The tallit (prayer shawl) is usually put in the coffin as now the need to keep the mitzvot is over. This is indicated by the fringes being cut.

The funeral

- The body should be buried in a single grave.
- The burial should, if possible, take place within 24 hours.
- The mourners will place the soil on the coffin.
- In some parts of the world Orthodox women are not encouraged to go to the funeral.
- Flowers are not usually placed on the grave.

Mourning

1st week (shiva)

- Certain rituals are observed: Orthodox Jews sit on low stools, mirrors are covered and prayers (kaddish) are recited.

Mirrors are covered or turned around

2nd–4th week (shloshim)

- No shaving or cutting of hair takes place.
- No parties are attended.

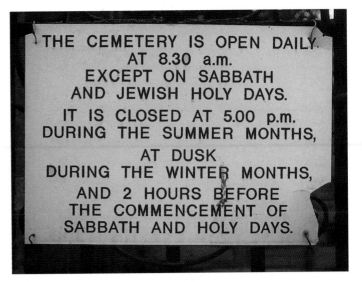

Each Jewish community usually maintains its own cemetary

The rest of the year

- All joyous events should be avoided.
- Kaddish prayers are said daily by children of the deceased (see page 219).
- Stones are placed on the grave when it is visited. It is believed that Abraham used a pebble to mark the spot where Sarah was buried.

Stones showing that visits have been made to the grave

Tombstone consecration

- Before the end of the year psalms are recited.
- There is a brief eulogy and the cover over the tombstone is removed.
- The tombstone will be horizontal if the deceased was a Sephardi and vertical if the deceased was Ashkenazi (see page 154).

1st anniversary and beyond

- Each year on the anniversary of the death (yarzheit), sons of the family will recite kaddish and candles are burned for 24 hours (see page 176).

- At various times of the year a small stone is left on the grave and special memorial services (**yizkors**) are held. Each year at Yom Kippur – and often also at the festivals of Pesach, Shavuot and Shabbat – prayers are said in memory of the departed.

The Yarzheit candle symbolizes the departed soul and burns for 24 hours

---

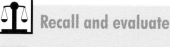

Recall and evaluate

1 What is the mitzvot? (1)

2 Do you think it is helpful to have a pattern of mourning rites spread over a period of time? Give reasons to support your answer. (5)

3 Select one photograph and give four details concerning the traditions used. (4)

The Messianic Age

Jerusalem in the evening

Jews believe that people will be redeemed when God's kingdom is established on Earth. A time will come in the future when the present world order will end and a specially chosen leader will usher in a new age of universal peace. People will live in harmony and without fear. This leader is known to Jews as the **Mashiach** or Messiah which means 'the anointed one'. It was taught by the prophet Isaiah that he would be descended from the house of David and his coming would be for the whole world when Israel fulfilled the role of being loyal to God. He would be a leader of great goodness. *'He has been named "The Mighty God is planning grace; the Eternal Father, a peaceable ruler".' (Isaiah 9:5)*

Teaching about the Messiah was reinforced by later prophets and the belief was developed that the Messianic Age will be a time when people live in harmony with each other and there will be an end to all violence and wars. *'Nation shall not take up sword against nation; they shall never again know war.' (Micah 4:3)*

Throughout history Jews have waited and hoped for the coming of the Mashiach.

Despite people claiming to be him, the **Messianic Age** has not yet dawned. Jews do not accept the Christian claim that Jesus was the Messiah.

Although all Jews share their hope for the Messianic Age, they differ in certain aspects of their belief about it. Orthodox Jews believe that the Messiah will come to restore the Temple in Jerusalem and their obedience to the Torah and daily prayers will help bring this about. During the Yom Kippur service reference is made to a physical resurrection and an individual Messiah. Reform Jews put an emphasis on the Messianic Age rather than the individual.

•*Every day of my life as a Jew, every action that I make, every thought that I have, is lived in the knowing certainty that one day the golden age of universal peace will dawn.*•

(Moshe Aaron)

 Creative assignment

Write an essay entitled: 'Harmony: my vision for the twenty-first century'.

Prayers are constantly said at the tomb of Maimonides

The following questions give you a chance to re-examine the issues raised in the preceding units. Remember to look at the number of marks for each question and to develop your answer accordingly.

a What do Jews mean when they describe God as 'King of the Universe'? **(4)**

b Describe what is meant by forgiveness and teshuva in Judaism. **(4)**

c Explain the relevance of the Shema to Jewish daily life. **(7)**

d 'What Jews do is more important than what they believe.'

Do you agree? Give reasons showing you have considered other points of view. **(5)**

Index

Index

The publishers would like to thank the following for permission to reproduce photographs:
Robert Aberman p. 177; Sue Adler/Camera Press p. 94; Sultan Ahmed/Islamic Relief Worldwide p. 136, 138 (right); Stephen Alvarez/Britstock IFA Ltd. p. 8; John Angerson/Guzelian p. 117 (bottom); courtesy of Anglia Television p. 172 (centre right); courtesy of Anglican Pacifist Fellowship p. 75; Chris Ashford/Camera Press p. 46 (top); Ilena Balka p. 179; courtesy of Bank of England p. 52; Barry Batchelor/PA News p. 45; BBC Photo p. 29; BBC Tomorrow's World p. 20; courtesy of Ahsen Bhati p. 97; Tony Buckingham/The Independent p. 34; John Buckle/Empics p. 9; Adam Butler/PA News p. 36; CAFOD p. 67; Douglas Carpenter p. 86; Channel 4 Television p. 172 (centre left); Christian Aid Photo Library p. 63 (bottom); Roger Coleman/Clergy Services Inc. p. 35; Carole Cornish p. 49; Croydon Advertiser pp. 39, 129; Koos Delport/FLPA p. 78; Sean Dempsey/PA News p. 59; Raymond Depardon/Magnum Photos p. 142; F. Dickson/Camera Press p. 61; Christina Dodwell/Hutchison Library p. 116; Craig Easton/The Independent p. 33; Peter Fisher pp.199 (bottom), 205 (bottom); Steve Forrest/Guzelian Photography p. 113; Gamma Press/Frank Spooner pp. 77, 83, 108, 191; Mike Goldwater/Network Photographers p. 148; Tony Gudgeon p. 159; Guzelian Photography p.11 (right); Tom Haley/Sipa Press/Rex Features p. 146; Fiona Hanson/PA News pp. 47, 172 (left); Robert Harding Picture Library p. 64; Liam Holohan/Taller de Difusion Popular (TDP) p. 62; David Hosking/Frank Lane Picture Agency p.199 (top); Mick Hutson/Redferns Picture Library p. 82; Islamic Relief Worldwide p. 138 (left); Joods Historisch Museum, Amsterdam p. 190; Martin Keene/PA News p. 165; Herbie Knott/The Independent pp. 128, 195 (right); Chabad Lubivitch p. 169; Stewart Mark/Camera Press p. 44, 50; Jenny Matthews/Format Photographers p. 189; Steve McCurry/Magnum Photos p. 68; Methodist Homes pp. 37, 41; Methodist Recorder p. 40; Neil Munns/PA News p. 78; Sarah Murray/Hutchison Library p. 121; John Nathan p. 175; P. O' Donnell/Camera Press p. 74; PA News pp. 71, 122, 205 (top); Panos p. 118 (bottom); Michélle Partridge p. 38; Rebecca Peters/Format Partners p. 134; Tom Pilston/The Independent p. 195 (left); Popperfoto p. 125; Mike Powell/Allsport p. 120; Ulrike Preuss/Format p. 188; John Reardon/Katz Pictures p. 112; Rex Features p. 58; Carlos Reyes-Manzo/Andes Press Agency pp. 63 (top), 85 (both); RSPCA Photolibrary p. 11 (left); Peter Sanders pp. 100, 106, 114, 118 (top), 145, 151; Tom Scott/PA News p. 76; Sigma p. 10; courtesy of Sinclair House p. 178; Michael Stephens/PA News p. 171; Homer Sykes/Network Photographers p. 88; Jenny Taylor p. 9; The Kobal Collection p. 193 (top); The Associated Press Ltd. pp. 89, 107, 206; The Quaker Tapestry Scheme p. 43 (top); Ibrahim Brian Thomson pp. 115, 131, 144, 152, 153; Denis Thorpe/The Guardian p. 139; B. S. Turner/Frank Lane Picture Agency p. 57; Tony Stone Images p. 220; John Voos/The Independent p. 46 (bottom); Rosemary Wass p. 43 (bottom); Franklin Watts & Chris Fairclough p. 30; Tony White/Camera Press p. 172 (right); Justin Williams/PA News p. 204; Jeremy Young/Rex Features p. 60; Zefa Picture Library pp. 18; 192. All other photographs were supplied by the authors.